USAF HISTORICAL STUDIES: NO. 132

AIR INTERDICTION IN CHINA IN WORLD WAR II

By Dr. Joe G. Taylor

USAF Historical Division

Research Studies Institute

Air University

September 1956

Published at

Maxwell Air Force Base, Alabama

September 1956

Air University USAF Historical Division Study
(AU–132–55–RSI)

Personal views or opinions expressed or implied in this publication are not to be construed as carrying official sanction of the Department of the Air Force or the Air University.

In accordance with the provisions of AFR 205-1, Section III, paragraphs 45a, and 45b, this entire study is classified CONFIDENTIAL However, only Chapter VII contains classified material The remaining chapters, I-VI, contain no classified material.

FOREWORD

This monograph recounts the air interdiction operations of the Fourteenth Air Force in China proper and Indo-China during World War II. Detailed attention is given to a description and analysis of efforts to interdict ocean and river shipping, roads, and railroads. A final chapter attempts to apply some of the lessons learned in World War II to the present day (1955) transportation system of China.

This study was written by Dr. Joe G. Taylor, USAF Historical Division The original of this monograph and the documents from which it was written are in the USAF Historical Division, Archives Branch.

Like other Historical Division studies, this history is subject to revision, and additional information or suggested corrections will be welcomed.

Contents

		Page
	INTRODUCTION	vii
I	COASTAL INTERDICTION	1
	Importance of Coastal Shipping to the Japanese	1
	Inception of the Antishipping Campaign	1
	Types of Attacks	4
	Evaluation	11
II	INTERDICTION OF RIVER LINES OF COMMUNICATION IN CHINA	14
	Importance of River Transportation	14
	Types of Shipping on Chinese Rivers	16
	Weapons and Tactics	17
	Japanese Defense of River Shipping	21
	Campaigns against River Shipping	22
	Evaluation	32
III	ROAD INTERDICTION	34
	Introduction	34
	Tactics	36
	Road Interdiction Campaigns	39
	Conclusions	44
IV	RAIL INTERDICTION IN INDO-CHINA	46
	The Railroads of Indo-China	46
	Railroad Administration in Indo-China	48
	The Interdiction of Indo-Chinese Railroads	48
	Results	51
V	INTERDICTION OF CHINESE RAILROADS IN WORLD WAR II	53
	Introduction	53
	The Railroads of China	53
	Railroad Administration in Occupied China	61
	Interdiction Operations	62
	Evaluation of Railway Interdiction in China	77
VI	CONCLUSIONS	82
VII	TRANSPORTATION IN COMMUNIST CHINA	86
	Introduction	86
	Chinese Communist Waterways	87
	Road Traffic in Communist China	89
	Railroads of China	91
	Conclusions	101
	FOOTNOTES	103
	GLOSSARY	111
	INDEX	113

Maps

No.		Page
1.	Shipping Routes off China Coast	3
2.	Navigable Rivers of China	15
3.	Important Roads in China	38
4.	Roads and Railroads in French Indo-China	47
5.	Railroads in Occupied China	58
6.	Railroads in Communist China	99

INTRODUCTION

United States Army Air Forces in China received a great deal of publicity during World War II, but this publicity was in the tradition of the "Flying Tigers" of the American Volunteer Group, with emphasis on deeds of derring-do. In the years since the end of the war, attention has been directed to conflicts in personalities and policies which were apparently as lively and bitter as the conflict with the Japanese Individual heroism, spectacular forays, and fights against odds were a definite part of Fourteenth Air Force operations, and it was just that they should receive public acclaim. Likewise, the conflicting policies of Lt. Gen. Joseph W. Stilwell, American theater commander in China, and Maj Gen. Claire L. Chennault, Fourteenth Air Force commander, deserve study because they had a definite bearing on subsequent events in Asia. However, other aspects of World War II operations in China are also worthy of attention and probably will be more useful than those mentioned above in planning for possible future operations against targets on the Asiatic mainland.

Those air operations which were directed against Japanese lines of communication in and adjacent to China are especially worthy of note This study attempts to describe and evaluate the attempted interdiction of coastal waterways, navigable rivers, highways, and railroads of China during the war with Japan. The tactics used and the targets attacked will be considered, and special attention will be given to the actual accomplishments An effort will be made to point out the reasons for success in some endeavors and for failure in others.

Since the basic Chinese transportation system, though improved, remains largely what it was during World War II, the conclusions reached regarding interdiction during that conflict should have pertinent application today. Therefore the study includes a discussion of possible interdiction of lines of communication in Communist China, based on World War II experience and on known changes and improvements in those lines of communication.

CHAPTER I

COASTAL INTERDICTION

IMPORTANCE OF COASTAL SHIPPING TO THE JAPANESE

SHIPPING ROUTES along the coast of China were of vital importance to the Japanese if they were to preserve the empire they had seized during the first months of World War II.* The war economy of the home islands depended directly upon oil from the East Indies, and to a lesser degree upon such raw materials as rubber and tin from Malaya, iron ore from Hainan Island, bauxite from Indo-China, and tungsten from China. The defense of the conquered areas was dependent upon arms, ammunition, and troops from Japan. The raw materials bound for the industries of Japan and the men and supplies directed to the islands of the empire could be transported only by shipping.

A glance at the map of the western Pacific Ocean reveals that the natural route for ships sailing between Japan and the south lay close to the China coast. Although it was possible for a ship sailing from Japan to the Philippines, the Indies, and Singapore to remain far enough out to sea to avoid exposure to attacks from World War II aircraft based in China, such a route afforded few ports of call and was dangerously exposed to submarine attack.

The usual route for south-bound Japanese shipping was to Shanghai and then south and east down the coast of China, or directly to Formosa and then east along the China coast. This route had a number of advantages. So long as the Japanese Air Force was strong, air cover from Shanghai, Formosa, Canton, Hainan Island, and Haiphong hampered Allied submarine operations. Naval bases at Shanghai, Takao, Hong Kong, and Hainan Island facilitated the operations of short-range patrol boats against submarines. Finally, the route afforded many harbors and anchorages—Shanghai, Wenchow, Foochow, and Amoy along the east coast of China, Kiirun and Takao on Formosa, Mako in the Pescadores, Swatow and Hong Kong between Formosa and Hainan Island, Kiungshan and Samah Bay on Hainan, and Haiphong, Vinh, Tourane, and Cap St Jacques on the coast of Indo-China—where ships might refuel or seek refuge from storm or Allied attack.

Even as merchant shipping through these lanes was vital to the Japanese Empire, so coastal shipping made up of smaller craft was vital to the Japanese military forces in south China and in Indo-China. For practical purposes, land communications between China and Indo-China did not exist, so only coastal shipping bound the two areas together. The internal economy of Indo-China depended upon coastal shipping between the northern and southern parts of the colony. Normally, the occupied ports of China had no land communications with one another or with Japanese forces in the interior; they too depended upon the sea for supplies and reinforcements.[1]

INCEPTION OF THE ANTISHIPPING CAMPAIGN

The advantages offered by Chinese bases for attacks against Japanese merchant shipping were so obvious that they must have been considered by military leaders from the beginning of the Pacific war, if not before. Indeed, Chinese aircraft had attacked Japanese naval units before Pearl Harbor. The rapid Japanese conquests in the Pacific and Asia during the first six

*See Map No 1, p 3

months of the war made it necessary for Allied leaders to give most of their attention to defensive measures, however, and little attention could be given to offensive plans. By the middle of 1942, this situation no longer prevailed; defense still had top priority, but the time had come to begin striking back at the enemy.

Insofar as China was concerned, defense had been the mission of the American Volunteer Group, and when the China Air Task Force (CATF) was activated, 4 July 1942, defense of Kunming and the eastern part of the air transport route across Burma to Kunming was its first task. During the same month, however, Brig. Gen. Claire L. Chennault, CATF Commander, suggested to the American theater commander, Lt. Gen. Joseph W. Stilwell, that attacks on shipping be given a priority after destruction of enemy aircraft and destruction of enemy military and naval establishments in China. A still higher priority was given to shipping attacks by a plan produced by Stilwell's staff in September 1942; only defense of the ferry terminal and Chungking was placed ahead of antishipping operations Separate plans presented to Generalissimo Chiang Kai-shek in late September 1942 by Stilwell and Chennault accorded priority to anti-shipping strikes after defense against enemy air attacks and destruction of enemy aircraft and air installations.[2]

Although, as noted above, General Chennault had recognized shipping as a high priority target, he seems to have believed, during this early period, that attacks on shipping would be a means of forcing the Japanese Air Force to come out and fight rather than a means for hastening Japanese defeat in itself. At any rate, such was the idea conveyed in a letter to Wendell L. Willkie in October of 1942. Chennault's main objective was to defeat the enemy air force (in which attacks on shipping would play their part), then to commence attacks on Japanese industrial targets from China bases. He thought of the bombing of Japanese industry, rather than the sinking of merchant vessels, as the means of cutting off supplies to Japanese forces in the Pacific.[3]

In April 1943 General Chennault went to Washington for a conference on the China-Burma-India Theater (CBI) and presented for air operations from China bases a plan which envisioned a counter-air campaign to commence in July and continue through August. During the latter month, medium bombers would begin the destruction of ports and shipping along the China coast, on Hainan Island, and in the Gulf of Tonkin while B-24's neutralized the Nanking-Shanghai area. By the end of November, according to this plan, the coastal sea lanes would be patrolled from Korea to Camranh Bay, and attacks upon Japan proper could begin.[4]

Perhaps President Franklin Delano Roosevelt was responsible for shipping's becoming a major objective in its own right. According to Chennault, who had a personal conference with the President before returning to China, Roosevelt was "particularly appreciative of the strategic possibilities of shipping strikes in the Formosa Strait and South China Sea He was convinced that Japanese merchant shipping was the key to the enemy war effort." The chief executive's enthusiasm for attacks on merchant shipping led Chennault to assert that his Fourteenth Air Force (which had replaced the CATF on 10 March 1943) could sink or severely damage 1,000,000 tons of Japanese shipping a year if given 10,000 tons of supplies a month in China.[5]

Shipping was therefore a prime objective of the Fourteenth Air Force from mid-1943 until the end of 1944, and attacks continued well into 1945. Fourteenth Air Force plans in 1944 gave priority to strikes against shipping targets second only to the maintenance of air supremacy in the missions of those units based within range of Japanese shipping lanes. Only when the main airfields within range of ocean shipping were lost to the enemy was emphasis shifted to attacks on land lines of communication.[6]

A successful campaign against shipping along the coasts of China and Indo-China depended upon the receipt of adequate supplies from India and the successful trans-

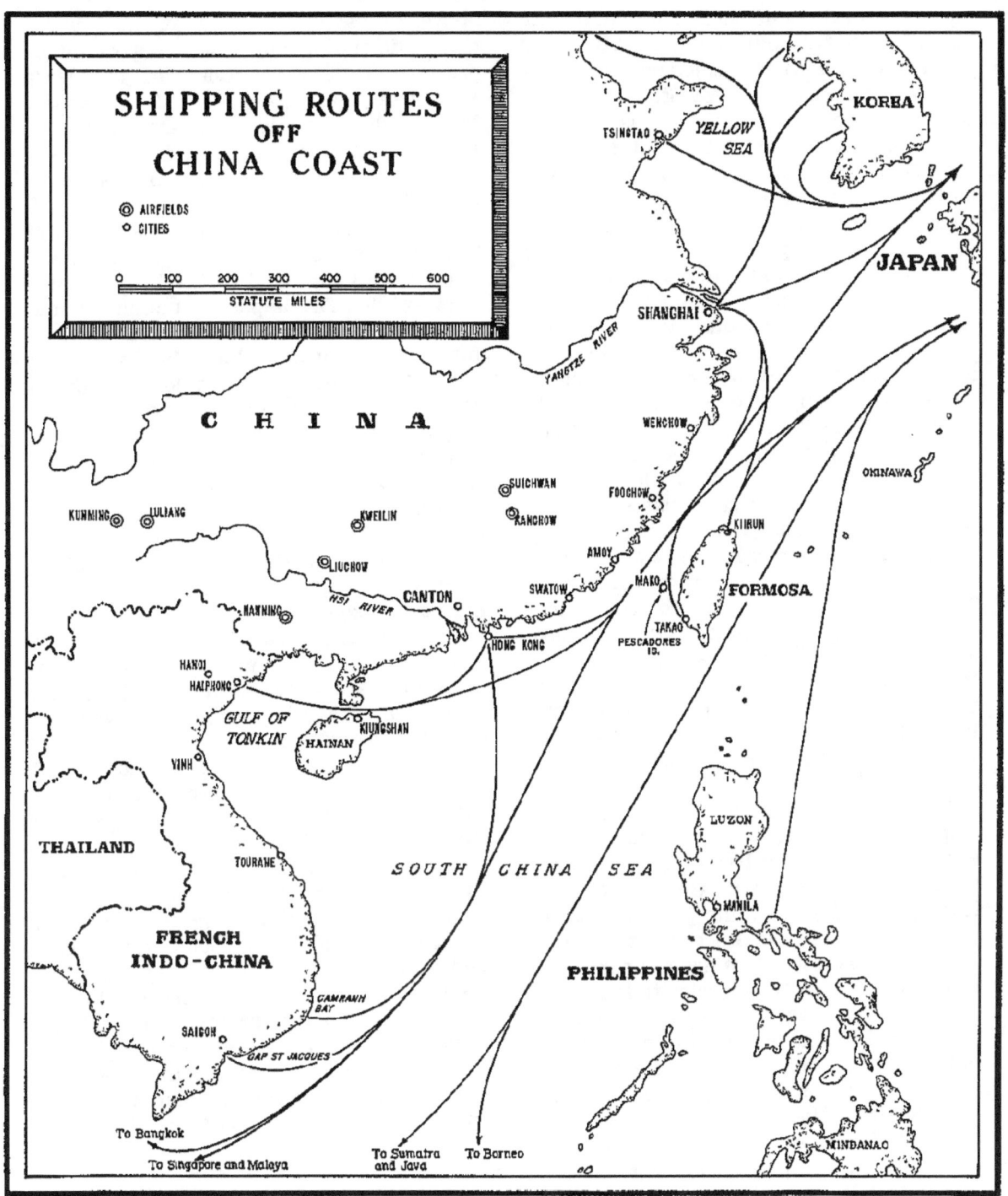

Map No 1

port of a portion of those supplies to air bases in east and south China, particularly to Suichwan, Kweilin, Liuchow, and Nanning. The Fourteenth Air Force did not receive the desired tonnage of gasoline and other items from India during 1943 or 1944 Adequate amounts of fuel were received at Kunming to fly antishipping strikes, in view of the priority these operations enjoyed, but delivery at Kunming was only half the story. Gasoline, bombs, and bullets for use against ocean shipping had to be transferred from Kunming to the eastern and southern bases, distances ranging from approximately 400 airline miles to Nanning to approximately 750 airline miles to Suichwan; the distance by road, railroad, or river was greater. Surface transport in China was never able to move all the necessary tonnage to the eastern bases, and the use of air transport was tremendously costly, amounting sometimes to as much as two tons consumed for each ton delivered. The inability of American forces to adequately supply the forward bases did have an inhibiting effect on shipping strikes. Even had General Chennault's demands for tonnage across the Hump been granted, the intra-China transportation weaknesses would still have hampered operations of all kinds.[7]

Absolutely essential to an effective antishipping campaign was retention of the eastern and southern bases from which sea sweeps could be flown General Stilwell feared, correctly as events proved, that an air offensive from eastern bases would provoke the Japanese into a ground campaign which would deny the airfields to the Allies. Chennault's answer to this was: "I will repeat what I have always maintained, namely, that I believe the Chinese ground armies can withstand any Japanese invasion, provided they are given adequate air support. This has been proven on many occasions and I am confident that this condition still holds."[8] The Japanese did, of course, capture the airfields, and this led to a controversy between Chennault and Stilwell partisans which has continued to this day. In his memoirs, General Chennault states that in making statements like the above, he "assumed . . . that the Chinese troops defending our . . . bases would be provided with some American lend-lease equipment," and that he did not expect that "Stilwell would . . . bitterly oppose sending a single American bullet to any Chinese army not under his direct supervision."[9]

Even if eventual loss of the eastern bases had been expected, the campaign against coastal shipping might still have seemed worth-while. The Japanese merchant marine was the strategic Achilles' heel of Japan, and any loss which the Fourteenth Air Force could inflict would be a direct contribution to the final defeat of the island empire. Every ship sunk, whether on its way south with men and munitions or returning to Japan with the products of the Indies, was a direct blow at Japan's war economy. The real question was whether air operations against shipping would be effective enough to justify the fuel and munitions expended

The campaign also promised returns in a tactical sense The absence of land communications between Occupied China and Indo-China made it possible to prevent cooperation between the two areas by sinking coastal shipping. Likewise, reinforcement of the occupied ports on the south China coast could be hindered, and supply of those ports could be made so uncertain as to make reinforcement inadvisable even though the men could be moved. Attacks on shipping would give valuable support to Allied forces in the Southwest Pacific and, to the extent to which they were successful, would speed the return to the Philippines. Lastly, attacks on shipping would probably drive some vessels farther out to sea and lead to routing down the east coast of Formosa, facilitating the operations of Allied submarines.[10]

TYPES OF ATTACKS

The campaign against shipping off the China and Indo-China coasts may, for purposes of description, be divided into four types of operation. Attacks on shipping in harbor and on harbor installations were made by heavy and medium bombers and fighters Likewise, all three types of aircraft carried out visual sea sweeps, though this was, by and large, a function of the bombers Heavy bombers with special radar equipment (SB-24's) for low altitude bombing (LAB) of shipping made night sweeps of Formosa Strait and the South China Sea Likewise, heavy bombers laid mines in Chinese, Indo-Chinese, and Formosan ports, and this mining campaign was strengthened by limited participation of B-29's of the XX Bomber Command.

Strikes on harbors and anchorages. From 1 January 1943 until the end of World War II, Fourteenth Air Force planes made 235 attacks on 30 harbors and anchorages, from Tsingtao in the north to Saigon in the south. Sorties per strike were few in number; sometimes only one aircraft hit a port, and many attacks were made by two P-40's or P-51's. The total number of sorties flown against harbor shipping and installations was in the neighborhood of 1,400, of which more than 350 were flown by B-24's, slightly more than 200 by B-25's, and more than 750 by P-40's, P-38's, or P-51's.

Hong Kong was the port hit hardest; it was the target for about 122 B-24, 75 B-25, and 167 fighter sorties. Haiphong, in Indo-China, was struck by some 99 B-24's, 12 B-25's, and 90 fighters. Hongay, attacked 29 times by a total of 11 B-25 and 103 fighter sorties, and Campha Port, struck 25 times by a total of 7 B-24, 12 B-25, and 67 fighter sorties, were the next most frequent targets. Samah Bay, Chikhom Bay, Fort Bayard, Nam Dinh, and Canton were other popular objectives [11]

In attacks on harbors and anchorages, B-24's generally bombed from medium altitude, and their strikes were more often directed against installations than against shipping One of their most successful attacks, however, was made at low altitude and sank four Japanese merchant ships anchored at Cap St Jacques, off Saigon. At Hong Kong, the Liberators cooperated with B-25's by bombing installations from medium altitude while the Mitchells swept in at mast height to skip-bomb shipping. While bombing harbor shipping alone or with fighter escort, B-25's always operated from minimum altitude, using their forward firepower to beat down opposing anti-aircraft fire Radar-equipped SB-24's returning from night sea sweeps in which they had discovered no shipping sometimes dropped their bomb loads on harbor installations, particularly Hong Kong.[12]

In the number of strikes flown, fighter aircraft played a major part in Fourteenth Air Force operations against harbors. P-40's, P-51's, and P-38's struck frequently from Kwangsi bases, Nanning in particular, at the many small ports along the east coast of Indo-China. Few large merchant ships were found by these fighter aircraft, but they made many attacks on coastal steamers, launches, and junks. The usual procedure was to make a sweep over the Gulf of Tonkin, then to attack a harbor if no shipping was found in the gulf In the harbors, shipping had first priority, but installations were bombed and strafed if no worth-while vessels were present. Often fighters would attack two or more Indo-China ports on the same mission By early 1944 these fighter strikes and the infrequent B-24 and B-25 strikes in the northern Indo-China area had driven larger shipping from the Gulf of Tonkin and, combined with attacks on Indo-China's railroads, had largely nullified the value of Indo-China to the Japanese. The loss of Nanning to Japanese forces in early 1945 reduced the pressure on Indo-Chinese harbors, but the pressure was renewed when Allied planes returned to this base in June of the same year

At the end of 1944, the Japanese occupation of major Allied bases in east China made Allied air attacks against harbors on the southeast coast more difficult. Strikes were continued, however, by using Suichwan and Kanchow airfields in Kiangsi Province. These fields were cut off from the main part of Free China by Japanese forces in the Canton-Hankow Railroad corridor, but they had been partially stocked with fuel and munitions before being isolated, and they received additional supplies by air transport. The tonnage consumed in supplying these bases was great, and operations were limited as a result, but SB-24 sweeps over Formosa Strait were continued for three more months, and a number of fighter strikes against Hong Kong and Swatow were made. The P-51 attacks on Hong Kong brought greatly exaggerated claims of ships sunk, probably sunk, and damaged. Nonetheless, the use of Hong Kong was greatly reduced after these attacks, though the generally desperate situation of the Japanese merchant marine and mines were probably more important in bringing about this reduction.[13]

According to a Joint Army-Navy Assessment Committee Report, Japanese Naval and Merchant Ship Losses During World War II (JANAC), which is the most authoritative analysis available on the subject, Fourteenth Air Force attacks on coastal harbors resulted in the sinking of only 16 merchant ships of 500 tons or over during World War II. This amounts to 40 percent of Fourteenth Air Force claims of ships sunk in such attacks. If, for lack of a better yardstick, claims of damage are discounted to the same extent, then perhaps 30 merchant ships were damaged by these strikes. JANAC is not without error, and the results of attacks on harbor shipping may have been slightly better than indicated. Similar discounting of claims leads to an estimate of 50 vessels of less than 500 tons sunk or damaged. Thus, though attacks on harbors were effective enough to be a constant hazard to Japanese shipping, the results were not nearly so good as was believed while the attacks were going on. As might be expected, bombing by B-24's and B-25's was much more effective against shipping than attacks by fighters. Six of the 16 ships credited as sunk were sent down by B-24's, nine by B-25's. So far as can be determined, fighters sank only one merchant ship of over 500 tons in attacks on harbors.[14]

Visual sea sweeps. All types of combat planes operational in China except P-47's and P-61's flew sea sweeps during World War II, but the fighters were effective only against small craft. Though P-40's and P-51's were effective in harassing junk, steamer, and launch traffic on the south China coast and the coast of Indo-China, the sinking of merchant ships of 500 tons or more was a prerogative of the medium and heavy bombers. The fighters now and then claimed to have sunk larger ships, but where these claims can be checked against JANAC, they prove erroneous

Sea sweep operations from China bases were originally assigned to the Mitchell bombers of the 11th Bombardment Squadron. The medium bombers ordinarily operated in pairs, flying parallel courses within sight of one another. When an enemy ship was sighted, one bomber flew slightly to the side and ahead of the other, using its machine guns and cannon to beat down antiaircraft fire, thus allowing the pilot and bombardier of the trailing plane to concentrate on the bombing problem. When a second run was necessary, or if a second target was found, the attacking aircraft exchanged places. Searches were made from rather low altitude—400 to 500 feet—and bomb runs were made at mast height. In China, as in the Pacific, the B-25 was efficient at this sort of work, and its effectiveness increased as later models with additional forward firepower became available. Operating from Kweilin, Suichwan, Kanchow, and, to a lesser degree, Nanning, the medium bombers could cover the Formosa Strait, a zone extending out more than a hundred miles into the South China Sea, and the Gulf of Tonkin. Enough planes, bombs, and gasoline for daily coverage of all these areas was not available, even had weather permitted such constant operation, but during late 1943 and early 1944 one or more teams of Mitchells were sent out nearly every day of good flying weather.[15]

B-24's of the 308th Bombardment Group arrived in China in March 1943 and began flying sea searches in May. Searches were not numerous during 1943, however, and most B-24 anti-shipping effort was devoted to the bombing of harbors. At the beginning of 1944, daylight sea sweeps were emphasized. Like the B-25's, the B-24's ordinarily hunted in pairs, making their searches on parallel courses as far apart as possible while maintaining visual contact with one another. The search altitude was normally 500 feet, and the heavy bombers came down as low as the faster B-25's to deliver attacks on shipping at sea. One plane bombed at a time, the second making a run if the first failed to sink the target. The B-24's ranged up the coast of China as far as Shanghai, over the Formosa Strait, and up the Ryuku chain almost as far as Okinawa. Farther south, they covered the South China Sea between southern Formosa, northwestern Luzon, and Hainan Island, and the coast of Indo-China as far south as Cap St. Jacques.[16]

Except for fighter sweeps in the Gulf of Tonkin and along the Kwangsi coast, daylight sea sweeps practically came to an end in June of 1944. After that time, the B-25's were needed for attacks on inland targets in direct or indirect support of the Chinese ground forces. The arrival of radar-equipped SB-24's enabled the 308th Group to search for and attack shipping by night, and this system, because more ships were found, was believed to be superior to daylight searches. The fall of major east China bases to the advancing Japanese made resumption of regular B-25 sweeps impossible, though sporadic medium bomber searches were flown from the isolated bases at Suichwan and Kanchow until they fell into Japanese hands.

Crews on visual shipping sweeps through 1943 and the first five months of 1944 claimed 48 merchant vessels sunk, 15 probably sunk, and 34 damaged. Checking these claims against JANAC reveals that only 25 ships of 500 tons or more* were actually sunk, or 52 percent of those claimed. If this same percentage factor be applied to the total of 23 vessels erroneously claimed as sunk, 15 claimed as probably sunk, and 34 claimed as damaged, an estimate of 40 merchant ships damaged seems reasonable. By use of the same factor, it is estimated that 35 smaller craft were sunk or damaged during the same period. This latter category was augmented considerably, however, by fighter sweeps during the remainder of the war, probably reaching a total of more than 400 powered craft, barges, junks, and sampans sunk or damaged. Much of the damage to these smaller craft, being from strafing alone, must have been superficial.[17]

Night sea sweeps. The most disappointing phase of the air war against shipping off the coast of China was the SB-24 campaign, although at the time the operations were carried out, they were believed to be highly successful. There was much dissatisfaction with visual sea sweeps because so many sorties discovered no shipping; fruitless consumption of gasoline was a serious problem for an air force afflicted with a chronic shortage of fuel. Maj. Gen. Howard C. Davidson, later commander of the Tenth Air Force, had recommended in June 1943 that B-24's with radar search equipment be made available for search of the waters within range of China-based aircraft.[18] "Visual search was at best of narrow range, subject to poor visibility and errors of omission."[19] On effective B-25 sea sweeps between 1 October 1943 and 26 May 1944, only 154 enemy ships were sighted, and only 45 of these were claimed as sunk. From January to April 1944, B-24's flew 52 effective sea search sorties, sighted only 13 enemy ships, and claimed only two as sunk. The narrow area covered by visual searches was believed to be partly responsible for the small number of ships sighted, but it was also believed that Japanese ships were taking advantage of the cover of darkness to move through the Formosa Strait.[20]

The arrival of SB-24's appeared to offer a solution to both of these problems, and insofar as the location of enemy shipping was concerned, this appearance was justified. The SB-24's flew 206 effective sorties between 24 May and 31 October 1944 and made radar contact with 620 vessels, 222 of which were attacked. The location of so many enemy ships was accomplished by the installation of SCR-717 radar search equipment in the SB-24's. At the common search altitude of 2,500 to 5,000 feet, the SCR-717 radar on occasion picked up targets as far away as 50 miles, and it was quite reliable within 30 miles.

The special equipment of the SB-24 was not limited to the search radar. It included an absolute altimeter which made it possible for the big bombers to make low alti-

---
*JANAC reports on only ships of 500 tons or more

tude runs against shipping at night without danger of flying into the water. The bombing equipment enabled the bombardier, by synchronizing his bombsight with the blip on the radar scope, to make blind bombing runs at shipping targets. Since night searches were more productive of targets, and since LAB attacks were believed to be accurate, practically all sea searches from June 1944 to early June 1945, when all except fighter sweeps came to an end, were flown by SB-24's at night.[21]

Blind bombing of shipping targets made it essential that precautions be taken which were not necessary for visual attacks; otherwise, the SB-24's might well attack an American submarine. To avoid this, certain areas were reserved for blind bombing operations.* Submarines were forbidden to enter these zones, and the SB-24's were forbidden to make attacks outside the zones. One of the two areas reserved for Fourteenth Air Force bombers was in the form of a semi-circle of 100 miles radius with Shanghai as its center. The other was an irregular area off the south China coast bounded by a line which, beginning on the coast approximately 100 miles northeast of Amoy, ran due east to Formosa, down the west coast of that island to a point south of Takao, then east southeast to a point about 100 miles east of Hainan Island, then southeast to the Indo-China coast just south of Tourane. Within this latter zone lay the Formosa Strait, the South China Sea approaches to Swatow, Hong Kong, and Hainan Island, and the Gulf of Tonkin. These zones were patrolled by Fourteenth Air Force SB-24's until the spring of 1945, at which time the search of the area became a responsibility of Far East Air Forces (FEAF) bombers based in the Philippines.[22]

Until the fall of Liuchow to the Japanese, SB-24's normally staged through that base for their missions. From November 1944 through January 1945, a number of searches were flown from Suichwan. Thereafter, the bombers had to fly from Luhang or Kunming, bases which were so distant from productive waters that the time spent in actual search was greatly reduced. Lack of bases and the ever-stringent supply situation led to abandonment of SB-24 missions from China bases in the spring of 1945.

During most of 1944, the searches ordinarily followed one of three courses, though there were many deviations. The first went from Liuchow to Swatow, then across the Formosa Strait and up the west coast of Formosa to the zone boundary; if no shipping was found bombs were often dropped on a secondary target in the Amoy or Swatow areas. A second route went from Liuchow to the waters in the Hong Kong area, then to Takao, then back down the China coast to Hong Kong, which usually served as a secondary target if no shipping was found. The third flight path went across the Gulf of Tonkin, then around Hainan Island to the south, then northeast to the China coast. Few flights were made to the Shanghai area.[23]

Usually two SB-24's departed on search, and one or more remained at Liuchow on alert ready to proceed to any good target which the searchers discovered and left afloat. When the radar operator on a searching plane located an enemy ship, the pilot turned toward it, gradually letting down to 400 feet altitude. At a range of 10-15 miles, the bomber flew a circle around the target in order to allow the radar operator to determine its size and, if a convoy, its composition. If a convoy was found, stragglers were preferred as targets. An attempt was made to make bomb runs at an angle of 45 degrees to the longitudinal axis of the enemy ship, but this was seldom achieved because it was difficult to determine the target's course before a run had been made, and after the initial attack the ship might take evasive action.

The bomb run was made at an indicated airspeed of 170 miles per hour at an altitude of 400 feet, and three or four bombs, fuzed for 4-5 seconds delay, were dropped 70 feet apart. The SB-24's carried either 10 or 12x500-lb. general purpose bombs (depending upon whether take-off had been accomplished by day or night), so three runs could usually be made. Ordinarily the first run took the enemy by surprise, but

---
*See Map No 1, p 3

antiaircraft fire was often encountered on second and third runs, making it important to choose a course which would permit as little fire as possible to bear on the bomber.[24]

Fourteenth Air Force intelligence officers realized that determination of results of bombing done in darkness presented a difficult problem Sometimes, though not often, the flash of a bomb's explosion might reveal a hit Crews believed that they could tell by the concussion of a bomb whether it had exploded on the target ship or in the water, but hits on a rock or reef might give the same effect. Since radar was not reliable for determining the size of the vessel attacked, there was a strong possibility that a junk might be mistaken for a merchant ship. It was decided to allow no claim of sinking or damage by night bombing unless there had been visual observation of the sinking, large fires were visible, the target blip disappeared from the radar screen and the set continued to operate perfectly; or a return to the area of bombing revealed that the target had disappeared and lifeboats were observed either visually or by radar [25]

Exactly what procedures intelligence officers used in applying these criteria is unknown, but a comparison of mission reports with Fourteenth Air Force claims leaves no doubt that the rules were interpreted very liberally. This tendency, combined with the unreliability of radar as a means of confirmation of damage and the natural tendency of crewmen to overestimate their accomplishments, led to gross exaggeration of the effectiveness of SB-24 strikes. From 1 June 1944 until the end of the war, LAB missions were credited with sinking 83 ships not in harbor or on the Yangtze River Actually they sank only 22 ships, little more than a fourth of the number claimed. Discounting the remainder of their claims to the same extent leads to an estimate of only 30 merchant ships damaged [26]

A better conception of the exaggerated nature of these claims may be gained by considering a statistical summary prepared by Fourteenth Air Force for the purpose of demonstrating the efficiency of LAB operations. According to this summary, LAB bombers flew 243 sorties between 24 May and 31 October 1944, attacked 222 ships, and sank 67 with a total estimated tonnage of 248,665, an average of 1,097 tons per sortie dispatched. In reality, the SB-24's succeeded in sinking only 10 ships during the period for a total tonnage of 28,569 Instead of the supposed average of 1,097 tons sunk per sortie dispatched, the bombers destroyed only 117 tons per sortie. In other words, the LAB missions were only one-ninth as effective in terms of tonnage sunk as was indicated by claims. Instead of the cost in bombs expended being under 4 tons per ship sunk, it was more than 30 tons. Likewise, the cost in fuel per ship sunk was more than 40,000 gallons rather than 5,600 gallons.

The responsibility for unrealistic claims of shipping sunk by LAB operations cannot be assigned to any one person, nor can any one factor be isolated as the principal cause for exaggeration Rather did one error compound another until gross inaccuracy resulted. Crews in China as elsewhere tended to overestimate the success of their efforts and therefore to exaggerate their accomplishments. The fact that LAB operations were carried out in darkness made accurate visual or photographic assessment of results impossible, even for the most conscientious assessor. Some known attacks were made on reefs and rocks, and no doubt there were others, some of which may have been reported as ships sunk or damaged. The size of ships was a difficult matter to determine by radar, and almost certainly some junks were destroyed and reported as merchant ships. Claims based upon radar observation were allowed, and under the best conditions radar was not a dependable means of determining whether a ship was hit or sunk When attacks were made in the neighborhood of thunderstorms, islands, or shoreline, radar observation was even more fallible. No doubt there was some duplication of claims, in attacks on convoys in which a ship was sunk after being attacked by two SB-24's, it was highly possible that each crew might claim a ship as sunk. Finally, Fourteenth Air Force intelligence officers failed to make allowances for these factors, failed to discount crew claims, and failed to check carefully for duplication. An example of the latter failure is evident in the assessment of a daylight mission by seven B-24's against six Japanese ships at anchor off Cap St Jacques Four of these vessels were sunk in a highly effective attack, but failure to allow for duplication resulted in claims that all six were sunk. If this could happen when the mission was flown in broad daylight, it was almost inevitable when attacks were made by radar at night.[27]

The completely unrealistic contemporary assessment of LAB attacks on merchant shipping off the China coast emphasizes the need for constant evaluation of the effectiveness of air operations In the case of night operations against fleeting targets, such evaluation may be difficult if not impossible, but the fact that completely accurate evaluation cannot be attained should never be an excuse for assuming effectiveness. In the case of the Fourteenth Air Force, such serious overestimation of the number and tonnage of ships sunk by LAB sweeps might have led to errors in strategic planning for the defeat of Japan though, happily, this was not the case. Quite probably, however, the effectiveness of Fourteenth Air Force operations as a whole were reduced by erroneous belief in the efficiency of night attacks on shipping. If the more than 3,000 tons of gasoline and more than 500 tons of bombs expended by the SB-24's during the Japanese offensive of 1944-1945 had been devoted to river shipping, interdiction of the roads and railroads, railroad repair shops, or to ground support, much more might have been accomplished. Of course the antishipping campaign was one of the factors determining the allocation of supplies to Fourteenth Air Force, and so it is possible that the bombs and gasoline would not have been available for other types of operation. In that case, however, all indications are that much better results could have been attained by devoting the effort expended on LAB sweeps to mining harbors. Perhaps, on the other hand, the actual sinking and damaging of Japanese shipping on the open sea was worth the effort expended—certainly the LAB sweeps had considerable value as a source of information on ship movements. But the fact remains that Fourteenth Air Force operations for a year, from the spring of 1944 to the spring of 1945, were based upon an erroneous estimate of the effectiveness of SB-24 operations.

Mining. In addition to the types of operation discussed above, the Fourteenth Air Force attacked enemy shipping by means of a mine-laying campaign. In proportion to the effort expended, mining was without question the most effective form of attack on merchant shipping. Probably mines laid in the Yangtze River were most effective of all, but the mining of ports was also highly successful.

The first mining mission from China was flown on the night of 16/17 October 1943, when three mines were laid in the approaches to Haiphong. Four more mines were laid in the same area on the night of 11/12 November. These mines sank two ships, making a strong case for continuation of the mine-laying campaign. In all, including 22 B-29 sorties to Shanghai, China-based aircraft laid 731 mines in seaports within their range. After FEAF bombers had moved forward to bases on Mindoro and Luzon, they added 517 mines to ports along the China coast. Mines laid in harbors were 1,000-lb. size, both magnetic and acoustic types. These were the only 1,000-lb types available to Fourteenth Air Force, and though either type could be swept by Japanese equipment, use of both types in the same harbor made sweeping much more difficult. Channels shallow enough for mines laying on the bottom to damage shipping and busy enough that mining would disrupt Japanese maritime schedules were selected as mining targets.[28]

Mine-laying was carried out on moonlight nights at low altitude—usually the mines were released from about 300 feet above the water. Bombers proceeded to the target singly and flew a predetermined course from a predetermined checkpoint in order to assure the placing of their loads in the desired area. Interception by the Japanese was seldom if ever attempted, and antiaircraft fire was weak and inaccurate when encountered at all B-24's flew 225 mining sorties over the Yangtze and coastal harbors from China bases, and only four were lost. None of the 22 B-29's which laid mines in the Shanghai area failed to return.[29]

The combined Fourteenth Air Force and FEAF effort laid 1,224 mines in 12 ports on or near the China coast. Hong Kong received the most attention, with 346 mines laid, and Shanghai ranked second with 292, thanks in the main to the 22 B-29 sorties. Hainan Strait was the dropping zone for 130 mines Takao received 116, and 114 were laid at Amoy. Other harbors mined were Canton, Haiphong, Kiirun, Mako, Swatow, Wenchow, and Samah Bay.[30]

"In considering the accomplishments of the mine laying campaign, it should be recognized that ship losses are but incidental to the primary objects of mining which are to delay and disrupt the enemy's shipping, disorganize his maritime supply system, and thereby deprive him of essential military and economic materials."[31] These purposes were served by the mining of Chinese coastal waters. After mining commenced, Haiphong was rarely if ever used by large enemy ships Mining of Chinese and Indo-Chinese ports seriously interfered with attempts to reinforce and supply the Japanese forces in Burma. Mines carried by a single aircraft, according to the Japanese, could close a port for a long period, due to the fact that their naval units were poorly equipped for sweeping. The mining of Takao in February 1944 closed that harbor for a week, and mines laid at Shanghai seriously interfered with the supply and reinforcement of Amoy, Foochow, Hong Kong, Formosa, and Hainan Island.[32]

Although the chief beneficial effect of the mining campaign, from the Allied point of view, was to disrupt Japanese maritime traffic, mines were also efficient in sinking and damaging ships Some 37 ships, amounting to more than 50,000 tons, were sunk by mines in Chinese coastal waters Fourteen of these were merchant ships of more than 500 tons, aggregating more than 45,000 tons. Some of the remaining vessels were small naval patrol craft, and the rest were merchant ships of less than 500 tons. An additional 37 ships, amounting to more than 110,000 tons, were damaged by mines Japanese naval officers noted that the fact that mining took place in shallow water was the only factor which kept many of these damaged vessels from sinking, particularly in Hong Kong Harbor. Shanghai, where 22 ships, some 36,000 tons, were sunk and 24 ships of 73,200 tons were damaged was the most fruitful area. However, 10 small ships totalling 4,500 tons were sunk at Hong Kong, and 12 vessels with a tonnage of 47,000 were damaged.[33]

EVALUATION

On the basis of the most reliable sources used in this chapter, it appears that Fourteenth Air Force, with some aid from FEAF and XX Bomber Command in mine laying, sank 77 merchant ships of 500 tons or more in Chinese and Indo-Chinese coastal waters. Adding 14 more such merchant ships sunk in the Yangtze River gives a war total of 91 merchant ships of approximately 238,000 tons. This amounted to 4.1 percent of the Japanese merchant tonnage sunk during World War II and 3 percent of Japan's total merchant fleet Additional credit must be given for seven small naval craft with a combined tonnage of perhaps 5,000 tons.

Compared with Fourteenth Air Force claims of 994,389 tons sunk, 441,700 tons probably sunk, and 861,600 tons damaged, and 32 naval vessels sunk or damaged, the above total seems ridiculously small The validity of the sources used then comes into question. Final authority for crediting or not crediting a sinking to Fourteenth Air Force has been JANAC This compilation is not without error, and since the directive setting up the committee stated that "Findings of the anti-Submarine Warfare Assessment Committee will be included in the overall evaluation of enemy losses without further review,"[34] the error probably lies in giving too much credit to submarines and not enough to air Careful study, however, leads to the belief that this error was small in the area in which Fourteenth Air Force operated Where Fourteenth Air Force claims give exact coordinates, no conflict with a submarine claim has been discovered. In no case where JANAC lists the cause of sinking as unknown or gives a submarine as the probable agent is there a claim by China-based planes in the area where the ship went down Since nearly all Japanese merchant ships over 500 tons are accounted for, there is little likelihood that China-based aircraft sank more than one or two such ships which do not appear in the assesssment. In other words, the Fourteenth Air Force sank little more, if any more, merchant shipping than has been credited to it in this study.

As indicated earlier, many claims of ships sunk were simply the results of errors in observation on the part of crews, the inability of radar to afford accurate information on damage, and the failure of intelligence officers to allow sufficiently for duplication of claims. Another highly probable cause of error was over-estimation of the size of the ships attacked. In night attacks, it is more than probable that many junks were bombed and reported as merchant ships. Even in daylight, crews might overestimate the size of ships attacked. When ships of more than 500 tons were attacked, overestimation of their size led to exaggeration in the claims of tonnage destroyed

In view of the fact that crews attacking in daylight could usually see whether or not their bombs struck the target, it seems probable that the proportion of damage in relation to sinkings was greater than they claimed; however, claims of damage were still greatly in excess of the number actually damaged. The aerial bomb, which could make a shambles of the inside of a ship without breaching the hull, was not as effective a weapon as torpedos or mines insofar as sinking ships was concerned. A bomb exploding under the water a few feet from the side of a vessel was more likely to sink it than a direct hit, but the crews were seeking direct hits, and they were no doubt tempted to assume that one or more direct hits meant that the ship would go down.

No doubt a number of ships hit so hard that the bomber crews believed they must surely sink managed to remain afloat and bring damage under control A compilation of damage inflicted on Japanese naval ships shows that many of them, even small craft, were damaged by air attack many times before being finally destroyed by a torpedo or a mine.[35] The same was probably true to a lesser degree of merchant ships Attacked in shallow harbors ships which suffered damage severe enough to have sunk them in deep water often merely settled to the bottom and could be pumped out and repaired later.

Allowing for all these factors, the tonnage of ships over 100 feet* in length sunk in the China Theater by Fourteenth Air Force attack or by mines laid by air may have amounted to one-third of the 994,389 tons claimed, though this allowance is probably too generous. The tonnage of ships over 100 feet claimed as probably sunk and damaged was 1,276,300 tons. No matter how much the claims and other sources are studied, there can be no hard estimate of the tonnage actually damaged, but a very plausible figure would be in the neighborhood of 500,000 tons, not counting damage inflicted by strafing alone.

Certainly these air operations from China against Japanese shipping were not essential to the Allied victory in the Pacific. A certain amount of support was given to Allied operations in Burma and the Southwest Pacific by these attacks, and a certain amount of damage was inflicted on the Japanese economy. Closing of the port of Haiphong was a real blow at Japan, and so was the attrition of shipping, however small it may have been. But it is self-evident that victory would have been delayed but little, if at all, had no China-based ocean shipping strikes been flown. It seems probable, moreover, that had the blind bombing zone been open to submarines, with Fourteenth Air Force efforts confined to mining of ports, the attrition of Japanese shipping could have been greater.

---

*Fourteenth Air Force used 100 feet in length rather than 500 tons as the breaking point between merchant shipping and small craft

Assuming the political and military necessity for maintaining Allied airpower in China, it is still necessary to question whether the effort devoted to ocean shipping was justified. The gasoline and munitions used for sea sweeps and bombing attacks on harbors might well have been expended more wisely on other targets. In keeping with the antishipping program, heavier attacks on river shipping would have sunk or damaged some merchant ships and might have helped the almost helpless Chinese ground forces. Much of the bomb and fuel tonnage devoted to sea sweeps and harbor strikes could profitably have been applied to an intensified mining campaign. With the advantage of hindsight, and taking into account the remarkable success of B-29 mining of Japanese home waters, the student of the war in the Pacific can suggest that had all the bomber effort expended on sea sweeps and harbor attacks been devoted to mine laying, the Yangtze River and all ports from Shanghai to Saigon could have been closed to Japanese shipping by September of 1944. Such concentration on mining might well have destroyed as much or more shipping than was destroyed by the Fourteenth Air Force in all types of operations, and the adverse effect on Japan's economy and the defense of her empire would have been great—far greater than the effect achieved by the antishipping campaign as it was executed.

CHAPTER II

INTERDICTION OF RIVER LINES OF COMMUNICATION IN CHINA

IMPORTANCE OF RIVER TRANSPORTATION

CHINA HAS TENS of thousands of miles of navigable rivers, of which four streams, the Yangtze, the Hsiang, the Hsi, and the Pei,* carried the main burden of supplies in China during World War II. Chinese highways were primitive in construction and poorly maintained at best; the neglect and sabotage resulting from the war made it impossible to use them for transferring material any great distance. Further to limit the usefulness of the roads, vehicles were scarce and fuel was not available for those in use. The railroads were far more useful than the highways, but the rail net was thin, its capacity was low, and in many areas the lines had been systematically destroyed. Therefore the rivers, whenever they were available, were used for the transport of both civilian products and military supplies.

Thus the rivers were extremely important to the Japanese war effort in China. The Japanese were a maritime people, and the rivers made it possible for men and munitions to be delivered directly from Japan to armies in the interior of China. Likewise, the rivers served as routes by which raw materials, mineral ores particularly, could be sent from the Chinese interior to Japan. Finally, when the Japanese mounted an offensive in China away from the railroads, it was necessary that they use a navigable river as the axis of their advance in order that a supply line might be available until roads and railroads to the rear could be put into operation.

The Yangtze is the most important of the four main rivers; it rises in northern Tibet and flows in a generally eastern direction past Chungking, Ichang, Hankow, and Nanking into the East China Sea just north of Shanghai. Over 3,000 miles long, the Yangtze was the main Japanese route into central China. The famous gorges between Ichang and Chungking were a barrier to deeper penetration by this route, but 3,000-ton ships could reach Hankow in low water, 5000-ton ships at high water. This city became the main Japanese supply base in central China. At high water, 3000-ton ships drawing 14 feet could proceed upstream as far as Ichang, and this port could be reached by 1,000-ton craft drawing 7 feet at low water stage. Until air operations successfully closed the Yangtze to large vessels, it was the main line of supply to the Japanese forces along its course. Downstream traffic on the river carried iron ore and other raw materials from China to Japan.

The Hsiang River rises near Kweilin and flows northeast to Hengyang and then north via Changsha to Tungting Lake, through which the channel of the Yangtze also passes. Large river steamers could ply between Changsha and the Yangtze most of the year, and steam launches could reach Hengyang during the high water season. Small native craft carried goods as far upstream as Hsingan. The Hsiang passes through the heart of rich Hunan Province, and it served as the supply route for the Japanese against Fourteenth Air Force bases along its course during the summer and fall of 1944.

The Hsi River rises in southern Yunnan Province and flows eastward past Nanning, Wuchow, and Samshui. Several channels

---
* See Map No 2, p 15

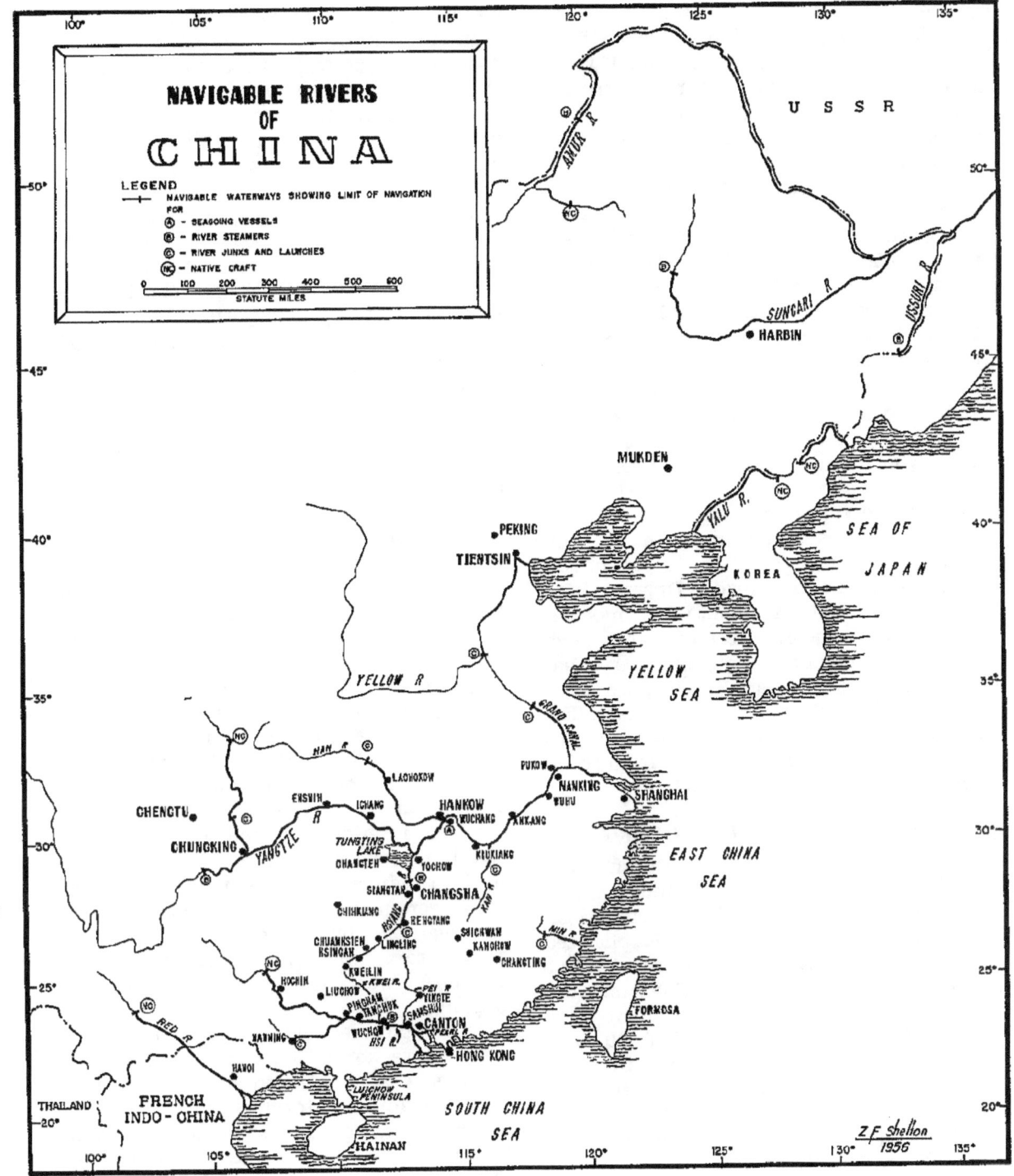

Map No. 2

in the delta below Canton afford access to the sea. The Kuei, a tributary which flows into the Hsi at Wuchow, rises near Kweilin and is connected by a canal with the Hsiang. During the high water season vessels drawing 13 feet ascend the Hsi to Wuchow, and steamers drawing not more than 7 feet reach this river port all year. Throughout the year, also, junks and gasoline launches can navigate the Hsi to Nanning and the Kuei to Kweilin. The Hsi and its tributaries served as the supply line for Japanese forces advancing north from Canton against Fourteenth Air Force bases in the summer and fall of 1944.

The Pei River, which rises south of Hengyang and flows south to the delta below Canton, was not so important as the rivers already mentioned, though it has served for centuries as part of the trade route between the Yangtze Valley and Canton. It did serve the Japanese as an alternate line of communication for part of the length of the Canton-Hankow Railroad. During high water, a period of about five months, launches drawing five feet of water could proceed upstream to Yingte, but above that point shallows and rapids restricted navigation to the smallest of native craft. The Japanese made considerable use of this stream during their withdrawal from south China in the summer of 1945.[1]

TYPES OF SHIPPING ON CHINESE RIVERS

For the sake of convenience, the shipping used by the Japanese on Chinese inland waterways may be divided into four classifications, though it must be emphasized that the distinction between the various types was not always sharp. The first category, of course, would be merchant shipping. Theoretically, ships of 5,000 tons could make use of the Yangtze as far upstream as Hankow, and smaller ocean-going ships might proceed as far as Ichang. The *Marus** plying the Yangtze included freighters, transports, colliers, small tankers, and, especially, vessels designed to carry both passengers and cargo.

Smaller powered craft of various kinds

—river steamers, steam, gasoline and diesel launches, and tugboats—may be considered a second category. The line dividing steamers and steam launches was not a clearly defined one, though generally the distinction was a matter of size. In June of 1944 there were nine large passenger steamers on the Yangtze, 310 feet to 360 feet in length, ranging from 2,800 to 4,100 tons, for an aggregate of almost 30,000 tons. These craft could, of course, carry cargo as well as passengers, but their most important function was as troop transports.

Smaller river steamers, ranging from 50 feet to more than 200 feet, were to be found on the Yangtze, and after the summer of 1944, on the Hsiang and Hsi. Many of these were small colliers, designed to carry coal down to Shanghai. The total number available is unknown, but those located on the Yangtze west of Nanking were estimated to total more than 50,000 tons in June of 1944.

The term launch was used to describe any small conventional vessel with steam or internal combustion propulsion. Some of these were lighters used for unloading larger vessels, but most were designed for commerce on Chinese rivers in those upper reaches where larger steamers could not go. These craft, which could move supplies much more rapidly than native boats, were very useful to Japanese troops advancing into the interior of China, but they were not numerous enough to bear the whole load in waters suited to their draft, and there were many parts of the smaller rivers in which they could not operate. Pilot reports leave the impression that these launches were especially vulnerable to strafing.

Other powered craft found on Chinese rivers were not so important to the Japanese as those mentioned above. Tugs, used for propelling and towing barges and sometimes junks, were fairly common and were often attacked. There were a few self-propelled ferry boats. Powered barges, junks, and sampans were encountered occasionally, as were motor boats of small size.

Barges were a third category of craft used by the Japanese on China's rivers.

---
*Japanese merchant ships

Barges had the advantages of shallow draft and great carrying capacity, but since they had to be pushed or towed by deeper-draft tugs or pulled by steamers, the advantages of shallow draft were more apparent than real. Barges ranged in size from small 40-foot affairs to huge 200-foot types which could be used only on the Yangtze. As noted above, a few barges were self-propelled.

Native craft, the fourth and final classification, varied greatly in size and description, but generally were classified as junks or sampans. Junks, which carried sails, were the largest, and ranged from more than 100 feet to less than 50 feet. Those junks found on the rivers were easily identified by their square bows and square lug sails. Often the sails were of bamboo matting rather than sailcloth. Junks drew little water, and the smaller ones were light enough to be poled on shallow streams when the winds were unfavorable. Gasoline engines were installed in a few junks.

Sampans might be 80 or 90 feet long, but were more commonly 30 to 40 feet. These were the typical light boats of Chinese rivers and their cargo capacity ranged up to 10 tons for the larger sizes. Sampans were easily identified because the center and after part were usually covered by an awning of bamboo matting. They were normally propelled by a large scull which projected over the stern, but internal combustion engines were sometimes installed.

All of these craft were used by the Japanese in moving troops and supplies over Chinese rivers. The larger steamers remained on the Yangtze, but smaller ones might go up the Hsiang to Siangtan or up the Hsi to Wuchow. Launches and barges used the same waters plied by steamers and also were found in shallower parts of the rivers, but not many of them made the voyage all the way to the supply head. Ordinarily men and munitions were transported aboard junks and sampans during the last stages of a river journey.

The crews of nearly all river craft were Chinese, though Japanese captains and officers might direct the activities of the steamers. Even for smaller craft it was advisable to have some Japanese personnel aboard to prevent pilfering of supplies and to check the tendency of the Chinese crews to turn back or go into hiding when attacked by Allied aircraft.[2]

WEAPONS AND TACTICS

At one time or another, every type of Allied combat aircraft in China except the B-29's was used for attacking river shipping, but B-25's, P-40's, and P-51's bore the main burden of this type of attack. These bombers and fighters used demolition, fragmentation and incendiary bombs, machine guns, cannon, and rockets against river craft.

B-24's, which were the most favored aircraft for sea sweeps, proved unsuited for bombing river shipping. Because of their low speed and weak forward firepower, which made them too vulnerable to ground fire during daylight, they were never used for daylight sweeps over the rivers. The 308th Bombardment Group did attempt night sweeps of the Yangtze, using LAB radar, but the equipment proved to be unsuitable for this type of work. The radar often failed to reveal shipping near the river banks until it was too late for a bomb run to be made. Furthermore, the necessity for flying an ever-changing course in order to follow the river prevented efficient use of the radar. Therefore attacks on river shipping were left to lighter aircraft.[3]

Both P-47's and P-38's were used now and then against shipping, but these fighters were secondary to the P-40's and P-51's. The P-38's of the 449th Fighter Squadron were based in west China during most of the war and therefore had little chance to attack river shipping except on an occasional flight over the Hsi River. When detachments of P-38's were based on eastern airfields, they were too useful as top cover for bomber formations to be diverted to shipping targets. The P-47's of the 312th Fighter Wing were based in the north for defense of the B-29 bases and could find few shipping targets within range, since Japanese shipping seldom went above Yochow during 1944 and 1945.[4]

B-25 bombers of the 341st Bombardment

Group and the Chinese-American Composite Wing (CACW) made many attacks on river shipping. For strikes against large craft, the B-25's carried 500-lb bombs and flew up or down the course of the river in pairs, the lead plane about a mile ahead of the wingman When a target was sighted, the lead plane went in at mast height, using machine guns to beat down defensive fire from the ship. Usually three bombs were dropped in trail, increasing the likelihood that one would strike the target. If further attacks were needed, the trailing B-25 swept over the target, repeating the tactics of the leader. Unless the ship was patently defenseless, the B-25's did not make a second pass; the medium bombers, like the B-24's, had good reason to fear ground fire, and an attack without benefit of surprise was asking for trouble. Ships and large rivercraft on the Yangtze had little room for evasive action, and the first pass often succeeded in inflicting damage.⁵ Against smaller craft. the B-25's flew in the same manner, but they used machine guns, fragmentation bombs, and cannon.

When the cannon-carrying Mitchells, the B-25G and B-25H, came off the production lines, there were high hopes that they would prove useful in China. General Chennault sent a special request for G's for use against boats The aircraft were forthcoming, but the results of their employment were far below what had been expected. The B-25G was not maneuverable enough to follow the winding courses of the Chinese rivers at low altitude and therefore had to make a high approach which alerted defending gunners. The B-25H was more maneuverable than the G, but it was slower, tended to be nose-heavy, and carried no co-pilot. This last feature might well mean the loss of an aircraft and crew when the pilot was hit by ground fire at low altitude. The necessity for a long low-altitude run for a cannon attack on shipping made ground fire all the more dangerous

Use of the 75-mm. cannon had drawbacks in addition to the hazards involved. In combat, pilots found it difficult to attain any great degree of accuracy Statistical analysis showed that a B-25 attacking a ship with the cannon had 18 to 33 percent expectation of scoring hits. This compared unfavorably with the expectation of 25-35 percent hits with 500-lb. bombs, especially when the greater destructive power of bombs was taken into account.

Finally, there were few targets well suited to the cannon. Demolition bombs brought much better results against ships and river steamers. Machine guns and fragmentation bombs were just as effective against smaller craft. Thus the cannon was "only an occasionally useful adjunct to the armament and rarely a necessary one "⁶

Before the end of 1943, river sweeps had forced the Japanese to halt daylight movement of large shipping on the upper Yangtze, except when bad weather afforded protection from air attack. Likewise, during the offensive up the Hsiang Valley in the summer of 1944, road and river sweeps soon put a halt to daylight movement. When this development became apparent, the Mitchells of the CACW and the 11th Bombardment Squadron, already accustomed to night harassment of Japanese airdromes, began night sweeps of the roads and rivers. For night search and attack the Yangtze was divided into two target areas, one from Yochow to Hankow, the other from Hankow to Kiukiang. On nights of clear weather and bright moonlight B-25's covered these assigned sectors and often discovered Japanese shipping by sighting the wake of a moving vessel or the shadow cast in the moonlight by an anchored ship. Once a worth-while target was discovered, a conventional low-level attack was made. The 11th Bombardment Squadron and the 68th Composite Wing reported good results from these missions.

On the Hsiang, few ships were to be found which were large enough to justify the expenditure of a 500-lb. bomb. Mitchells which swept this river used fragmentation bombs and machine guns against the launches, barges, junks, and sampans which night searches revealed. Typical of successes achieved was a CACW report of 12 direct hits, 10 near misses, and 10 misses with bombs on 100 sampans north of Hengyang on the night of 10/11 August 1944 and claims of more damage by strafing. A later night sweep from the same base resulted in claims of a dozen motor launches sunk The 491st Bombardment Squadron, which flew similar sweeps over the Hsi River, reported no results comparable with those obtained on the Hsiang. Night sweeps of the Hsiang Valley from Chihkiang continued until the end of the war, but as the Japanese repaired the roads and railroads to their rear, trains and motor transport were attacked more often than shipping.[7]

Because of their speed, maneuverability, strafing power, and comparatively low gasoline consumption, the P-40 and P-51 were the planes used most often for daylight attacks on river shipping. P-51's eventually replaced the P-40's completely, but the older plane had one advantage over the newer; it could take punishment sufficient to bring down the P-51, fly home, and be ready to fly again in a short time. For this reason, many pilots preferred the P-40 for low altitude strafing and bombing attacks. The advantages of the P-51 more than offset its vulnerability to ground fire, however. It had armament and bomb-carrying capacity equal to that of the P-40, was much more maneuverable, was a superb dive-bomber, and had a much longer range.[8]

Dive-bombing was a frequent tactic of China-based fighters in attacks on shipping. The nature of the target controlled the procedure used, and dive-bombing was usually employed against shipping in river ports known to be heavily defended, such as Yochow, Wuhu, Hankow, and Kiukiang. The fighters normally approached such a target at an altitude of 10,000-12,000 feet. Just before diving, they climbed a bit to lose air speed, then winged over into a 60-80 degree dive. Pilots normally released their bombs at 5,000 feet, an altitude which permitted a pull-out above effective range of most small-arms fire. On occasion, however, pilots came down to 2,000 feet before releasing their bombs, then left the target area at minimum altitude, utilizing the speed built up in the dive as a means of escaping defensive fire.

Dive-bombing had a second advantage in addition to protection from ground fire. Since planes waiting their turn to bomb the target served as top cover for those committed to the dive, attacks could be made when enemy fighters were in the vicinity. This was not true of minimum altitude bombing, because such attacks gave the enemy fighters a decided altitude advantage.[9]

Most of the fighters engaged in dive-bombing carried demolition bombs, usually 500-pounders, so only fairly large river vessels were suitable targets. Minimum altitude attacks could deliver delayed-action demolition bombs, parafrags, or incendiaries. Minimum altitude tactics were almost always the ones employed against ships in motion, away from the protection of shore-sited antiaircraft guns. Often, too, attacks against shipping in river ports were delivered from mast height. The attacking fighters sought surprise by approaching as low as possible and by building up speed to approximately 300 miles per hour when 25 miles or so away. After bombs were released the fighters continued on the deck until clear of the target area. Some pilots averred that this type of attack on a heavily defended area afforded more safety than dive-bombing.

Small demolition bombs, parafrags, and, in 1945, napalm tanks were used in attacking small craft from minimum altitude. Single junks, sampans, or small powered craft made poor targets for bombing of any kind, though they were highly vulnerable to strafing. It was not unusual, however, to find scores and even hundreds of small river craft moored side by side along the banks of the Yangtze, Hsiang, and Hsi Rivers during periods of large-scale enemy movement. These made worth-while bombing targets, especially for fragmentation bombs and napalm.

Until late in the war, it was necessary to provide fighter escort of practically all low-altitude river sweeps in China, but this was accomplished without loss of striking power. The planes assigned to a mission were divided into two equal flights. While one flight bombed and strafed, the other remained aloft on watch for enemy interceptors. When the attacking flight had expended its bombs and three-fourths of its ammunition, it climbed back to altitude and provided cover while the second flight dropped down to bomb and strafe. When fighters escorted B-25's on low-altitude river sweeps, they usually went down and strafed after the bombers had completed their attacks and turned back toward base.

As may be judged from the above, strafing was the tactic most often used by fighter aircraft against shipping and was an important part of B-25 attacks. Fighters had six forward-firing .50-cal. machine guns. B-25's had as many forward-firing machine guns, the 75-mm. cannon, and four more machine guns, located in the top turret and the tail, which could be brought to bear on occasion. Some Fourteenth Air Force fighters were equipped with rockets, but these weapons proved inaccurate and highly prone to malfunction.[10]

Other than attempts to intercept enemy night bombers over Fourteenth Air Force bases, there were few efforts in China to use conventional day fighters for night attack on Japanese targets. When the 5th Fighter Group sent two P-40's over the Hsiang Valley from Chihkiang on the night of 25 September 1944, one failed to return, and the experiment was not repeated. When P-61's arrived in the theater, they flew some night intruder missions and attacked shipping as well as other targets. The P-61's were very few in number, however, and even then the planes available were restricted in their operations because of the chronic gasoline shortage in China.[11]

Against merchant ships and large river craft found on the Yangtze, the 500-lb bomb was the most effective weapon used by the Fourteenth Air Force for direct attack. Whether delivered by dive-bombing or by minimum-altitude attack, the explosive effect of this bomb was sufficient to guarantee sinking or heavy damage when hits were made on the target. Near misses with this bomb occasionally sank ships on Chinese rivers and effected damage more often. Smaller demolition bombs, 250-lb. and 100-lb., were used to some extent. They were effective against small steamers, tugs, launches, and barges, but were not nearly so effective as the 500-pounder against larger vessels.

As related above, the early rockets proved unreliable. Whether from lack of knowledge and experience on the part of pilots or because of faults in the rockets, they seldom hit the targets at which they were aimed. The tubes mounted under the wings of P-40's or P-51's reduced the speed and maneuverability of the aircraft, adding to the discontent of pilots. Malfunctions were almost always reported after rocket attacks. Finally, the destructive power of the new weapons was not great enough to make them a substitute for bombs against large boats, and machine guns gave better results than rockets against small craft.

Parafrags, 20-lb. fragmentation bombs equipped with parachutes which delayed their fall long enough for the attacking aircraft to get out of range of fragments, were used against small craft by both B-25's and fighters. Such bombs seldom sank the flimsy sampans and junks against which they were directed, though they might seriously damage boat and cargo and inflict casualties on personnel. "The probabilities are that the combined .50-cal. machine gun fire of fighters and B-25's . . . damaged far more enemy river traffic than all the frags used by the same planes."[12]

Strafing was surprisingly effective against powered craft. Small steamers, launches, and tugs were quickly brought to a halt by persistent strafing, and .50-cal. bullets damaged larger vessels. Several times it was observed that the crews of powered craft ran their vessels aground and sought shelter when strafing attack commenced. These grounded vessels, according to reports, were frequently attacked and burned by Chinese guerrillas, who secured considerable equipment from them.

Like fragmentation bombs, strafing was more likely to damage than to sink the sampans and junks which were the most frequently discovered targets on Chinese rivers. Pilot reports indicate, however, that personnel aboard such craft often either were killed by the strafing or drowned when they found dubious safety by jumping into the water. Strafing was most effective when the targets carried some inflammable cargo; at any rate, when such was the case, pilots could see some visible results of their work.

Napalm might have been the ideal weapon for use against the large concentrations of river craft so often attacked in the summer and autumn of 1944. Unfortunately, this incendiary mix was not available for widespread use in China until the spring of 1945, and by that time large groups of river craft were hard to find. When such concentrations were discovered, however, napalm proved an effective weapon. On 1 June 1945, for example, 18 P-51's found at Yochow a great number of junks, most of them loaded with supplies According to claims, 53 of these junks were destroyed by fires set by napalm, and 114 were damaged by fire and strafing.[13]

As was true in regard to attacks on ocean shipping, mines were the most effective weapon used against large river shipping by the Fourteenth Air Force. Mining was confined to the Yangtze River because only in that stream were targets suitable for mines likely to be found All told, some 508 mines, all delivered by B-24's, were laid in the Yangtze, the great majority of them above Nanking. More than half were 1,000-lb. mines, and of the 1,000-pounders, most, if not all, were magnetic The number of acoustic type mines was negligible, if any at all were laid The remainder of those laid were 550-lb. contact mines which were set to drift downstream under the surface. All mine-laying in the Yangtze was carried out at night.

The mining campaign was so successsful that the river above Nanking was closed to metal-hulled ships for several periods during 1944 and was closed completely to such ships in the spring of 1945. Thus the usefulness of the Yangtze as a supply route was greatly reduced.

The river could never be completely closed by mining because a significant proportion of the Japanese supplies were transported on small wooden vessels. Magnetic mines had no effect on such craft, the contact mines sank some of them, but the remainder continued to ply the river. General Chennault felt the need for a small floating contact mine which would be effective against such shipping, but the 550-lb. Mark 19 was the only available type which approached his specifications, and its weight made it impossible to lay them in great enough numbers to significantly reduce the amount of light shipping. Throughout 1944 and 1945 junks and sampans operated on the Yangtze at night with considerable freedom [14]

JAPANESE DEFENSE OF RIVER SHIPPING

Japanese defenses against attacks on river shipping were conventional, fighters, ground fire, and passive measures. Enemy fighters frequently intercepted U.S. aircraft during 1943 and 1944; U.S. airmen were usually victorious in these encounters to the extent of inflicting losses on the interceptors greater than those sustained. On the other hand, these interceptions did seriously interfere with the attacks on shipping By the summer of 1944, Japanese fighter strength in central China was almost exhausted, and the resulting increased effectiveness of shipping strikes gave serious concern to Japanese commanders. To counter this development, the enemy in September transferred the 29th and 22d Air Regiments from Japan and Formosa to China and gave air cover to traffic on the Hsiang River. This support greatly aided the Japanese advance by making it possible to move supplies by river to Siangtan But the newly arrived air units withdrew to Japan and Formosa in early October, leaving the air over the battle area completely dominated by the Fourteenth Air Force. This condition continued to the end of the war, and attacks on river shipping were seldom interfered with by the Japanese Air Force after October 1944 [15]

Antiaircraft fire was responsible for most losses suffered by planes attacking shipping. Heavy antiaircraft guns (75-mm.) and 40-mm. guns were sited at the major Yangtze ports, such as Hankow, Kiukiang, and Nanking, but these weapons caused little damage to dive-bombers and were almost useless against minimum-altitude attacks. Much more effective were 20-mm. and smaller automatic weapons sited on shore and on the larger river vessels. These weapons, and the rifles and machine guns carried by well-trained ground units often found in the vicinity of river targets, could be quickly brought to bear on attacking aircraft, and frequently shot them down. Gunboats, usually found at the main river ports, bristled with automatic weapons and were rightly feared by attacking pilots. A statistical analysis of losses of fighter aircraft from July 1944 through February 1945 showed that "attacks against water transportation targets were much more costly per 1,000 sorties than those against land transportation targets."[16]

As Japanese airpower decreased in effectiveness, ground fire improved. All Fourteenth Air Force units which operated over the Yangtze and Hsiang Rivers during the autumn of 1944 noted the increased volume and accuracy of the Japanese antiaircraft fire. The rate of loss from this opposition increased, but it never reached such a level as to pose a threat to continued operations. Losses of the 23d Fighter Group, 68th Composite Wing, were 50 aircraft from all causes during the last three months of 1944, but 3,572 sorties were flown by the group during those three months. Losses of CACW units were somewhat higher, but not alarmingly so. In a majority of cases, pilots whose planes were shot down were sheltered by the Chinese and eventually returned to their units.[17]

Passive defense measures were probably more helpful to the Japanese than either interceptors or antiaircraft fire. Under air attack the enemy simply stopped moving during daylight hours, except when the weather was so bad that air attack was improbable, but this relinquishment of daylight movement did not give full protection, because boats might be attacked by B-25 intruders, or they might be found and destroyed in their daytime hiding places. Dark and cloudy nights afforded much more protection to shipping than periods of bright moonlight. Boats left in the open during the day were quite likely to be attacked, but the Japanese were adept at camouflage and soon learned to run river boats in to the shore at dawn and cover them with green foliage. When so concealed a boat, even a fairly large one, was hard to detect by an observer in a fast-moving airplane.[18]

Against mines, the Japanese along the Yangtze were almost defenseless. No sweeping equipment whatever was available when the first mines were laid. Eventually a few sweeps were obtained from Japan, but they were too few to keep the river clear. Usually the mine-laying aircraft went undetected, and the existence of the minefield was unknown until a ship was hit. This led, understandably, to a great deal of confusion, especially when a drifting mine exploded, leading to a false conclusion that a minefield was located in the area. Even when a real minefield was discovered, mud and the river currents hampered sweeping to such a great extent that some ships were sunk by mines in supposedly cleared areas.[19]

CAMPAIGNS AGAINST RIVER SHIPPING

Attacks on Yangtze shipping. Throughout its wartime existence, Fourteenth Air Force waged war on Yangtze River shipping. Shipping on the Yangtze was a prime strategic target because raw materials for Japanese factories came down the river on their way to Japan. During 1943 and 1944, the Japanese were engaged in a great effort to increase the transportation of raw materials from China. Thus blows at shipping on Yangtze were direct blows at the Japanese economy.[20]

Likewise, until late in the war, the Yangtze was the chief supply route for Japanese armies in central China. The city of Hankow became the chief base for offensive operations, and to this city all supplies from Manchuria and Japan were brought by river until the opening of the Peking-Hankow Railroad provided a tenuous alternate supply line at the end of 1944. Fortunately for the Japanese, they were able to obtain most of their food and forage in the occupied areas of China. Nonetheless, clothing, replacements, gasoline, and all types of munitions had to be moved to Hankow by means of the river during 1943 and 1944. Thus blows against shipping on the Yangtze had a direct tactical bearing on the Japanese armies in central China.[21]

Fourteenth Air Force efforts during 1943 were feeble in comparison with later years, but along the Yangtze strikes were numerous and effective enough. Claims during the year amounted to 8 ocean-going ships, 9 powered craft, and 1 gunboat sunk; vessels probably sunk and damaged were 9 ships, 4 gunboats, and 31 powered craft. As early as June of 1943 daylight movement of large ships above Nanking came to a halt, and smaller vessels moved at considerable risk.[22]

From Fourteenth Air Force bases in Hunan Province, chiefly Kweilin and Hengyang, attacks on Yangtze shipping continued during the first five months of 1944. Claims for the period were for 3 ships, 17 powered craft, 9 barges, and 58 junks and sampans sunk. Vessels claimed as probably sunk and damaged included 10 merchant ships, 41 powered craft, 3 gunboats, 7 barges, and 32 junks and sampans. Though pilots engaged in river sweeps regarded the hunting as poor, these attacks convinced the Japanese that a railroad should be opened between Hankow and north China, and they confirmed the Japanese in their belief in the necessity for eliminating American airfields in east China. These attacks did not, however, prevent the buildup at Hankow of troops and supplies destined to be used in the offensive against the airfields.[23]

From June through November 1944, the Fourteenth Air Force was struggling desperately to check the Japanese drive on its east China bases. Therefore the greater part of its effort was devoted to support of the Chinese ground forces and attacks on lines of communication leading from Hankow to the battle zone. Most sorties were directed against shipping on the Hsiang River and Tungting Lake until the companion drive north from Canton made the Hsi River a prime target area. The roads which supplemented these waterways also received attention. Planes based at Hengyang, Kweilin, Liuchow, Lingling, and Chihkiang carried out these strikes.

From other bases, however, Suichwan, Kanchow, and especially Enshih, some fighter missions were directed at the Yangtze, supplemented by a few bomber sorties from Kweilin. In all, 46 missions, amounting to 7 B-24, 33 B-25, and about 275 fighter sorties struck shipping on this river between 1 June and 30 November 1944. No ocean-going ships were claimed as sunk, but 14 powered craft, some of them large river steamers, 3 barges, 2 gunboats, and 39 sampans were claimed. Claimed as probably sunk or damaged were 6 merchant ships, 35 powered craft, 4 gunboats, 38 barges, and 66 sampans. Though these attacks did not destroy any great amount of shipping and represented only a small proportion of Allied air effort in China during the period, the commander of the Japanese forces in China stated after the war that June 1944 was the turning point in Yangtze shipping. From that month on, the arrival of supplies shipped up the river could not be depended upon, and construction of the Peking-Hankow Railroad was pushed.[24]

If the Japanese had expected the capture of the main Allied bases in east China to bring a halt to attacks on the Yangtze, they were doomed to disappointment. Cut off from the rest of Free China by the Japanese occupation of the Canton-Hankow Railroad, Suichwan and Kanchow airfields remained in Allied hands. These bases were partially stocked with gasoline and munitions, and air transport was expected to supplement the stocks on hand. With the fall of the bases farther west, a detachment of B-25's and two squadrons of P-51's moved east to Suichwan and Kanchow. Flying missions against coastal harbors as well as the Yangtze, these units operated with considerable success during December 1944 and January 1945. Exhaustion of fuel and munitions eventually halted their operations, but by that time the Japanese armies were only a few miles away, and their missions would have come to an end even had the supply situation been better.

Twenty-eight missions and 168 sorties, all but 2 by P-51's, were flown against Yangtze shipping from Suichwan and Kanchow during the two month period. Good targets were discovered, and attacks pressed home at low level brought good results. Claims for the period were 1 merchant ship, 12 powered river craft, 4 barges, and 1 gunboat sunk. Six merchant vessels, 28 river steamers, 15 barges, and 2 gunboats were claimed as damaged. As these missions came to an end with the evacuation of the airfields, P-51's were already reaching out from Laohokow* to continue the aerial blockade of the Yangtze.[25]

Laohokow lies on the Han River approximately 200 miles northeast of Hankow. Thus the Japanese-occupied section of the Yangtze from Ichang to Nanking was within easy range of P-51's based at Laohokow. Eight P-51's from this base on 31 December 1944 sank two river steamers and damaged two more on the Yangtze. This was the first of 25 missions, about 116 sorties, which harried boatmen on the Yangtze until 9 March. These strikes brought claims of 6 merchant vessels damaged, 15 powered craft sunk and 47 damaged, 6 barges sunk and 11 damaged, 1 gunboat sunk and 3 damaged. This damage to the Yangtze line of communication stung the Japanese into retaliation, and the airfield at Laohokow was occupied by enemy infantry in March. From 9 March until 1 April 1945, shipping on the Yangtze was not molested by Allied bombing, though mines continued to be a great danger.[26]

April and May 1945 saw the last Japanese offensive in China halted, and the beginning of a retreat toward the north. The enemy was unable to press far past Laohokow in the north, and an attempt to capture Chihkiang was bloodily repulsed. In Kwangsi Province, Chinese armies began to move eastward, content to follow the enemy as he gave ground. Yangtze shipping was no longer a target of prime importance; mining and submarine activity had made it less vital than the Chinese railroads as a Japanese line of communication. It was still used to a considerable extent, however, and during April and May 1945, 130 sorties by P-51's were directed against shipping on the river.

The Mustangs making these strikes flew from Ankang, west of Laohokow, and from Chihkiang. One mission staged through Changting in the pocket east of the Canton-Hankow Railroad. Chihkiang and Ankang were not so conveniently located as Laohokow had been, but the Yangtze as far down as Nanking was still within P-51 range. The missions flown during April and May were more productive, if claims form a valid basis of comparison, than those of earlier periods. No ocean-going ships were sunk, but three were damaged. No fewer than 28 powered craft were reported sent to the bottom, though these vessels were generally smaller than those attacked earlier, and 55 were damaged. Four gunboats were sunk and as many damaged, and 7 barges were sunk and 33 damaged. Fourteenth Air Force planes began to systematically attack junks and sampans on the Yangtze during this period—mainly in the Hankow area—and claimed 29 sunk and 216 damaged.[27]

Air strikes against shipping on the Yangtze from 1 June 1945 to the end of the war were devoted to a different purpose than those which had been made earlier. Heretofore such attacks had been tactically devoted to reducing the strength of Japanese offensives. The strategic objective had been accomplished—mines and air attacks had closed the river to metal-hulled ships above Nanking, and mines had practically closed the port of Shanghai. Thus it would have been impossible to get raw materials out of China via Shanghai even if it had been possible to get them across the East China Sea to Japan. Air attacks on the Yangtze during June, July, and August 1945 were intended to harry an enemy in retreat and prevent his establishing a firm line of resistance along the river.

During this period approximately 170 sorties were flown, all by fighters. Four missions were flown from Enshih, the remainder from Chihkiang. Good targets were not so abundant as they had once been; only one ocean-going ship was claimed, and this was probably a large river steamer. Twenty-five powered craft were claimed sunk and 69 damaged, but most of

---

*See Map No 2, p 15

these were tugs and motor launches; the few river steamers claimed were small ones No gunboats were attacked, and only 9 barges were claimed as sunk and only 26 damaged. The shortage of good targets was evidenced by the number of junks and sampans claimed, a total of 728 sunk and damaged.[28]

The Changteh offensive of 1943. In November 1943 the Japanese Eleventh Army launched an attack against the city of Changteh The objectives of the offensive were to destroy the bases and troops of the Chinese Sixth War Area armies in the Changteh region and to prevent the transfer of troops from that front to Yunnan where they might be used against Burma in coordination with an offensive from India. A secondary objective was seasoning of Mongolian and Chinese puppet troops. The Japanese had no intention of holding Changteh at this time, and the plans for the attack provided for return of the attacking forces to their original positions [29]

The Changteh campaign was not decisive in any sense Its importance lies in the fact that it served both the Japanese and the Fourteenth Air Force as a rehearsal for the crucial Hunan-Kwangsi campaign of 1944. Since Japanese troops and supplies for the offensive had to be moved across Tungting Lake, Allied airmen gained experience in attacks on light shipping in support of ground forces.

On 18 November 1943 Col. Clinton D. Vincent, commander of Fourteenth Air Force Forward Echelon with headquarters at Kweilin, was directed to support the Chinese ground forces in the Changteh area as a mission second only to defense of forward airdromes. Vincent was given some discretion as to the type of support he would give, but was instructed to furnish tactical support upon request by the proper Chinese authorities whenever possible. Before formally receiving this directive, Vincent had sent Lt. Col. M. F. Taber to Hengyang to command a Tungting Task Force of 9 B-25's, 16 P-40's, and 15 P-51's based at Hengyang and Lingling. The B-25's were to devote their main effort to Yangtze shipping and supply centers while fighters not required for base defense were to engage in "offensive reconnaissance with instructions to strafe any target of opportunity such as small boats ... road transport ... and troops."[30]

Fighters from Hengyang and Lingling flew a total of 1,039 sorties during the period of the Changteh offensive. Fifteen B-25 and about 280 fighter sorties attacked shipping on Tungting Lake, but many of the attacks were made with ammunition left over after other missions had been carried out. Few powered craft were used by the Japanese on Tungting Lake; only two tugs were claimed as sunk and five small steamers and tugs damaged during the offensive. Pilots made little or no distinction between barges, junks, and sampans in their reports, but claims for all three types amounted to 90 sunk and at least 380 damaged. Many of the boats attacked were loaded with troops, and it was believed that heavy casualties had been inflicted on the Japanese.[31]

The Changteh operation gave the Fourteenth Air Force valuable experience in the tactical interdiction of water lines of communication in China. However, it gave the Japanese equally valuable experience in mounting and supplying an offensive under the conditions which prevailed in Hunan Province. The withdrawal of the Japanese armies from Changteh was according to plan and was not forced upon the enemy by Chinese troops or American air action, but American airmen in China were not aware of this fact They came to believe, not unnaturally, that American aircraft and Chinese infantry had thrown the Japanese back from Changteh. This led to overoptimistic conclusions as to the effectiveness of air attacks against advancing ground troops and as to the fighting quality of the Chinese. These illusions were thoroughly destroyed during the Hunan-Kwangsi campaign of 1944 [32]

The Hunan-Kwangsi campaign. Before the end of 1943, Japanese forces in the Pacific were being driven back from their most advanced positions. The fall of Guadalcanal and New Georgia in the Solomons, of Buna, Lae, and Finschhafen in New Guinea, of

Attu in the Aleutians, and of the Gilbert Islands in the central Pacific were important defeats in themselves and prophesied further Allied advances. In China the Japanese had nothing to fear from a Chinese ground offensive, but United States airpower threatened the Yangtze line of communications, and Allied aircraft and submarines were making sea communications from China to the home islands of Japan more and more hazardous. Finally, the Japanese knew that American B-29's would soon be in operation, and that all industrial targets in Japan were exposed to attack if these long-range bombers staged through airfields in east China.

Thus a campaign into east China offered a number of worth-while results to the Japanese. Heavy losses could be inflicted on the Chinese armies, but this was a secondary consideration. More important, capture of the Fourteenth Air Force bases in east China would relieve pressure on the Yangtze River and on the shipping lines along the China coast. Furthermore, when these bases were in Japanese hands, the B-29's would be forced to operate from bases in the Chengtu area, leaving only Kyushu as a suitable target in the home islands.

Capture of the east China airfields alone would have made an offensive worth-while, but there were two other advantages to be gained. Capture of the railroad corridor through Changsha, Hengyang, Liuchow, and Nanning* would afford direct land communications between Japanese forces in China and Indo-China and would provide right of way for a railroad connecting Japanese-occupied areas from Korea to Burma and Singapore. Since realization of this ambition would have required more railroad construction than the Japanese were likely to be able to accomplish, it remained merely a hope for the future.

Opening of through communications from Peking to Hankow and from Hankow to Canton, however, had immediate practical advantages. If these rail lines could be opened, Chinese raw materials destined for Japan and men and munitions sent from Japan to China could be routed through Manchuria and Korea. Much shipping space could be saved, for only a short voyage to Korea would be necessary, over a route much less exposed to submarine attack than the longer routes across the East China Sea.

A final consideration inclining the Japanese toward an effort to eliminate the east China airfields was fear of an Allied amphibious landing on the south China coast. Fourteenth Air Force aircraft could support such a landing from east China bases; therefore the bases should be neutralized. Possession of the Peking-Hankow, Canton-Hankow, and Hunan-Kwangsi Railroads, moreover, would permit rapid Japanese deployment to meet an invasion of south China if it did take place.[33]

Although the Japanese offensive had as one of its objectives the opening of land lines of communication, except for the opening of the upper Peking-Hankow Railroad in mid-1944, it depended upon rivers for supply until land lines could be established. The first phase plan, somewhat simplified, was for the Japanese First and Twelfth Armies, with some assistance from the Thirteenth, to occupy the railroad corridor from the Yellow River to Hankow as a preliminary to the Hunan drive. The Chinese armies of General Tang En Po, "a poorly disciplined mob, hated as much by the Chinese peasants whose food they confiscated as the Japanese,"[34] offered little resistance, and the few CACW units based within attacking distance could offer little more. By the middle of May 1944 the railroad bed from the Yellow River to Hankow was in possession of the Japanese, and reconstruction of the line had begun. Months were required for reconstruction, but when it had been accomplished; rail connections between Japanese forces in Hankow and those in north China and Manchuria were an accomplished fact.

The second phase of the offensive was a drive by the Japanese Eleventh Army south from Hankow to Changsha and Hengyang. This advance was up the Hsiang River, and the river was the main supply line throughout. Until roads could be built and the rail-

---

*See Map No 5, p 58

road restored, it was the only supply route Since the Hsiang was within reach of the east China airfields at Hengyang, Lingling, Kweilin, Liuchow, and Chihkiang, the Fourteenth Air Force could operate effectively against the Japanese supply lines.

The Japanese plan was to continue to the southwest toward Liuchow after the capture of Hengyang. In cooperation, the Twenty-third Army was to move northwest from Canton against the same objective. The Eleventh Army would still depend upon the Hsiang for most of its supply, and the Twenty-third would move its supplies up the Hsi River from Canton. The rivers would continue to be the main supply routes when Nanning was captured to establish land communication with Indo-China, and when the Eleventh Army drove south from Hengyang to open the remainder of the Canton-Hankow Railroad and to occupy the Allied airfields at Suichwan and Kanchow.[35]

Despite attacks on Yangtze River shipping, the Japanese had accumulated troops and supplies at Hankow. Whether this mobilization could have been prevented if more supplies had been available to the Fourteenth Air Force is doubtful The ships which moved up the Yangtze route traveled by night and took refuge in well-defended ports by day. As noted earlier, interception and antiaircraft fire interfered with the air attacks which were delivered along the river Apparently, also, the Japanese had a surplus of men and munitions for the drive until heavy resistance was encountered at Hengyang

Chinese defensive tactics against the Japanese in previous campaigns had been to offer little resistance to the advance until the enemy's lines of communication were well extended, then to defend a fortified city to the front and to attack from the flanks against the communications. Against limited offensives such as the drive on Changteh in November of 1943, such tactics had worked very well. However, when the same tactics were tried against the Japanese offensive in May and June of 1944, they failed miserably The Japanese used far greater strength in this drive than they had used in the past, and their troops were the best available. "Numerous units of Japanese and puppet plainclothesmen" preceded the infantry and cavalry These soldiers in civilian dress infiltrated the fluid lines and demoralized the rear areas. Instead of piling up against the fortified cities of Changsha and Hengshan, the Japanese bypassed these strongpoints and continued on toward Hengyang The Chinese garrisons in the bypassed cities lacked the strength and mobility to take the offensive and were soon starved into submission. Changsha capitulated on 18 June, Hengshan on the 22d, but by that time units of the Eleventh Army were approaching Hengyang. "Unprepared Chinese towns, deep behind the forward lines, were attacked and frightened. There was evidence of military disintegration in the lowest echelons and a growing sense of helplessness at the highest echelons."[36]

The chief resistance against the Japanese was by the Fourteenth Air Force and CACW aircraft under its control. As of 1 June 1944, 535 aircraft were assigned to Fourteenth Air Force and CACW; of these, 377 were fighters, 82 were medium bombers, 36 heavy bombers, and 40 other types. Of the 495 fighters and bombers, 420 were assigned to operational units, and 354 of them were operational. Because the first priority missions of the Fourteenth Air Force were defense of the Kunming ferry terminal, defense of the B-29 bases in northwest China, and support of the Chinese armies in the Salween, only a part of the available strength could be used against the Japanese in Hunan

Deployed at bases within range of the Japanese forces in east China were 37 Mitchell bombers of the 11th Bombardment Squadron and of the 1st Bombardment Group, CACW. Twenty-seven of these B-25's were operational on 1 June 1944. Also established on eastern bases (including Nanning) were 126 fighters, mainly P-40's of the 23d Fighter Group and the CACW. On 1 June 1944, 103 of these fighters were operational

The 308th Bombardment Group, with 31 operational B-24's, was also in China and based within range of the Hsiang Valley. Nevertheless, except for strikes at supply bases, the B-24's were not available for use against the Japanese supply lines in the valley. There were other targets for which the Liberators were better suited, and their gas consumption was so high that they were restricted to essential missions

Fourteenth Air Force strength was to grow before the end of 1944—by the end of October, 524 fighters and 152 bombers were assigned. During the summer, however, losses more than offset the number of new aircraft received, and the strength listed in the paragraphs above is approximately what was available during the crucial period of May through August 1944. It was that strength which contested the Japanese advance to Hengyang.[17]

The Japanese began their drive south from Yochow on 20 May 1944. During the remaining days of May, few communications targets were available in the battle area, though strikes on the Yangtze continued. The 155 fighter and 12 B-25 sorties flown in opposition to the offensive during May attacked troops and horses in the main In June river boats on the Hsiang River, which was reaching high water level and thus was well-suited to navigation, became an important target for the defense of Hengyang. During the month more than 1,900 sorties, 218 of them by B-25's, were flown against the advancing Japanese; 73 bomber and 993 fighter sorties attacked shipping. Early in the month most missions took off from Hengyang, but as the Japanese pressed closer, operations retreated to bases at Lingling, Kweilin, and Liuchow. Also, some strikes were delivered from Chihkiang and Suichwan, bases on the flanks of the enemy advance Claims of shipping sunk on Tungting Lake and the Hsiang River during June amounted to 22 steamers, tugs, and motor launches, 5 barges, and 199 sampans. Damaged shipping was listed as 32 powered craft, 57 barges, and 690 sampans The Japanese found these air attacks galling, and their fighters frequently intercepted, but interception seldom forced complete abandonment of the attack.[18]

Though aircraft losses during June, July, and August 1944 were more than equal to the replacements received by Fourteenth Air Force (by the end of August only 323 fighters were available as compared with 377 in June), from 1 July through 8 August, when Hengyang fell, the medium bombers flew 291 sorties against the advancing Japanese and the fighters more than 2,600. More than 1,300 sorties, 96 by B-25's, struck at shipping in the Hsiang Valley. Again claims indicated good results, amounting to 143 steamers, tugs, and launches, 128 barges, 410 junks, and 2,176 sampans sunk or damaged. These air attacks made it impossible for the Japanese to bring up supplies and reinforcements as fast as had been planned, with the result that the advance fell behind schedule. From the end of June until 8 August, Japanese forces were unable to advance or to capture Hengyang Even when the latter task had been accomplished, the Eleventh Army was spent and required rest and replacements before it could renew its drive to the west.[39]

Restoration of the Eleventh Army's strength posed serious problems to the Japanese command Air attack and mining of the Yangtze had reduced traffic on that stream to 20 percent of the normal level. "If the amount of coal, salt, motor fuel, aviation and railway materials transported is excluded from this figure the transportation of ordinary war supplies was, for all practical purposes, nil."[40] Rail repairs from Wuchang to Hengyang would take many months to complete, and shortages of motor fuel and the poor condition of the roads made motor transportation most difficult. It was still necessary to depend upon the Hsiang for moving supplies forward. The Japanese had about 100 powered craft available at this time (including 80 small steamers), 41 barges, lighters (usually called barges by Allied airmen) with a total capacity of 3,000 tons,* and 2,500 privately owned sampans and junks with a total capacity of about 10,000 tons. The Japanese commanders might well be hesitant as to their ability to deliver supplies to the Eleventh Army, for during the period 20 May-

---

*Number of lighters unknown

8 August 1944, 50 percent of the 20,000 tons sent out from Hankow had been destroyed by air attack or consumed on the way. During August and September, replacements marching to the front had to forage for food in territory already ravaged by combat units. Because of this, replacements were late arriving at the front and suffered many losses from sickness and straggling. After arrival, they were found to be in poor physical condition

Late September and October saw a significant improvement in the Japanese supply situation. Exceedingly bad weather in Hunan Province and loss of the bases at Hengyang and Lingling drastically reduced Fourteenth Air Force attacks. Temporary aerial reinforcement from Japan and Formosa afforded some protection to the enemy's supply lines. Higher water levels in the Hsiang made it possible to move supplies as far as Hengyang entirely by water. Ripening of the harvest in Hunan made subsistence of troops and horses easier, and considerable quantities of Chinese war supplies were captured Finally, the fact that after the fall of Hengyang the Chinese offered little or no resistance greatly reduced the Japanese expenditure of munitions.

It should also be mentioned that the absence of Chinese resistance reduced the effectiveness of air attack on the Japanese supply lines. Such Chinese opposition to the Japanese as was offered before the fall of Hengyang had made it possible for the limited airpower available to bring the offensive almost to a halt The disorganization and demoralization of the Chinese armies after 8 August made it possible for the Japanese to operate almost without supplies and to disperse their forces to a much greater extent than had been possible before. Therefore the Eleventh Army was much less vulnerable to air attack.[41]

The second phase of the Hunan-Kwangsi campaign of 1944, which resulted in the loss of Allied airfields at Kweilin, Liuchow, and Nanning, began at the end of August. The Japanese Eleventh Army drove southwest from Hengyang, forcing abandonment of Lingling on 4 September and reaching Chuanhsien by the middle of the month. Here a halt was made while supplies and reinforcements were brought up. In the meantime the Japanese Twenty-third Army in the Canton area began a drive up the Hsi River, and had occupied Tanchuk, Pingnam, and Taiping by 1 October. Meeting little resistance the Twenty-third Army drove west toward Liuchow while the Eleventh Army encircled Kweilin. As soon as Kweilin was neutralized by encirclement, Eleventh Army troops, disregarding orders which assigned the capture of Liuchow to the Twenty-third Army, plunged southwest to Liuchow, which was occupied on 11 November. Nanning fell on 24 November, and Japanese forces moved northwest of Liuchow to Hochih, where the lines were stabilized.[42]

During the period from 9 August to the end of September, more than 3,000 fighter sorties and 750 B-25 sorties were flown against Japanese communications in the Hsiang Valley Attacks upon motor transport and bridges received more emphasis as the Japanese improved the roads, but more than 900 bomber and fighter sorties attacked shipping, either as a primary target or as a strafing target of opportunity after bombing. Crews reported 138 powered craft, most of which were small steamers, sunk or damaged. In addition, bombing and strafing attacks were reported to have sunk or damaged 92 barges and more than 2,000 junks and sampans on the Hsiang. All of this effort failed to halt the offensive

After the beginning of the Twenty-third Army's drive up the Hsi, planes from Liuchow and Nanning began to seek out targets on that river. Between 9 September, when Samshui was bombed, and 17 November, when the Hsi River offensive had merged with the advance of Eleventh Army in the Liuchow area, 420 missions were flown against the Twenty-third Army. Fighters, with approximately 2,000 sorties, and bombers, with 164 sorties struck at troops, motor transport, and river shipping nearly every day during this 10-week period. Almost 850 sorties hit shipping on the river, and claims of sinking or damage included 166 steamers and motor launches, 364 barges, and more than 1,250 junks and sampans.

During October, when the greatest Allied success was being attained on the Hsi, bad weather, coupled with the loss of advance bases, was considerably reducing the effort exerted over the main supply route in the Hsiang Valley. Weather, though still bad, improved somewhat in November, but the fall of Kweilin and Liuchow left only Chihkiang as a base for interdiction operations by fighters and medium bombers. During the two-month period, approximately 1,275 fighter and 31 bomber sorties were flown against targets in the valley, but many of them were directed against areas above the head of Hsiang River navigation. Only about 240 sorties, all by fighters, attacked shipping. Claims resulting from these strikes were for 21 steamers and motor launches, 12 barges, and about 500 junks and sampans sunk or damaged.[43]

In nine months, the Japanese had succeeded remarkably well in accomplishing the immediate objectives of their offensive. Land communications with Indo-China were established, though the only result for the Japanese command in China was the loss of two good divisions which marched into Indo-China to reinforce the garrison of that French colony It was completely beyond Japanese resources to establish rail connections between China and Southeast Asia.

Rail connections between Peking and Hankow and Hankow and Hengyang were established, however, and thus complete dependence upon submarine-infested seas and the mined course of the Yangtze was ended. Soon after the beginning of 1945, the Canton-Hankow rail corridor south of Hengyang was secured, but time and material for restoring this section of railroad to through operations were lacking A gap still existed between Hengyang and Canton when the war ended. The Japanese were to discover that even when rail lines were restored, they too were vulnerable to air attack.

Likewise, the Japanese succeeded in destroying the effectiveness of the armies of the Chinese Ninth War Area. The troops which remained to the Chinese commanders were without artillery, short of ammunition, and in many cases lacked even rifles. Perhaps more important, their morale, low at the beginning of the campaign, was completely destroyed by seemingly endless retreat. This condition gave but a temporary advantage to the Japanese, however, for the return of American-trained Chinese troops from Burma and the long-delayed issue of American equipment to troops facing the Japanese in China was to restore the strength of the Chinese armies. No such restoration was possible for the Japanese, who were to be stunned by defeat at Chihkiang in the spring of 1945. As the war ended, the Chinese were ready to launch an offensive which had every promise of driving the Japanese north of the Yangtze.

Finally, the Japanese captured the major Fourteenth Air Force bases in east China. Thereafter, Allied air operations against the Yangtze and the sea lanes were carried on through much of January from the isolated bases at Suichwan and Kanchow, but when these fields fell, only Chihkiang remained operational in east China. Surprisingly enough, capture of the air bases brought little benefit to the Japanese in China. LAB and B-25 searches of Formosa Straits and the South China Sea continued from Philippine and west China bases. Attacks on the Yangtze continued from Laohokow, Ankang, and Chihkiang Lastly, the Hsiang corridor, vital to the supply of both the Kweilin-Liuchow area and the south coast, became a gauntlet to be run, because it was under attack day and night from Chihkiang.

Attrition in the Hsiang Valley, December 1944-April 1945. With the close of the Japanese Hunan-Kwangsi campaign in November 1944, air strikes at the Peking-Hankow and other north China railroads, and at shipping on the Yangtze River, were more profitable for the Allies than strikes at transportation in the Hsiang Valley. However, planes based at Chihkiang, though they made occasional forays against other areas, kept pressure on the railroads, roads, and waterways between Hankow and Liuchow.

During the five months between 1 December 1944 and 30 April 1945, about 1,700 fighter and 120 bomber sorties struck at communications in the corridor. Almost 800 of these sorties attacked shipping, resulting in claims of 29 tugs, steamboats, and motor launches, 134 barges, and more than 1,900 other craft sunk and damaged.

This harassment of transportation in the corridor, especially of water transportation, had a number of results, none of which were favorable to the Japanese. Damage to river craft made it impossible to divert shipping, badly needed in the Hankow area, from Hunan. Only the most essential supplies could be sent to the forces south and west of Hankow, and 20 percent of these were destroyed on the way. Therefore no reserves of men or material could be built up. Finally, more than 10,000 tons of war material captured from the Chinese during the offensive could not be removed from the places where they were stored. The inability of the Japanese to build up reserves or use this captured material, in conjunction with increased lend-lease supplies to Chinese forces and extensive air support given by the Fourteenth Air Force, was responsible, for the failure of the Japanese effort to capture Chihkiang in April and May of 1945. After the failure of the Chihkiang campaign, the only course open to the Japanese was retreat from South China. Yet the retreat exposed more men and material to the air attacks which had made retreat necessary [44]

River interdiction during the Japanese retreat to north China, May-August 1945. The Japanese retreat in China during the late spring and summer of 1945 followed several routes Troops moved down the Hsi River to Canton, and those on the Luichow Peninsula moved overland to the Canton area. From Kwangtung, these and other units moved either up the Canton-Hankow Railroad corridor to Hengyang and then north to Changsha and Hankow, or northward through the Suichwan-Kanchow area to Nanchang. In the one case they made use of the Pei River part of the way, and in the other they made use of the Kian River

Forces retiring from the Liuchow-Kweilin area had no choice but to move down the Hsiang Valley through Hengyang, from whence they went on to Changsha and Hankow. Thus the river corridor between Hengyang and Yochow was a bottleneck through which almost all had to pass. This bottleneck and the routes leading to it and from it were harassed day and night by the Fourteenth Air Force. So serious was the damage to men and materials moving between Hengyang and Hankow that one division abandoned the well-established route and moved from Changsha to Nanchang in an attempt to avoid such punishment

The battle for Chihkiang came to an end by mid-May, and Japanese troops began withdrawing from that front. At the same time, the beginnings of the move northward were evident in Kwangtung Province. Allied aircraft found good hunting along the Hsi and Hsiang Rivers. Fighters flew more than 500 sorties against communications south of the Yangtze during May, and B-25's flew 65 sorties, mostly night intruder. Over half of the fighters and 10 of the bombers attacked shipping Junks and sampans suffered the most, more than 1,900 being claimed as sunk or damaged. Thirty-six powered craft and 20 barges were also claimed.

June was another hazardous month for shipping on the rivers being used by the retreating Japanese. Approximately 450 fighter and 18 bomber sorties were flown against southern communications, and 198 sorties attacked shipping. Claims were for 67 powered craft, 75 barges, and 825 junks and sampans.

From 1 July 1945 until Fourteenth Air Force operations came to an end on 11 August, the Japanese retreat from south China was in full swing Targets were abundant, but as had so often been the case in the past, supply restrictions limited the effort which could be made, however attractive the targets. Despite the diversion of hump tonnage to building up supplies for the Tenth Air Force and to equipping Chinese forces for a ground offensive, almost 900 fighter and 79 B-25 sorties were directed against communications south of the Yangtze. Of these, 560-odd sorties attacked shipping. During the seven-week period, claims were made for 125 powered craft, 163 barges, and more than 2,600 sampans sunk or damaged.[45]

EVALUATION

The first problem which must be faced in any evaluation of the interdiction of inland waterways in China is the matter of claims. The problem is more difficult than that encountered in evaluation of claims of shipping sunk in salt water because, except for ocean-going ships on the Yangtze, there is no authoritative source, such as the Joint Army-Navy Assessment Committee (JANAC) report, Japanese Naval and Merchant Losses during World War II, against which claims can be checked. Therefore, there can be no firm conclusions as to numbers of vessels, tonnage, or amount of cargo destroyed or damaged. On the other hand, examination of the evidence available immediately makes it apparent that Fourteenth Air Force claims were too high. The question remains, how much too high?

Total claims were as follows: ocean-going merchant ships, 20 sunk, 69 probably sunk or damaged; gunboats, 9 sunk, 27 probably sunk or damaged; powered craft, 312 sunk, 914 probably sunk or damaged; barges, 285 sunk, 1,026 probably sunk or damaged; junks and sampans, 4,032 sunk, 13,432 probably sunk or damaged. The records indicate that 110 merchant ships, 42 gunboats, 1,485 powered craft, 1,765 barges, and 21,879 junks and sampans were attacked.[46]

Even for assessing merchant shipping sunk on the Yangtze, JANAC cannot be accepted without question. This report credits Army aircraft with sinking only six merchant ships on the Yangtze. The United States Strategic Bombing Survey (USSBS) report, "The Effect of Air Action on Japanese Ground Army Logistics," on the other hand, names 11 ships sunk on the Yangtze by bombing attacks. These ships include the six credited to Fourteenth Air Force by JANAC, three which JANAC credits to other agents, and two which JANAC does not mention. Finally, a Japanese monograph lists 14 merchant ships sunk on the Yangtze by bombing and strafing attacks. Resolution of these conflicts is impossible, but the higher estimate of 14 ships sunk has in its favor the fact that with one exception Fourteenth Air Force attacks coincide roughly in time and place with the sinkings listed.[47]

For obvious reasons, Fourteenth Air Force made no definite claims as to numbers of ships sunk by mines. JANAC credits mines with sinking seven ships over 500 tons on the Yangtze (excluding the Shanghai area) for a total of 17,026 tons. The USSBS report on "The Effect of Air Action on Japanese Ground Army Logistics" credits mines in the Yangtze River with eight ships totalling 18,392 tons. Another USSBS report, "The Offensive Mine-Laying Campaign against Japan," states that 36 ships with a total tonnage of 25,087 tons were sunk by mines on the Yangtze, and that 10 more ships, 10,764 tons, were damaged. Many of these 36 vessels were, of course, of less than 500 tons and would not have appeared in JANAC. Here again the larger total seems more plausible; it is at least doubtful that the Japanese would have abandoned the use of the Yangtze had losses amounted to only seven ships.[48]

The question of gunboats sunk is not so obscure. Despite the claims of nine, no source credits more than two, one sunk by bombing, the other by a mine. It should be noted that eight other gunboats were damaged, some of them more than once. It may be that the Fourteenth Air Force claims in this category included five small (under 100 tons) miscellaneous naval craft sunk on the Yangtze by air attack during the course of the war.[49]

When an attempt is made to evaluate claims of lesser shipping, nothing definite can be stated. There is no record of how many powered craft, barges, junks, and sampans the Japanese controlled in China or of how many were left at the close of the war. That claims were in excess of accomplishment can be demonstrated fairly conclusively in regard to the Hankow-Hengyang supply line along the Hsiang River. At about the time of the fall of Hengyang (8 August 1944), the Japanese had on this route some 100 powered craft, perhaps 200 barges and lighters, and 2,500 junks and sampans. Since the Japanese thereafter desired to withdraw shipping from the Hsiang, it is improbable that any significant number of vessels was added to this fleet. Yet Fourteenth Air Force claimed to have sunk or damaged 315 powered craft, 561 barges, and 9,725 junks and sampans on the Hsiang during the remaining year of the war. Since a vessel might be damaged any number of times, these claims are not mathematically impossible, but they are, to say the least, rather improbable.[50]

The fact that Fourteenth Air Force claimed too much does not mean that too little was accomplished. On the contrary, shipping on the Yangtze River was reduced to one-fifth of normal by mid-1944, and the river above Nanking was closed to steel vessels in the spring of 1945. The first achievement was mainly accomplished by bombing and strafing, the second largely by mines. Likewise, attacks on Hsiang River shipping at times reduced by half supplies to Japanese forces advancing to the west, making it necessary for reinforcements moving toward the front to forage for sustenance, thus delaying their arrival in the fighting zone and bringing about reduced efficiency when they did arrive.

The fall of Hengyang was almost certainly delayed a month or more by the air strikes on Hsiang River shipping. This delay, and the period of recuperation which the Japanese found necessary before the offensive could be renewed, at least made it possible for Fourteenth Air Force aircraft to operate longer from east China airfields and thus increase Japanese losses. Had ground defenses been in the hands of a less demoralized and less exhausted army, the Japanese delay at Hengyang might have afforded an opportunity to prepare a successful defense of bases to the east.[51]

Attrition of shipping and other means of supply in the Hsiang Valley during the winter of 1944-45 certainly contributed toward frustrating the Japanese attempt to capture Chihkiang. Losses exacted from the Japanese during the summer retreat of 1945 did not, as it turned out, hasten the end of the war, but had the enemy decided on a fight to the death, this attrition would have been important.

Fourteenth Air Force interdiction of Japanese river shipping in China accomplished a great deal. That it did not accomplish more was due not to poor execution or insufficient weight of attack, but to the fact that tactical benefits could not be gained when the Chinese armies were unable to take advantage of the opportunities created by air action. With the partial exception of attacks on Yangtze River shipping, river interdiction in China was a tactic designed to aid friendly ground forces. By the summer of 1944, the Chinese armies in east China were beyond any help that Fourteenth Air Force could give.

CHAPTER III

ROAD INTERDICTION

INTRODUCTION

*Roads in China** Roads were the least important lines of communication in China during World War II They were merely supplements of the vital rail and water routes and therefore received far less attention from the Fourteenth Air Force than the railroads and waterways. Roads were little-used for two reasons: first, the Japanese suffered from a shortage of motor transport and, especially, motor fuel; second, the condition of the roads was such that they were unusable during much of the year.

Before the Japanese invasion, China had no all-weather road network—90 percent of the "modern" roads in China were of simple earth construction and became quagmires in rainy weather. A few paved roads radiated out from the larger cities, but no farther than 40 or 50 miles at most. The main highways between cities had at one time been surfaced with crushed rock, and these were considered all-weather routes. The passage of years in which little or no maintenance was possible reduced the quality of these highways toward the level of those which had never been surfaced.

One factor which contributed to the deterioration of the already poor road net was deliberate destruction of the roads by retreating Chinese armies It was Chinese policy to maintain a zone as much as 50 miles wide of practically impassable communications in front of the Japanese positions. In this zone all bridges were torn up or blown down, and deep ditches, as much as ten feet deep and at least as wide, were cut across the roads at right angles The completeness of destruction probably reached its zenith in Honan Province. Fourteenth Air Force reconnaissance of that area revealed that long stretches of the former road and rail lines had completely disappeared under the crops of land-hungry Chinese farmers.

The degree to which the destruction carried out by the Chinese was effective varied from region to region and season to season. In flat Honan, during the dry months, military vehicles could make their way across the open fields, as was demonstrated during May of 1944. In Kwangtung Province, on the other hand, men afoot or on horseback made their way with difficulty during the dry season unless the roads had been rebuilt. In wet weather, travel of any kind was impossible on unrepaired roads. In Hunan Province in 1944 the Chinese retreat was so rapid and the armies so demoralized that there was little attempt to destroy the highways. Even so, the Japanese had great difficulty in moving supplies to the front by motor transport in wet weather.

The Japanese restored only those roads essential for military traffic in Occupied China, and those only to a limited extent. By and large, a road paralleling the Yangtze below Hankow was kept open, as were short sections paralleling or supplementing the main railroad lines. When rails and ties were removed from railroads—as was often the case when the Japanese believed they could be put to better use elsewhere—the naked railroad bed was sometimes used as a highway. The few attempts the Japanese made to use roads far removed from rail and river lines ended in failure; any length left unguarded was quickly cut by Chinese guerrillas.

*See Map No 3, p 38

Thus the roads in China were so poorly built and maintained, so often destroyed by the Chinese, and consequently so little used by the Japanese, that they were a far less vital transportation target than shipping or railroads. Attacks on roads, road bridges, or road transport, then, were usually mounted only as a means of delaying a Japanese advance or striking some particularly lucrative target discovered by reconnaissance.[1]

Roads in Indo-China.* French Indo-China was a target area for the Fourteenth Air Force, and the colony had a road net much better than that of China. Approximately 5,000 miles of asphalt or macadam roads were in existence before the war began, and a good part of the remaining 15,000 miles of roads boasted crushed rock surfaces. Two surfaced highways extended north-south the length of the colony, and these were intersected by five east-west highways.

The most important of the Indo-Chinese roads was *Route Coloniale* Number One, which extended from Hanoi south to Saigon. It was along this highway and access roads leading to it that Fourteenth Air Force strikes took place. Strikes directed primarily against the roads were few in number because road traffic in Indo-China was of minor importance. Road bridges did receive considerable damage, but this resulted from the fact that since many of the bridges were combined road-railroad structures, bridge strikes directed primarily against the railroads often also interdicted roads.[2]

Roads in eastern Burma. A primary mission of American forces in the India-Burma area was to open a ground supply route from India to China across northern Burma. In 1942 the Japanese, following up the conquest of Burma, had advanced up the Burma Road from Lashio to the Salween River. From India, the Allies pushed the Ledo Road across Burma to Bhamo, then eastward to join the old Burma Road into China and on to Kunming. Opening the final section of the Ledo Road-Burma Road supply route to Kunming depended upon an offensive by Chinese forces from China to drive the Japanese back from the Salween until a juncture could be effected with the Chinese-American forces in Burma.

The wisdom of this plan was at least open to question. It resulted in the diversion of a great amount of American and Chinese effort to the opening of a supply route which, even when it became operational, carried only a fraction of the tonnage carried by airlift across the Hump. It is probable that after the capture of Myitkyina an expenditure of equal effort toward improving the airlift would have increased the amount of supplies which reached China considerably beyond the increase brought about by opening the road. More important, the supplies would have reached China sooner, and a ton of supplies in China in 1944 was worth far more than the same amount in 1945.

It must also be mentioned that the Salween campaign required air support from the Fourteenth Air Force. The effort expended against the Japanese in the Salween could have been most useful in the east during the Japanese offensive of 1944. It must be remembered, however, that sorties flown from bases in Yunnan used fuel put down at Kunming after being brought over the Hump. Sorties flown from eastern bases used fuel which had been transported, at great cost, from Kunming to eastern bases. Thus a sortie flown against the Japanese in the Salween, though its results may have been less important, was not nearly so expensive as a sortie in the east in terms of supplies.

The Japanese had no railroad beyond Lashio, nor was a water line of supply available. Therefore the Japanese in the Salween were dependent upon roads for their supplies. Two main roads were used, one the old Burma Road from Lashio, the other a road from northern Thailand opened by the Japanese. Thus roads and road traffic, which were minor interdiction targets in east China and hardly targets at all in French Indo-China, were the only interdiction targets in the Salween area. The Fourteenth Air Force bombed bridges, attempted

*See Map No 4, p 46

to start landslides, strafed motor transport and pack horses along the Japanese supply routes, and sought targets of opportunity along the trails which led to Japanese strongpoints along the line.¹

TACTICS

Attacks on road bridges. During 1943 there were few attempts to destroy road bridges in China and eastern Burma by bombing. The few attacks made were delivered by B-25's operating from medium altitude or by dive-bombing fighter aircraft. Road bridges were usually small targets, and such tactics brought few hits. During 1944 and 1945, B-25's practically always bombed road bridges from minimum altitude. If the Japanese defenses at a particular bridge were known to be strong, fighters might be sent with the bombers to strafe defensive gun positions before or during the bomb run, but ordinarily the forward firepower of the medium bombers was considered sufficient to beat down antiaircraft fire without help.

After 1943, fighters also made minimum-altitude attacks in most instances, though heavy defenses might dictate a dive-bombing attack. On minimum-altitude strikes, fighter pilots sought to imitate the bridge-busting approach of the B-25's, pulling up slightly an instant before bomb release, then pushing the nose down just as the bomb fell This method of delivery lessened the likelihood that the bomb would skip away from the target.

Active Japanese defenses at road bridges were seldom formidable. Most were completely undefended, and the more important bridges seldom boasted more than one or two automatic weapons. Attacking aircraft were in greatest danger when Japanese ground troops were in the area of a road bridge. Small-arms fire from infantrymen scattered along the road leading to the bridge was likely to score some hits on a plane making a minimum-altitude bombing run, and occasionally it brought a plane down. Losses were not high, however. Fourteenth Air Force lost only 56 aircraft in attacks on road transportation targets throughout the war.

Japanese passive defenses were much more effective. Most of the road bridges were small, uncomplicated structures, and the Japanese rebuilt them within a few days. In the Salween area they did even better Bypass bridges were built near the original sites, as many as three at some crossings, so that two or more bridges had to be bombed out at once if traffic was to be interrupted.

Quarter-ton demolition bombs were the preferred ordnance for attacks on road bridges, though, in order to save weight, some attempts were made to use 250-lb. and even 100-lb. bombs against some of the smaller spans It was discovered in China as elsewhere that the use of anything smaller than a 500-lb bomb was uneconomical because direct hits with the smaller bombs sometimes failed to damage bridges. No half-ton bombs were used on road targets, though they were used on rail bridges now and then. A trial of napalm against wooden bridges brought little success.⁴

Creation of road blocks. The Fourteenth Air Force made numerous attempts, some of them successful, to block the Burma Road with landslides This tactic was possible in the area between Lashio and the Salween because the road looped through mountainous country. A bomb detonated against the hillside above the road sometimes did set off a fall of rock and earth which either blocked the roadway or, even better, carried it away Direct hits on the roadbed produced craters which had to be filled before traffic could proceed.

Some of the bombing to achieve this object was done by fighters, but a greater weight of bombs was dropped by B-24's Ordinarily such a mission would have been considered unworthy of a heavy bomber, but in China tactics were dictated by the supply situation. In order to operate from Chinese bases, B-24's had to fly-in part of their own fuel and other supplies. Their route to India for these supplies took them near Burma Road targets. Therefore it was quite economical for a B-24 to drop a few bombs along the road on its way to India, a few more on its return to China⁵

During the Japanese offensive of 1944,

there were attempts by fighters and bombers to create road blocks in the east China areas of action In a few places, where the roads ran along hillsides, demolition bombs were dropped to bring about landslides as in the Salween area. Sometimes bombs were aimed at the roadbed for the sake of their cratering effect, though such damage was quickly repaired Late in the war, M-29 fragmentation clusters (butterfly bombs) were used to make road blocks. These small missiles usually had three kinds of fuzing, all dropped together: some were fuzed for instantaneous detonation, to inflict casualties on personnel and to damage vehicles in the area when the bombs fell, others were fuzed for one or more hours delay, so as to present a hazard to traffic on the road for some time after the attack; still other bombs were set as "boobytraps" with anti-disturbance fuzes which caused them to explode if an attempt was made to remove them. These bombs were not used extensively enough for any evaluation of their effectiveness to be possible [6]

Attacks on road traffic. The most frequent type of interdiction attacks on the roads carried out by Fourteenth Air Force was direct bombing and strafing of motor transport, horses, and horsedrawn vehicles. Such targets were fairly numerous during the first stages of Japanese offensives, and they were encountered with some regularity throughout the war

For attacks on traffic on the roads during daylight, fighter aircraft were the usual instrument, though low-flying B-25's often took part. Sometimes the fighters carried parachute-suspended fragmentation bombs which were dropped from minimum altitude, but main reliance was upon the .50-cal. machine gun. Whether the target was a truck convoy, a cavalry column, a pack train, or a convoy of horse-drawn vehicles, the attacking aircraft strafed the length of the column, sometimes flying exactly over the axis of the target, sometimes approaching at an acute angle.

Many attacks on road traffic were supplementary to strikes against other targets. The main roads often paralleled railroads or rivers, so trucks and horses were often sighted in the course of attacks on railroad bridges and, to a lesser degree, on shipping When such was the case, fighters or medium bombers with ammunition remaining would give their attention to strafing road traffic when the strike on the primary target had been completed In the Hsiang Valley, bombers and fighters often made sweeps and shot up any target discovered. Thus a group of aircraft on a single mission might attack river shipping, rolling stock on a railroad, and trucks on a highway.

Throughout 1943 and 1944, Japanese interception was always a possibility during attacks on roads. Often therefore part of the attacking formation would remain aloft as top cover while the remainder bombed and strafed. When the initial attacking element had expended its bombs and half its ammunition, it would climb to take over the covering detail while the element which had originally provided cover went down to bomb and/or strafe.

This type of attack was usually not feasible against motor pools. Such concentrations of motor vehicles were likely to be defended by antiaircraft weapons, which made minimum-altitude strafing a risky business. When reconnaissance or intelligence revealed the location of a motor pool, a bombing attack usually preceded strafing. When the target was an especially lucrative one, B-24's might be called in to do the bombing, but ordinarily four or six B-25's drew this detail. Sometimes, too, fighters dive-bombed such targets then went down to strafe in the confusion created by their own bombs

During the Hsiang Valley offensive of 1944, the Japanese learned that daylight movement of trucks was too expensive, and soon large convoys were observed only during the hours of darkness. The Fourteenth Air Force never succeeded in inflicting losses at night comparable to those claimed during daylight hours, but every effort was made to harass night traffic and to do as much damage as possible.

Though at least one experimental mission was flown in which B-25's dropped flares to illuminate targets for fighters, B-25's operating without the benefit of arti-

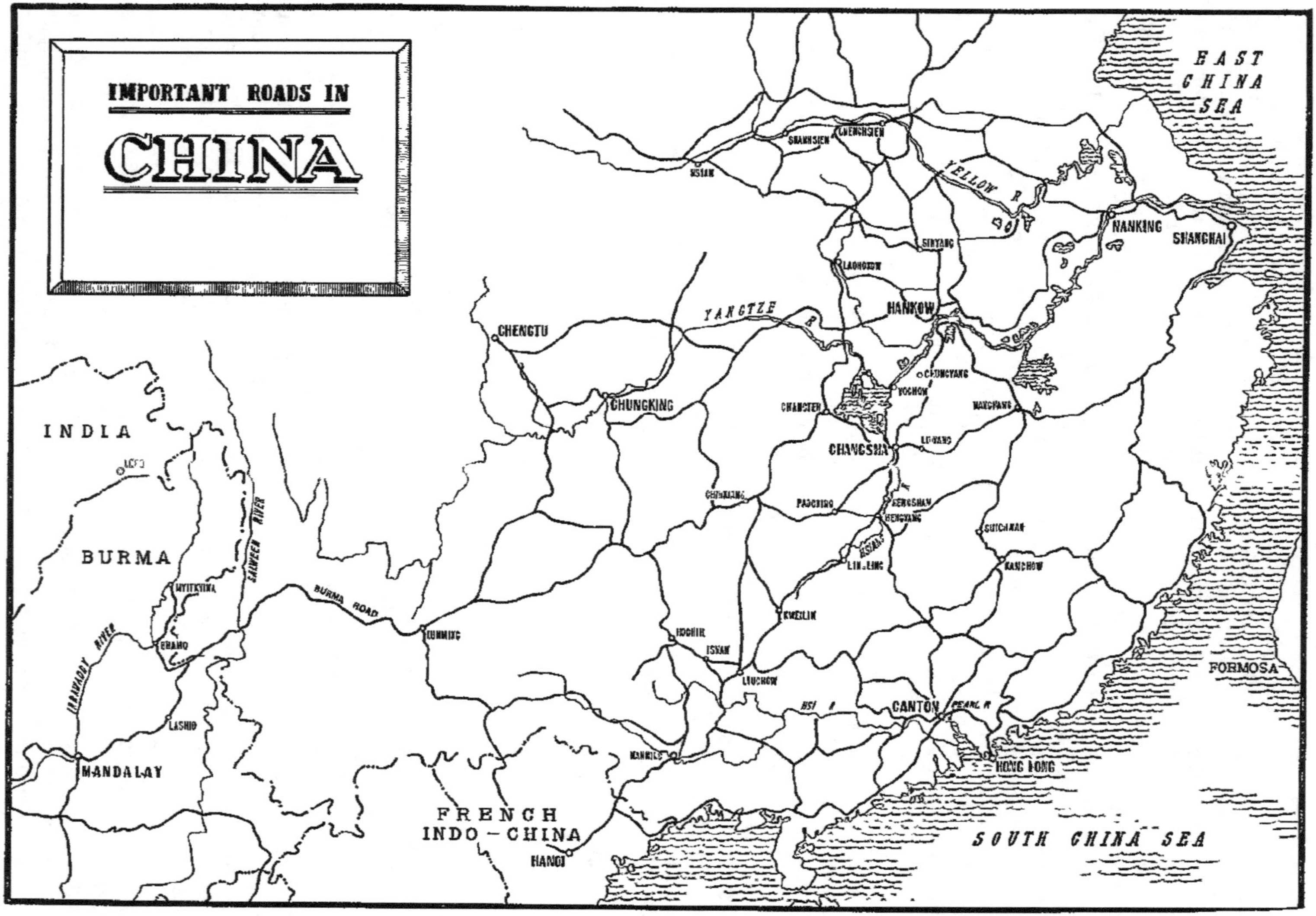
IMPORTANT ROADS IN
CHINA
EAST CHINA SEA
SOUTH CHINA SEA
FORMOSA
INDIA
BURMA
FRENCH INDO-CHINA
NANKING
SHANGHAI
HANKOW
CHENGTU
CHUNGKING
CHANGSHA
CANTON
HONG KONG
MANDALAY
LASHIO
BHAMO
MYITKYINA
KUNMING
HANOI
KWEILIN
LIUCHOW
YELLOW R
YANGTZE R
PEARL R
BURMA ROAD
SALWEEN RIVER
IRRAWADDY RIVER
KANCHOW
HSIAN
LAOHOKOW
SINYANG
YOCHOW
HENGYANG
PAOCHING
CHANGTEH
ISHAN
HSI R

Map No. 3

ficial light were the chief instruments used for night intruder work. In level terrain, the medium bombers often strafed motor convoys revealed by their headlights—especially was this possible in the Hsiang Valley. The more usual method of attack, however, was to bomb the convoy from 1,000-4,000 feet altitude, using fragmentation or small demolition bombs Sometimes incendiaries were used to mark targets for a second bombing run. There was expectation that proximity fuzes, which became available toward the end of the war, would increase the effectiveness of night attacks on truck convoys, but the use of these new devices in China, if it existed at all, was very slight. In 1945 P-61 night fighters, better equipped for night flying, supplemented the B-25 effort with greater emphasis on strafing attack [7]

ROAD INTERDICTION CAMPAIGNS

Like almost all air operations, those of the Fourteenth Air Force were not neatly divided into campaigns either chronologically or geographically. Different phases of air action overlapped both in time and space. Moreover, the same aircraft could (and sometimes did) attack river shipping, road targets, and railroad targets on the same sorties. A somewhat arbitrary classification of operations into campaigns does make it possible to discuss road interdiction activities with less danger of confusion, but it is necessary to remember that at least two of the campaigns discussed below were going on at almost any given time

The Salween campaign, January 1943-January 1945. The Salween campaign, as related earlier, was the effort by Chinese forces to defend the western approaches to Kunming and, after May 1944, to move west from Yunnan to establish land communications with Allied forces moving east from India. Air activity in connection with the Salween campaign was mainly devoted to air defense and to direct support of the Chinese ground forces, but there were many attacks on communications between Lashio, northern Thailand, and the front. Bridges were the most common communications target, but after bombing bridges, or after a strike in support of the ground forces, aircraft might seek out trucks or other targets on the roads Also included in the Salween effort were the attempts, described earlier, to cause landslides on the Burma Road.

During the months between January 1943 and February 1945, Fourteenth Air Force bombing attacks were credited with destroying 34 bridges and damaging 25 on the approaches to the Salween front. Bridges destroyed were on the Burma Road or on the the supply route leading to the Salween area from Thailand It should be noted that the totals given above include the destruction of some individual bridges several times The Japanese proved very capable of quickly reconstructing bombed-out bridges; furthermore, many bypasses were constructed in order to minimize the effects of bombing Since aerial photography and/or reconnaissance confirmed most of the Fourteenth Air Force bridge claims and contradicted none of them, it may be assumed that the totals above are approximately correct. Further destruction of bridges on the Japanese supply routes was effected by Tenth Air Force fighters and bombers, particularly those based at Myitkyina after Allied occupation of that airfield. Yet so effective was Japanese bridge rebuilding, bypass construction, and utilization of fords and ferries that lack of supplies was never a serious obstacle to Japanese forces in the Salween area Lack of reinforcements was a serious problem, but this lack resulted from a shortage of troops in Burma as a whole rather than from inability to transport men to the front over the roads.

During 1943 and the first four months of 1944, Fourteenth Air Force fighters claimed to have destroyed 73 motor vehicles and to have damaged 70 in attacks on Salween communications. Pilots also attacked 102 horses and 9 carts. Although the number of sorties flown increased greatly after the Chinese offensive began in May of 1944, the number of motor vehicles claimed during the nine months of the offensive was only 108 destroyed and 130 damaged. As low as these claims are, it is quite possible that they are too high The Japanese had comparatively few vehicles on the

Salween front, and most of their movement was at night. The terrain was not suited to night operations such as were carried out in the Hsiang Valley during the same period. Being on the defensive in terrain they had occupied for two years, the Japanese needed less transport than would have been necessary for an offensive.[8]

Indo-China, January 1943-August 1945. With the exception of skirmishing between Japanese and French forces in March 1945, no ground campaign was fought in Indo-China in World War II. Early Fourteenth Air Force operations in this area were mainly strategic, designed to prevent the shipment of raw materials from Indo-China to Japan. Later operations were intended to cut communications between the northern and southern parts of the colony. Such being the case, shipping and railroads were the chief targets after air superiority had been established.

There was no campaign against road bridges in Indo-China. However, since many bridges were combined road-railroad crossings, attacks on the railroads had a secondary effect on the road system. As a supplement to railroad interdiction, through mistaken identity, or as targets of last resort, two road bridges not combined with rail bridges were destroyed and six were damaged in Indo-China during the war.

Destruction of motor vehicles was also incidental to other missions. B-25 bombers making low-altitude attacks on railroad bridges sometimes sighted trucks and destroyed them by strafing. Bombers or fighters which had failed to find shipping on sweeps of coastal waters occasionally attacked motor transport as a target of opportunity. Some trucks were destroyed by fighters whose primary mission was to attack enemy airfields. Claims of cars, trucks, and buses destroyed during the war totaled 106, with 89 claimed as damaged.[9]

East and north China roads, January 1943-April 1944. Fourteenth Air Force made no effort to interdict the roads in Occupied China before the beginning of the Japanese offensive in 1944. Japanese communications followed water routes during the Changteh offensive of November-December 1943, so there was no call for effort against road traffic. The attacks which were made against motor vehicles, horses, and road bridges in Occupied China prior to May 1944 were incidental to strikes on other targets—usually accomplished by escorting fighters after the bombing force had turned toward home. Under such conditions, the damage inflicted was naturally slight. Claims for the period amounted to 33 trucks destroyed, 21 trucks damaged, 40 horses killed, and 1 pontoon bridge damaged.[10]

Interdicting the Honan Offensive of 1944. The first step in the great Japanese offensive of 1944 was the drive across Honan Province with the object of occupying the Peking-Hankow Railroad zone from the Yellow River to Hankow. The occupation of this railroad was necessary in order to establish land communications between Hankow and North China, communications which were essential to Japanese plans in view of the constriction of supply up the Yangtze and the increasing depredations of Allied submarines in the East China Sea.

The Japanese offensive in Honan was quickly successful. Although the Chinese had earlier destroyed the roads and the railroads in the area, the level wheat fields of Honan sufficed for the movement of motorized equipment. Between the middle of April and the end of May, the Japanese had occupied the Peking-Hankow corridor from Chenghsien to Sinyang, which gave free access to Hankow when the railroad had been rebuilt. Also, control of the Lunghai Railroad from Chenghsien to Shanhsien had been secured, and effective Chinese resistance between the Yellow and Yangtze Rivers had been eliminated.

Occupied with the beginning of the Salween offensive in the west, with defense of their bases in the east against air attack, and plagued by an unusually severe fuel shortage, Fourteenth Air Force was unable to check or even seriously hamper the Japanese advance. A few Chinese-American Composite Wing (CACW) aircraft went into action in early May, after the enemy had already gained momentum. During the remainder of the month, these B-25's and P-40's claimed to have destroyed 164 motor vehicles, to have damaged 457, and to have killed 235 horses. The Japanese completed the campaign with the fighting effectiveness of the participating units largely undamaged.[11]

The Hunan-Kwangsi campaign of 1944. An outline of the Japanese offensive up the Hsiang Valley from Hankow and from Canton up the Hsi Valley to Liuchow has been given in the preceding chapter. The Hsiang and Hsi Rivers were the chief supply routes for this drive, but the roads were also used rather extensively.

During the first phase of the offensive, from 20 May 1944 until the fall of Hengyang on 8 August, the Japanese used two land routes. Pack trains moved along the abandoned railroad bed from Changsha toward Hengyang. Trucks moved along the road which roughly paralleled the railroad. The Japanese attempted to keep open two other roads (Chungyang-Liuyang and Hsinghiang-Changsha) from the Hankow area, but the rains which aided them in navigation of the Hsiang made these roads impassable and their improvement impossible. As a result, practically all of the Japanese vehicle units, including field artillery, had to pass over the Yochow-Changsha Road, which was itself so muddy that trucks preceeded at snail's pace.[12]

Fourteenth Air Force units based at Hengyang, Lingling, and Kweilin took full advantage of the opportunity this congestion afforded. During June and July and until 8 August, claims totaled 990 motor vehicles destroyed, 1,638 damaged, and 2,739 horses killed. No doubt the figures for motor vehicles were somewhat exaggerated, but the Japanese noted the loss of more than 10,000 horses from all causes, and troops in the line received few supplies of any kind before the end of July. Bridges were not a primary target system, but five were reported destroyed and eight damaged.[13]

As noted above, the Japanese soon learned to hide their vehicles during the day and to move them only at night. This passive defense measure, and bad weather which plagued Fourteenth Air Force operations, enabled the Japanese to move supplies west from Hengshan to Hengyang. Some 25-30 motor vehicle companies were used to move munitions to the front, and about 3,000 tons of supplies had reached Chuanhsien by the end of October. This heavy traffic in wet weather severely damaged the roads and led to serious difficulties as the battle line moved westward. The arrival of the Twenty-third Army from Canton at the front below Kweilin did nothing to improve the transport situation because that army had depended almost entirely on the Hsi River as a supply route during its advance.

Fourteenth Air Force attacks during the remainder of 1944 were intensely annoying to the Japanese, but motor traffic was not halted. Troops in the Kweilin-Liuchow area continued to be supplied by trucks until, in early 1945, the Hengyang-Kweilin section of the Hunan-Kwangsi Railroad was repaired to an extent which enabled it to assume part of the burden. Claims for the period from 8 August through September, a time which afforded many days of good weather, came to 763 motor vehicles destroyed, 1,747 damaged, and 1,744 horses killed in the Hsiang corridor. In addition, 13 road bridges were claimed destroyed and 14 damaged. In October, which brought exceedingly bad weather to the Hsiang Valley area, claims were reduced to 51 vehicles and 235 horses destroyed and 90 vehicles damaged. Seven bridges were destroyed and six damaged. Weather was good in the Hsi River area during September and October, but road targets were few. During those months and November, claims were for only 26 vehicles destroyed, 86 damaged, 4 bridges destroyed, and 6 damaged. Horses killed were listed as 575, but the number was that large only because one cavalry column was caught in a defile and slaughtered by relays of aircraft. During November and December, attacks on the roads from Hankow to Hochih resulted in claims of 1,490 horses killed, 229 motor vehicles destroyed, 420 motor vehicles damaged, 2 road bridges destroyed, and 7 road bridges damaged.

The campaign under discussion was the Fourteenth Air Force's most important attempt at road interdiction, though it must be remembered that it was only part of an over-all interdiction effort directed at railroads, shipping, and roads. It did not bring the Japanese armies to a halt short of their original objectives, though there is some evidence that their timetable may have been disrupted.

As noted in the discussion of the Salween campaign, claims of bridge destruction and damage were largely confirmed by aerial photography and/or reconnaissance. Japanese sources confirm the loss of more than twice as many horses as the Fourteenth Air Force claimed during the 1944 offensive. Therefore the total claims for the period June-December 1944 of 31 road bridges destroyed, 41 road bridges damaged, and 6,831 horses killed can be accepted as reasonably accurate.

The same cannot be said for the claims of 2,059 trucks destroyed, and 3,981 damaged during the same period. The Japanese had, at the most, 30 motor vehicle companies in the Hsiang Valley. It is highly unlikely that these companies had full table of organization equipment, but if they did, this amounted to only some 5,000 trucks. Perhaps 1,000 more trucks were attached to other than transport units, and perhaps (though not likely) 1,000 replacement vehicles arrived during the campaign. Thus not more than 7,000 trucks could have been available to the Japanese. Since no trucks were manufactured in China, since replacement from Japan had become more and more difficult, and since normal wear and tear without doubt had depleted the vehicles originally assigned, half of 7,000 would probably be a closer estimate of the number of trucks on hand and ready for use. If the attrition to be expected from wear and tear on the muddy Hsiang Valley roads be added to the number claimed damaged and destroyed by Fourteenth Air Force, the Japanese army in the corridor should have exhausted its truck supply before the end of 1944. In reality, trucks were still operating in the valley the last night of the war, and shortage of motor fuel was more of a handicap to the Japanese than a shortage of trucks. Almost certainly, not more than 1,500 trucks were destroyed by air action in China during 1944.[14]

Roads in north China, January - May 1945. As related in the earlier discussion of air attacks on Yangtze River shipping, Laohokow became an important base for such attacks after the fall of east China bases, and particularly after the fall of Suichwan and Kanchow in early 1945. Soon after the first of the year, the Japanese began gathering troops and equipment in the Yellow River area of Honan for a drive on Laohokow. Although most Fourteenth Air Force activity in North China was directed against shipping and the railroads, there were some strikes against road traffic. During January and February 1945, 49 motor vehicles were claimed destroyed, 40 damaged, and 60 horses were claimed as killed.

Early in March the Japanese began advancing against Laohokow across the Honan plains, and the airfield fell on the 27th of the month. Fourteenth Air Force fighters and bombers gave close support to the Chinese ground troops in their unsuccessful defense and also attacked Japanese transportation. Claims for the month came to 415 horses killed, 82 motor vehicles destroyed, and 415 motor vehicles damaged. Fighting continued in the Laohokow area throughout April, and during that month claims made were for 3,168 horses killed, 80 motor vehicles destroyed, 235 motor vehicles damaged, and 1,012 animal-drawn carts destroyed or damaged.

Ground activity was reduced in May, and as a result, though 95 trucks were claimed destroyed and 123 damaged, only 30 horses were claimed killed.

Interdiction effort in north China did not halt the Japanese drive on Laohokow, nor did it appreciably delay the capture of that base. However, interdiction, close support, and a comparatively strong effort by the Chinese ground forces prevented further advances which the Japanese may have contemplated. Chinese authorities feared for the safety of the Allied base at Hsian, and there is some evidence that the enemy did hope to add this airfield to his conquests, though the route to Hsian led through mountain passes which could have been defended easily by a small force. The Japanese certainly wanted to occupy a

they were, in many instances, better equipped than their opponents. The Chinese reserves, which were never committed, were those American-trained and equipped divisions which had fought their way across Burma to open the western portions of the Ledo-Burma Road. Finally, the Chinese defenders before Chihkiang had close air support on a scale far greater than had ever been seen before in China. Scores of fighter aircraft reported to liaison officers in the front lines and were directed to targets selected by the ground forces.

Interdiction of the roads behind the front also contributed to the Japanese defeat. All supplies had to be moved from Hengyang to Paoching and beyond by truck or horse, and Fourteenth Air Force aircraft attacked motor vehicles, bridges, and draft animals frequently. Many trucks, concealed during daylight, were destroyed by close support aircraft after the place of concealment had been discovered by ground force patrols. During April, claims in the area amounted to 38 trucks destroyed, 85 trucks damaged, 435 horses killed, 9 bridges destroyed, and 5 bridges damaged. During May the climax of the battle came as the Japanese reached their maximum penetration of the defenses and the Chinese switched from defense to offense. Trucks claimed as destroyed during May were 233, other claims included 244 trucks damaged, 812 horses killed, 8 road bridges destroyed, and 3 bridges damaged. During June, as the counterattacking Chinese drove the Japanese back to Paoching, only 50 horses were killed, but 103 motor vehicles were claimed as destroyed and 130 as damaged.[17]

The Japanese retreat, July - August 1945. Road interdiction was an unimportant part of Fourteenth Air Force operations against Japanese forces retreating from south China in July and August 1945. Although troop formations on the roads occasionally provided lucrative targets for strafing, attacks on river targets and the railroads brought, generally, a better return for a given effort. During the six weeks from 1 July to the end of the war, 277 horses were killed, 6 road bridges were destroyed and 1 damaged, 143 motor vehicles were claimed as destroyed, and 137 damaged.[18]

CONCLUSIONS

The Japanese in China used rivers, railroads, and roads to move men and military material. Because good roads were few in number and generally afforded a poor alternative to rail and water routes, they were not a prime target for interdiction. Bombs and bullets expended against rail bridges, locomotives, and shipping damaged Japanese lines of supply more than bombs and bullets expended against road bridges, motor vehicles, and horses. Only in the congested Hsiang corridor were roads and road traffic worth-while targets as communications. Of - course, when destruction of bridges and trucks was of direct help to Chinese ground troops, as was the case in the Salween, in the Hsiang corridor in 1944, in Honan in May 1944 and early 1945, and in the Paoching area in April and May of 1945, air attacks on road targets could be justified.

Fourteenth Air Force efforts against road targets brought rather extensive claims. For the course of the war, these claims amounted to 3,771 motor vehicles destroyed, 6,619 motor vehicles damaged, 96 road bridges destroyed and 90 damaged, 13,304 horses killed, and more than 1,500 animal-drawn carts destroyed or damaged. These claims resulted from more than 7,500 sorties by B-25 bombers and various types of fighter aircraft, but these planes frequently attacked other targets on the same missions, so the entire sortie expenditure cannot be charged to road interdiction. Probably less than 2,000 sorties operated exclusively against road targets [19]

In regard to these claims, it must be noted again that the claims of motor vehicles destroyed are undoubtedly too large —probably by 50 percent. Bridge claims are realistic, but involve the repeated destruction of a number of bridges after they had been repeatedly rebuilt by the Japanese. Claims of horses killed appear large, but since claims during the greatest campaign are more than confirmed by Japanese sources, it may be assumed that the total is approximately correct.

Except for the attrition exacted from Japanese transport capacity, road interdiction in China seems to have accomplished little Some fraction of the credit for delaying the capture of Hengyang until 8 August 1944 can be assigned to this type of air operation, and a still smaller share of the credit for the Japanese defeat at Chihkiang may likewise be assigned Elsewhere, the Japanese apparently went where they wanted to go when they wanted to go, perhaps inconvenienced, but certainly not halted or delayed by attacks on road transport. The story could have been different had the Chinese ground forces been able to offer stronger opposition. In a closely matched military contest, partial interdiction of the roads might have tipped the balance Under the conditions which existed, however, most of the air effort expended against the roads could just as well, if not better, have been devoted to other targets.

CHAPTER IV

RAIL INTERDICTION IN INDO-CHINA

THE RAILROADS OF INDO-CHINA*

IN FRENCH INDO-CHINA, the railroads were a supplement to water transportation, and were therefore not so vital a target for air operations as, for instance, the Peking-Hankow Railroad in China. The Indo-Chinese railroads did, however, offer targets to those Fourteenth Air Force bombers and fighters which were based in west China and which could not be used against targets in east or north China. For this reason, attacks were made on the system when opportunity arose throughout the period of Fourteenth Air Force operations. In 1945, after the Japanese had occupied a corridor which, at least in appearance, provided continuous land communications between Korea and Indo-China, a sustained campaign against Indo-Chinese railroads commenced

Because of range factors, practically all Fourteenth Air Force attacks were made against the rail lines north of Saigon. Inasmuch as a 170-mile gap existed between Saigon and Phnom Penh, Cambodia, which latter point was connected by rail with Thailand, Malaya, and Burma, the railroads from Saigon north were a separate system. For convenience, this system may be divided into four parts, like spokes of an eccentric wheel, with the hub at Hanoi.

The Hanoi-Na Cham line ran from Hanoi to within a few miles of the China border. It had little military significance, except that if the Japanese had been able to carry out their dream of extending the railroad from Hengyang to Liuchow, Nanning, and the Indo-China border, the Hanoi-Na Cham line would have been part of continuous rail communications from Korea to Saigon, if no farther.

The Hanoi-Lao Kay line extended 185 miles from Gia Lam, just outside Hanoi, to Lao Kay, practically on the border of Yunnan Formerly this railroad had run on north to Kunming, but when the Japanese occupied Indo-China, the Chinese destroyed 100 miles of track through some of the most forbidding terrain in China, making a Japanese advance north from Lao Kay practically impossible. Early in the war, phosphate was shipped to seaports over this railroad, but as Japanese shipping was sunk and ports were mined, this function came to an end. By 1945, the railroad served only as a means of transporting small quantities of agricultural products and as a line of supply for Japanese garrisons along the route.

The railroad from Hanoi to Haiphong gave access to the port of Haiphong and had considerable importance so long as that port was in use. After June of 1943, mining and air attacks made the port facilities useless, so the railroad lost its main purpose. The Japanese still made every effort to keep the line open because of its potential usefulness as a line of supply in case of an Allied landing in the Hanoi area.

The Hanoi-Saigon rail line was far longer than any of the above-mentioned Indo-Chinese lines, extending more than 1,000 miles down the coast to Saigon. This railroad, like the Hanoi-Na Cham, would have been an essential part of the Pusan-Singapore rail system had this idea ever been turned into reality. Even after the Japanese abandoned the Liuchow-Nanning corridor, this railroad was vital to the Japanese in Indo-China, being the only practical connection between their forces in the north and in the south after water transportation of men and supplies became imprac-

*See Map No 4, p 47

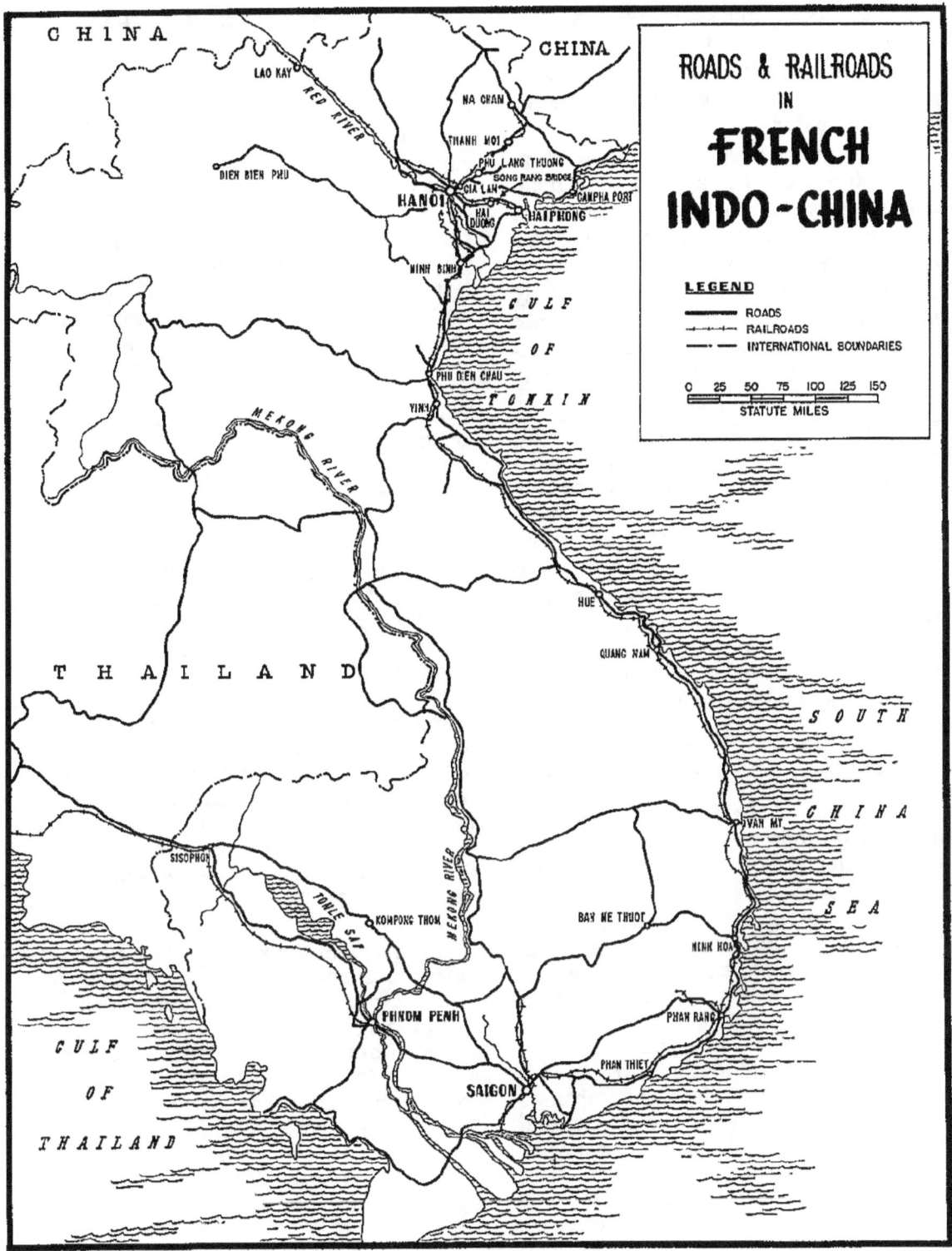

tical. Also, north Indo-China was a food-deficiency area, depending on food from the south, and much of this had to be sent by rail because of air and submarine attacks on shipping.

Designed only as a supplement to shipping, meter-gauge throughout, the Indo-Chinese rail system north of Saigon was of very limited capacity. In peacetime the Hanoi-Saigon section was capable of carrying only 1,500,000 tons a year, or slightly more than 4,000 tons a day, and other lines were rated considerably lower. By neglecting maintenance and overloading cars, the Japanese were probably able to exceed this figure for a while, but wear and tear, combined with air attacks, eventually brought the figure to a point far below peacetime capacity. Though rolling stock had been attacked only as a target of opportunity, the supply of locomotives had been reduced from 240 to probably 200 by 1 January 1945, and passenger and freight cars from 3,500 to a probable 3,000. During 1945, systematic attacks on Indo-Chinese railroads reduced rolling stock and capacity considerably more.[1]

RAILROAD ADMINISTRATION IN INDO-CHINA

Until March of 1945, the railroads in French Indo-China remained under French administration. The Japanese were content in Indo-China to leave the French authorities in control of the government and economy under the terms of agreements which satisfied Japanese needs. Thus the French ran the railroads and, insofar as any defense was offered, defended them. Japanese bases were, in general, well removed from the cities and main communication lines. In March 1945 the Japanese took over direct control of the colony and, eventually, set up a puppet government. For the last four months of the war, then, the Japanese were responsible for railroad administration and management. Even so, most French and native employees and supervisors were retained, and there was no material change in administration.[2]

THE INTERDICTION OF INDO-CHINESE RAILROADS

Introduction. The air campaign against railroads in Indo-China was undertaken neither to establish air superiority nor to support Allied ground forces. In 1943 and 1944 the main object of the campaign was to interdict the movement of raw materials from points of production to ports from whence they could be shipped to Japan. A few attacks on the separate rail system in western Indo-China and Thailand served the same purpose but also had some effect in hampering the movement of supplies and reinforcements from Indo-China and Thailand to Japanese forces engaged in the defense of Burma.

After the attrition of Japanese shipping by submarines, aircraft, and mines had curtailed the shipment of raw materials to Japan, attacks on Indo-China railroads continued. Through the latter half of 1944 and the first half of 1945, however, these attacks were intended more to separate the northern and southern parts of Indo-China from one another than to sever the colony from Japan. Indirectly, attacks on Indo-China railroads may have hampered Japanese efforts in Burma. There was also some hope that these strikes would be helpful to American forces in the Pacific, but in actual fact, the Japanese had no intention of reinforcing the Pacific from Southeast Asia. On the contrary, two divisions from China were added to the Indo-China garrison in early 1945.

Certainly an important reason for attacks on Indo-China railroad targets was the geographical fact that Indo-China was within range of Fourteenth Air Force bases in west China. Only a little more than half as much fuel was required to fly a sortie from Kunming or Yangkai as was needed to fly a similar sortie from Chihkiang. Moreover, the fuel was available as soon as it was flown over the Hump (or pumped in by pipeline in the last months of the war) in contrast to long delays encountered in moving it to north China bases. Indo-Chinese railroads may not have been so important to the Japanese as Chinese railroads in late 1944 and early 1945, but missions could be mounted against Indo-China without hampering the operations of fuel-starved units in east and north China

Strikes against marshalling yards and repair facilities. Attacks against marshalling yards and repair shops in Indo-China were a minor part of the air campaign. The shops at Vinh were put out of action by 24 B-24's on 13 February 1944, when three-fourths of the built-up area was demolished Minor facilities at Campha Port were bombed by four B-25's on 2 March 1944, and the minor shops at Phu Lang Thuong were bombed by six B-25's on 10 July 1945 and by 4 B-25's on 20 July 1945. The B-24 attack on Vinh was very effective, and each of the other strikes inflicted some damage, but little more was accomplished than inconveniencing the operators of the railroads, because shops were available in southern Indo-China out of effective range of all Fourteenth Air Force aircraft save B-24's.

Marshalling yards, though they received less attention than bridges and rolling stock, were hit harder and more often than repair facilities. B-24's flew 137 sorties against marshalling yards in Indo-China and Thailand from China bases. B-25's flew 35 sorties, and fighters flew 92 Planes sometimes strafed marshalling yards on sweeps of Indo-Chinese railroads, but only planes on those sorties detailed above dropped bombs.

The B-24's attacked yards at Haiphong, Chengmai, Lampang (twice), Bangkok, and Gia Lam. All targets were hit to some extent, and photographic interpretation revealed considerable damage. An intelligence report derived from French sources stated that the last of the B-24 strikes, against Gia Lam on 28 November 1944, destroyed 300 meters of track, damaged or destroyed all station installations, damaged or destroyed six locomotives which were left buried under debris, and damaged some 30 passenger and 100 freight cars.

Sixteen other yards were bombed by fighters or small formations of B-25's Four of these, Campha Port, Thanh Moi, Phu Lang Thuong, and Ninh Binh, were attacked two or more times. Considerable trackage was destroyed by these strikes, and in many instances rolling stock was damaged as well. Usually such missions were undertaken only when reconnaissance had revealed a concentration of rolling stock.[3]

Attacks on rolling stock Destruction of and damage to rolling stock on the Indo-Chinese railroads was a part of the Fourteenth Air Force interdiction scheme, though a minor part. Attacks on locomotives and railroad cars in Indo-China began in March 1943, but only ten such strikes, 44 sorties, were flown during that year Claims were for 6 locomotives destroyed and 11 damaged, and 33 cars damaged. Most of the claims resulted from strafing attacks. No doubt other rolling stock was damaged by bombs aimed at marshalling yards, but it was not always possible to make detailed claims in such cases.

Attacks on rolling stock were heavier during 1944, with 69 strikes, totaling some 300 sorties, of which more than 100 were flown by B-25's and the remainder by fighters Locomotives claimed destroyed numbered 26, and 39 were listed as damaged More than 300 cars were claimed as destroyed or damaged. Some of these missions were planned strikes against concentrations of rolling stock discovered by reconnaissance—concentrations which sometimes resulted from bombed-out bridges—but most of the damage to locomotives resulted from fighter sweeps searching for targets of opportunity. Some attacks on rolling stock were made by aircraft returning from sea sweeps over the Gulf of Tonkin.

It was estimated that as of 1 January 1945, there were 200 locomotives and 3,000 cars in service on Indo-Chinese railroads as compared with 240 locomotives and 3,500 cars in 1940. From January through July 1945, 83 strikes attacked rolling stock north of Saigon About 370 sorties, more than 150 by B-25's, were sent on these missions. Claims amounted to 29 locomotives destroyed, 148 locomotives damaged, 50 cars destroyed, and 386 cars damaged. These claims, in regard to locomotives, were an impressive proportion of the total in service in Indo-China. When the fact that these attacks were concentrated north of Saigon is taken into consideration, it becomes evident that the number of serviceable locomotives in northern Indo-China must have been drastically reduced, even though the claims were somewhat exaggerated.

In regard to the validity of these claims, no exact evaluation is possible. It must be remembered that they do not include all rolling stock destroyed or damaged by attacks on marshalling yards, so that factor compensates somewhat for undue optimism in assessment. On the other hand, the figures for locomotive destruction are undoubtedly too high One of the lessons of World War II was that anything less than a direct hit or very near miss with a heavy bomb seldom destroyed locomotives Since many of these claims were based on strafing attacks, it is almost certain that the number of locomotives destroyed was less than the number claimed The total destroyed or damaged, however, must have been 150 or more. This was certainly sufficient to greatly hamper operation of the railroad, especially since the capacity of the repair shops in northern Indo-China had been reduced.[4]

Attacks on Indo-China bridges Bridges afforded the best railroad targets in Indo-China and received the most concentrated attention from Fourteenth Air Force. The north-south railroad from the China border and Haiphong to Saigon ran along the coast and crossed hundreds of streams flowing into the Gulf of Tonkin and the South China Sea. On the 1,800 miles of track in the colony there were 74 bridges not less than 100 meters long, or an average of one major bridge to every 25 miles of track. Since no alternate railway routes existed, destruction of any one of these bridges effectively cut the railroad, giving the Japanese no choice but to unload freight, transport it across the stream by boat or truck. and reload it aboard a train on the other side. Since 23 of these major bridges were combined rail-highway crossings, their destruction interrupted road as well as rail communications

Because of distance, most bridge missions were flown against targets north of Saigon, but a few strikes ranged over into Thailand, attacking and eventually destroying the Dara, Chiengrai, and Kenghluang bridges in that country.

Over-all, the Fourteenth Air Force flew 105 missions, 643 sorties (18 B-24, 363 B-25, 67 P-40, 103 P-38, and 92 P-51) against bridges in Indo-China and Thailand. There were 141 attacks on bridges. Fifty-six of these attacks missed (or failed to damage) bridge targets, 51 inflicted some damage, and 34 destroyed one or more spans of the bridge attacked.

This over-all résumé does not give the whole story. Attacks on bridges in Indo-China began in February 1944 when the 22d and 491st Squadrons of the 341st Bombardment Group arrived in China. The tactical justification of the campaign, as suggested earlier, was to prevent the transfer of troops and material from southern to northern Indo-China. From February through April 1944, 19 strikes, most of them by B-25's, destroyed or damaged eight bridges between Hanoi and Hue, the latter located about half-way to Saigon. The Japanese moved slowly in repairing this damage, and only 22 more strikes were flown during the period May-October 1944, destroying one or more spans of three bridges, inflicting some damage on nine, and missing 18 Despite considerable inconvenience, the Japanese managed to keep a fairly steady flow of traffic moving over the line until September, when a low-level strike by B-24's completely demolished the large bridge at Hue. Transshipment around this gap greatly reduced traffic for several weeks, and the rate of freight movement never reached what it had been before the Hue bridge was destroyed.

In November 1944 it became apparent that the Japanese could open a corridor across south China into Indo-China, and there was some apprehension lest troops from Indo-China should move toward Kunming. During November and December of 1944, 28 strikes for a total of 120 B-25 and

80 fighter-bomber sorties made 36 attacks on bridges in Indo-China Fourteen of these attacks were unsuccessful, four destroyed bridges, and 18 inflicted damage

When the Japanese land corridor through Hengyang, Liuchow, and Nanning to Indo-China was an accomplished fact, the importance of Indo-Chinese rail targets was enhanced. From January through July 1945 the Fourteenth Air Force waged war on Indo-China railroad bridges with such success that the Japanese finally gave up attempts at repair.

A comparison of bridge attacks in Indo-China in 1944 with those of 1945 is instructive, showing the increased effectiveness of air operations when crews have gained experience and techniques have been perfected. During 1944, Fourteenth Air Force made 90 attacks on bridges in Indo-China. Almost half of these attacks, 42, inflicted no damage, 10 destroyed one or more spans of the bridge, and 38 inflicted damage to some degree. Percentagewise, 11 percent of the attacks destroyed bridges, 42 percent inflicted damage, and 47 percent missed. During the first seven months of 1945, China-based aircraft made 51 attacks on Indo-Chinese railroad bridges, missing 14, damaging 13, and destroying one or more spans of 24 In percentages, 47 percent of the attacks destroyed bridges, 25 percent inflicted damage, and 28 percent missed.]

RESULTS

As an example of what air action can do to an isolated railway system without alternate routes, the campaign against Indo-Chinese railroads, and the lines north of Saigon in particular, was a classic Through traffic was interrupted frequently during 1944 and the capacity of the lines, low under favorable conditions, was significantly reduced Chief emphasis in the campaign was on bridges, but repair shops in the northern part of the colony were demolished, and lack of repair shops made blows at rolling stock and locomotives all the more damaging Attacks on rolling stock and locomotives were sporadic, launched when reconnaissance revealed a concentration or incidentally while engaged in other operations until 1945. Beginning in January of that year, however, locomotives became a primary target, and a special effort was made to destroy or damage those in operation between demolished bridges. An estimated two-thirds of the locomotives operating north of Saigon were damaged Most of these damaged units could be repaired rather quickly when removed to shops, but at the least considerable time was lost. Very slight damage might put a locomotive out of action for a long time if it chanced to be between two demolished bridges when attacked

As for bridge cuts, the Hanoi-Na Cham line had at least one major bridge out continuously from 1 January to 13 March 1945, and from 13 March to the end of the war three combination road-railroad bridges remained out Between Hanoi and Lao Kay, an 880 foot bridge was destroyed on 15 April 1944 and was not repaired thereafter. Between Hanoi and Haiphong, the 1,245-foot Hai Duong bridge was severely damaged—one span destroyed—on 12 December 1944, and the nearby Song Rang bridge was rendered impassable on 12 March 1945. On this section the Japanese made no repairs in 1945. They did attempt to repair damage to bridges on the Hanoi-Saigon section, but through traffic on this railroad was never possible from 19 January 1945 until the end of the war The damage inflicted on this line was so great that it remains broken to the date of this writing, in the summer of 1955.

The Japanese made frantic efforts to keep goods moving across the gaps in the railroads. The most common method was to unload goods on one side of a broken bridge and transfer them by boat to another train waiting on the other side. This method had its drawbacks, the most important of which was the time consumed Since two trains were tied up for considerable lengths of time, there was acute danger that they would be discovered and strafed by Allied fighter planes. Also, this measure became impossible when no locomotive was available between two bridge cuts, as was sometimes the case after locomotives became a primary target in early 1945. At some bridge sites, warehouses were built at each end, so that freight could be stored after being transshipped across the gap, thus exposing only one locomotive at a time. This measure, however, brought even more delay in the delivery of goods to their destination.

Sometimes it was possible for the Japanese to unload goods from trains, load them on trucks, and circumvent two or more line breaks on highways parallel to the railroad. The opportunities for this sort of transshipment were limited, however, because so many bridges accommodated both the highway and the railroad that a break in one often constituted a break in the other. Even so, trucks could be ferried across streams, while trains could not.

Because transshipment by boat was usually possible, and because building a bypass bridge merely created another and more vulnerable target unless the main bridge was repaired, the Japanese built few bypasses in Indo-China as compared with Burma and China. A bypass was built at Do Len, 96 miles south of Hanoi, and an earth and stone causeway served as a bypass at Song Chu, a little farther south on the same line.

Though the damage inflicted upon Indo-Chinese railroads was great, it is difficult to determine how this damage had any effect on the over-all Japanese ability to wage war. By the time railroad strikes became effective, it would have been impossible for the enemy to have reinforced his garrisons in the Pacific from Indo-China. It is certain that the Japanese in Indo-China had no intention at any time of invading Yunnan; hence attacks on the railroads brought no help to Chinese ground forces. Probably Fourteenth Air Force strikes against the railroads in western Indo-China and Thailand did give some support to Allied forces in Burma, but this could have been accomplished from better-supplied air bases in India.

Nor did the attacks on Indo-China railroads have any particular effect in reducing the flow of raw materials from Indo-China to Japan. Shipping routes had been cut by air and submarine action and by the mining of Indo-Chinese ports long before the air campaign against the railroads became effective. If it had been possible to devote this Fourteenth Air Force effort to the campaign in east China, perhaps the Japanese offensive could have been halted sooner.[6]

CHAPTER V

INTERDICTION OF CHINESE RAILROADS IN WORLD WAR II

INTRODUCTION

AT THE BEGINNING of 1943, the railroads of Occupied China were the most important means of communication the Japanese had in north China, and they were secondary only to the rivers and coastal waterways in east and south China. As the Japanese shipping situation grew more and more desperate, the railroads in China grew in importance.

As the railroads' importance to the enemy increased, it could be expected that they would become a major target for Fourteenth Air Force operations. From the Fourteenth Air Force operational point of view, this was all to the good, because the Japanese offensive of 1944 choked off attacks on ocean shipping and added greatly to the difficulty of attacks on Yangtze River shipping. Thus the railroads became a vital target just at the time when it was necessary for the Fourteenth Air Force to give up its orientation toward shipping strikes and apply its capabilities in another direction. Railroad strikes were a part of Fourteenth Air Force operations throughout 1944, but they became the dominant type of operation only in 1945.

Compared to western Europe or the United States, the rail system of China proper hardly qualified as a network, since a comparatively few lines, with few connections one with the other, were in operation. Manchuria had a much more extensive rail system, but it was beyond the range of Fourteenth Air Force operations. Therefore rail interdiction operations in China ranged from Peking in the north to Tsingtao and Nanking in the east to Canton in the south. It should also be noted that a few strikes were made from China bases against the Mandalay-Lashio Railroad in Burma, though this target was never an important one for Fourteenth Air Force.

THE RAILROADS OF CHINA*

Canton-Kowloon This railroad ran 112 miles from the port of Kowloon, opposite Hong Kong Island, to the city of Canton in Kwangtung Province. Maintenance of this line was difficult in peace, since much of the track was laid in swampy terrain and part of it along a coastline subject to damage from tidal waves and typhoons. More than 130 bridges, ranging from small to large, were subject to air attack and sabotage. Steel rails and bridge members eroded rapidly due to the humid, salty atmosphere.

During the pre-occupation period (1936-1939), 28 locomotives, 90 passenger cars, and 199 freight cars, owned by the British and Chinese, had been operating on this line. By 1944, it was estimated that only 10 steam locomotives, an undetermined number of diesel trucks equipped with flanged wheels, and 250 freight cars were operating in all of Kwangtung Province. Shops located at Tashatou and Kowloon had more than adequate repair capacity for the rolling stock available.

The pre-war military freight capacity of the Canton-Kowloon Railroad was estimated at 4,800 tons each way per day. By 1944, because most of the sidings had been removed, locomotives were few in number, and the condition of the bridges and right of way was poor, the capacity of the line was considerably lower.

The Canton-Kowloon Railroad was connected with the Canton-Hankow line by

---
*See Map No 5, p 58

a branch which ran around the northern edge of Canton. A branch also served the airfield and a factory to the south, and one other ran to the port of Whampoa southeast of Canton.[1]

Canton-Samshui. Beginning at Shihweitang, across the Pearl River from Canton, this railroad led to Samshui, 30 miles to the west on the Hsi River. Originally the line was double-tracked to a point ten miles west of Shihweitang, but the Japanese removed the rails from one track for use elsewhere. The right of way ran over the alluvial plain of the Hsi and Pei Rivers throughout its length, and service was frequently interrupted by floods.

This line was believed to have been capable in peacetime of carrying only 2,000 tons each way per day, and by 1944 capacity was greatly reduced by the condition of the roadbed, the shortage of locomotives, and the less stringent shortage of cars. Minor repair facilities were available at Shihweitang. Also at this point a ferry carried passengers and goods but not locomotives and cars across the Pearl River. The Canton-Samshui had no branches and no connections with other lines.[2]

Canton-Hankow. The Canton-Hankow Railroad, which really ran from Canton to Wuchang, across the Yangtze River from Hankow, was never open to through traffic during World War II. The Japanese began operating a section north to Hsinchieh after their occupation of Canton, and they also operated a section south from Wuchang to Yochow. The Chinese continued to operate the line from Changsha south to Lokchong until the summer of 1944. The Japanese gained control of the line from Wuchang to Leiyang during their offensive in 1944, but the Chinese still ran trains from Chenhsien to Lokchong until early in 1945, when the Japanese overran the entire route. The Japanese hoped to open the line to through traffic and had succeeded in providing a service of sorts from Wuchang to Leiyang in the north and from Canton to Yuantan in the south by June 1945. Their decision to abandon south China, followed soon by the surrender, prevented restoration of through service. Indeed, in view of air attack and Chinese guerrilla activities, it is doubtful that the line could have been opened in any event.

The southern section of the Canton-Hankow Railroad connected with the Canton-Kowloon just outside Canton, and freight could be shipped across the Pearl River to the Canton-Samshui. A branch led from Hsinchieh to coal mines at Hushsien. In the north, the Canton-Hankow connected with the Hunan-Kwangsi Railroad at Hengyang and with the Chekiang-Kiangsi line at Chuchow. There was no physical connection between the Canton-Hankow and the Peking-Hankow, but goods could be transferred from one line to the other after being carried across the Yangtze River. No regular train ferry was established at this point, but cars were sometimes ferried across the river by barge.

The capacity of this railroad was low before the war. During the struggle the poor quality of original construction, poor maintenance, air and guerrilla action, and a stringent shortage of cars and locomotives held capacity on the southern portion to a mere fraction of the theoretical maximum of 4,200 tons each way per day. The capacity of the section south from Wuchang was lower still.[3]

Hunan-Kwangsi. The Hunan-Kwangsi Railroad ran southwest from Hengyang to Liuchow. From Liuchow one fork ran northwest through Hochih and Tuhshan; it had been planned that this fork should extend on north to Chungking, but a gap of approximately 300 miles still existed in 1944. A second fork ran southwest from Liuchow to the French Indo-China border. When the Japanese occupied Indo-China, the Chinese destroyed the railroad from Nanning to the boundary, but the remainder of the line remained intact under Chinese operation until the Japanese offensive of 1944. As the Japanese advanced, the Chinese demolished or seriously damaged considerable portions of this road.

The Japanese apparently succeeded in restoring the line from Hengyang to Kweilin during the period of occupation. Railroad cars and some locomotives abandoned by the Chinese were restored to usable condition, and a few more cars and locomotives may have been shipped across the Yangtze from Hankow and brought down the Canton-Hankow Railroad from Wuchang to Hengyang Flange-wheeled trucks provided some additional motive power.

The Japanese dreamed of a railroad from Korea to Singapore and made frequent reference to such a project in their propaganda. The successful offensive of 1944 gave them possession of a railroad bed for the part of this route which ran through China Nonetheless, the Pusan-Singapore railroad remained a dream New construction would have been required to bridge the gap between Saigon and Pnom Penh across 140 miles of difficult Indo-China terrain. Not only was this construction beyond Japanese capability, but no attempt was made even to repair the demolished section between Nanning and the Indo-China border The Hunan-Kwangsi served the Japanese as a means of moving limited amounts of material west from Hengyang, but for little more.[4]

Chekiang-Kiangsi Originally this railroad was built with light rails, but it had just been rebuilt with standard rails when the Japanese occupation began. At that time the line ran from near Hangchow to Chuchow on the Canton-Hankow Railroad Much of the road was demolished by the Chinese during the early years of the war. A section 116 miles long from Chiangpien to Kinhwa was restored by the Japanese and was in operation in 1944 At that time the railroad was estimated to be capable of carrying 4,000 tons a day, and was used mainly for delivering fluorite from the mines at Wuyi to Shanghai.

A section 50 miles long, from Shangjao in Kiangsi Province to Chiangshan in Chekiang Province was operated by the Chinese This section had very limited capacity; only one train ran a day, and freight was reported to amount to 2,400 tons of military supplies a month.

The remainder of the Chekiang-Kiangsi Railroad was not restored during World War II The Japanese-operated section had little military significance, and it was so distant from Fourteenth Air Force bases that it was an infrequent target for air attack[5]

Shanghai-Hangchow-Ningpo. This railroad originally extended from Markham Station in Shanghai 192 miles to Ningpo, near the south shore of Hangchow Bay. The Japanese removed the rails from the section between Hangchow and Ningpo and used the roadbed as a highway, but they continued to run trains between Shanghai and Hsiaoshan, a distance of about 119 miles. This line operated without a great deal of interference from air or ground, using motor coaches for passengers and steam locomotives for hauling freight During 1944 about eight trains a day with a combined freight capacity of 5,000 tons operated on this road. The Shanghai-Hangchow-Ningpo connected with the Shanghai-Nanking Railroad at Shanghai and with the Chekiang-Kiangsi near Hangchow. The Japanese removed the rails from all branches[6]

Nanchang-Kiukiang The Japanese made some use of this short rail line, which ran 76 miles from Nanchang to the Yangtze at Kiukiang. Because it gave garrisons in the Nanchang area access to the Yangtze, it had some military importance. It was reported to have had an annual freight traffic of less than 200,000 tons in peacetime, and its capacity under the stress of war was probably even less.[7]

Peking-Hankow (Pinghan) The Peking-Hankow Railroad, better known as the Pinghan, became one of the most important Fourteenth Air Force targets North of Sinsiang the road was reconstructed and put into operation by the Japanese soon after their occupation of China began On this section, express trains maintained an average speed of 35 miles per hour before the Allied interdiction campaign began. Ample marshalling yards were available at Peking, Shihmen, Shihchiachuang, Anyang, and Sinsiang, in early 1944 yards were built on the north side of the Yellow River for use in handling cars carrying construction materials for the rebuilding of the line south of the river.

The Pinghan connected at Peking with the railroads leading from that city to

Shanghai to the south and Mukden to the north. At Shihchiachuang a junction was made with the Chengtai Railroad which ran west to Taiyuan and with the newly-built Shihchiachuang-Tehsien Railroad which gave access to the Tientsin-Pukow (Tsinpu) line. From Sinsiang the Kaifeng Cut-off departed from the Pinghan to join the Lunghai at Kaifeng. The main line of the Pinghan crossed the Yellow River south of Sinsiang and connected with the Lunghai at Chenghsien. Eight or more branches led to mining areas.

Because the Japanese did not operate railroad lines as separate entities, the number of locomotives and freight cars on the Pinghan varied. The line was physically joined to other roads of north China and through them to the Manchurian system, so rolling stock could be transferred to the Pinghan from these other lines. At Changhsintien and Fengtai, in the Peking area, were large locomotive and repair shops, and shops of considerable capacity were also available at Shihchiachuang and Sinsiang.

To the south, the Japanese occupation of Hankow gave them control of the Pinghan north to Sinyang. The 237-mile section between Sinyang to the south and Sinsiang to the north was dismantled by the Chinese and continued nominally under the control of Chinese armies until the spring of 1944. As related earlier, the first step in the Japanese offensive of 1944 was a drive which crossed the Yellow River and moved down the Pinghan right of way to Sinyang. Reconstruction began as soon as the roadbed was occupied, and some freight moved to Hankow before the end of 1944.

Opening of the Peking-Hankow throughout its length gave the Japanese the means of shipping goods by rail from Pusan in south Korea to Hankow. The Hsiang Valley offensive of May-August 1944 and the reconstruction of the Canton-Hankow Railroad from Yochow to Hengyang extended this rail connection still farther. Though the Japanese were unable to extend this connection to Canton or Indo-China, the direct connection between Korea, Manchuria, Peking, and Hankow was a great advantage to them. A given amount of shipping could transport far more goods between Pusan and Japan than between Japan and Shanghai, and the short voyage to Pusan was far less exposed to submarine attack. Furthermore, precious shipping did not have to run a gauntlet of mines and air attack up and down the Yangtze River.

As will be seen, the Japanese were unable to realize the full benefits, theoretically possible, from the newly-established rail connections. Fourteenth Air Force could strike rails, bridges, repair shops, and rolling stock as well as shipping. The yards and shops on the Pinghan made good targets for B-24's and B-25's. Fighters strafed locomotives unmercifully, and fighters and medium bombers attacked bridges day after day. Traffic continued to move over the Pinghan, but it moved at a crawl and in a volume far below the theoretical capacity of the line. The Yellow River bridge, the railroad's most vulnerable point, was bombed out again and again, until it was out of service as much of the time as it was available for use.[8]

Lunghai. The eastern terminus of the Lunghai Railroad was at Laoyao, on the Yellow Sea, and the track ran almost due west through Tungshan (Suchow), Kaifeng, Chenghsien, Loyang, and Hsian to Paochi, in western Shensi Province. The Kaifeng-Chenghsien section was largely destroyed by the 1938 flood which changed the course of the Yellow River, and retreating Chinese troops finished the destruction of this section. During most of World War II, therefore, the Japanese controlled the Lunghai from Laoyao to Kaifeng, the Chinese from Loyang to Paochi. However, during the spring of 1944, the Japanese overran the section between Kaifeng and Loyang and reestablished the connection with the Pinghan Railroad at Chenghsien. This development was important, because it gave the enemy two crossings of the Yellow River—on the main Pinghan line north of Chenghsien and on the Lunghai between Chenghsien and Kaifeng. By means of the Kaifeng Cutoff, mentioned earlier, goods could be moved over the Lunghai bridge at Chungmow when the Yellow River bridge was bombed out, or over the Yellow River bridge when the Chungmow bridge was out. By March of 1945, the Japanese were operating 430 miles of the Lunghai, from Laoyao to Loyang.

The Lunghai was one of the better-built railroads in China with well-ballasted roadbed rising 13 feet above the swampy terrain along most of its route. Marshalling yards were available at Laoyao, Tunghai, Yunho, Tungshan, Kaifeng, and Chenghsien. Small repair shops were located at Laoyao, Tungshan, and Kaifeng, but during normal operations locomotives were sent to Pukow for major repairs. In addition to the already-noted junctions with the Pinghan at Chenghsien and the Kaifeng Cutoff at Kaifeng, the Lunghai had a connection with the Tientsin-Pukow Railroad at Tungshan, which gave access to Nanking and Shanghai to the south, and to Tsingtao, Tientsin, Peking, and Manchuria to the north.

In 1935-36, the Lunghai was equipped with 108 locomotives, 1,057 freight cars, and 207 passenger cars. Under Japanese control the rolling stock and locomotive pool of the entire north China-Manchuria system was available in case of necessity. The capacity of the road in 1944 was estimated at 4,000 tons per day, but the estimate was based on slight information, and capacity may have been as high as 10,000 tons per day.⁹

Tatung-Puchou (Tungpu). The Tungpu Railroad was in the main constructed by the Japanese after their occupation of Shensi Province in 1938. Standard-gauge track ran from Tatung in the north through Sinhsien, Yuanping, and Ningwu to Taiyuan; south from Taiyuan meter-gauge track ran through Yutze and Linfen to Puchou. The standard-gauge section was 217 miles long, the meter-gauge section 298 miles long; an important meter-gauge branch extended 92 miles from Tungkuan to Luan.

At Tatung the Tungpu was connected with the Peking-Suiyuan (Pingsui) Railroad and thus was joined to the north China and Manchurian systems. At Taiyuan there was a junction with the Shihchiachuang-Taiyuan (Chengtai) line, thus affording a connection with the Pinghan at Shihchiachuang. The standard-gauge Chengtai and the meter-gauge Tungpu paralleled one another south to Yutze, where the Chengtai turned east. In addition to the Tungkuan-Luan branch mentioned above, a number of branches led from the Tungpu to mines near the main line.

The standard-gauge section of the Tungpu, by virtue of its connections with the north China railroad system, participated in the north China pool of rolling stock and locomotives. In early 1944 70 locomotives and 1,200 freight cars were reportedly in use on the meter-gauge section. By April of 1945, according to photographic reconnaissance of the railroad, only 40-45 locomotives remained operational or reparable south of Taiyuan. Repair facilities on the northern section were at Tatung, Ningwu, Yuanping, and Sinhsien. On the southern section, major shops were located at Taiyuan, and lesser facilities at Taiku, Pingyao, and Linfen.

The capacity of the Tungpu, with its hastily constructed roadbed and varying gauge, was low, at best. Though the northern section had a theoretical maximum capacity of 5,750 tons of freight a day, there was never enough rolling stock available for the line to approach this figure in actual operations. On the southern section, which had a theoretical maximum of 2,500 tons a day, the effect of air attack had been sufficient by the spring of 1945 to reduce actual capacity to less than 600 tons per day.¹⁰

Shanghai-Nanking (Hainan). One of the more important Chinese railroads, the Hainan ran between Shanghai and Nanking, a distance of 311 single-track miles. The first 16 miles of the track north from Shanghai was doubled. Through most of 1944, this railroad was a vital part of the Japanese military economy. Raw materials moved from their points of origin in north and central China to Nanking where they could be moved by rail or the Yangtze River to Shanghai for shipment to Japan. The decimation of Japanese ocean shipping, which drastically reduced exports from Shanghai, had greatly reduced the importance of the Hainan Railroad by 1945.

In 1935-36, the Hainan was equipped with

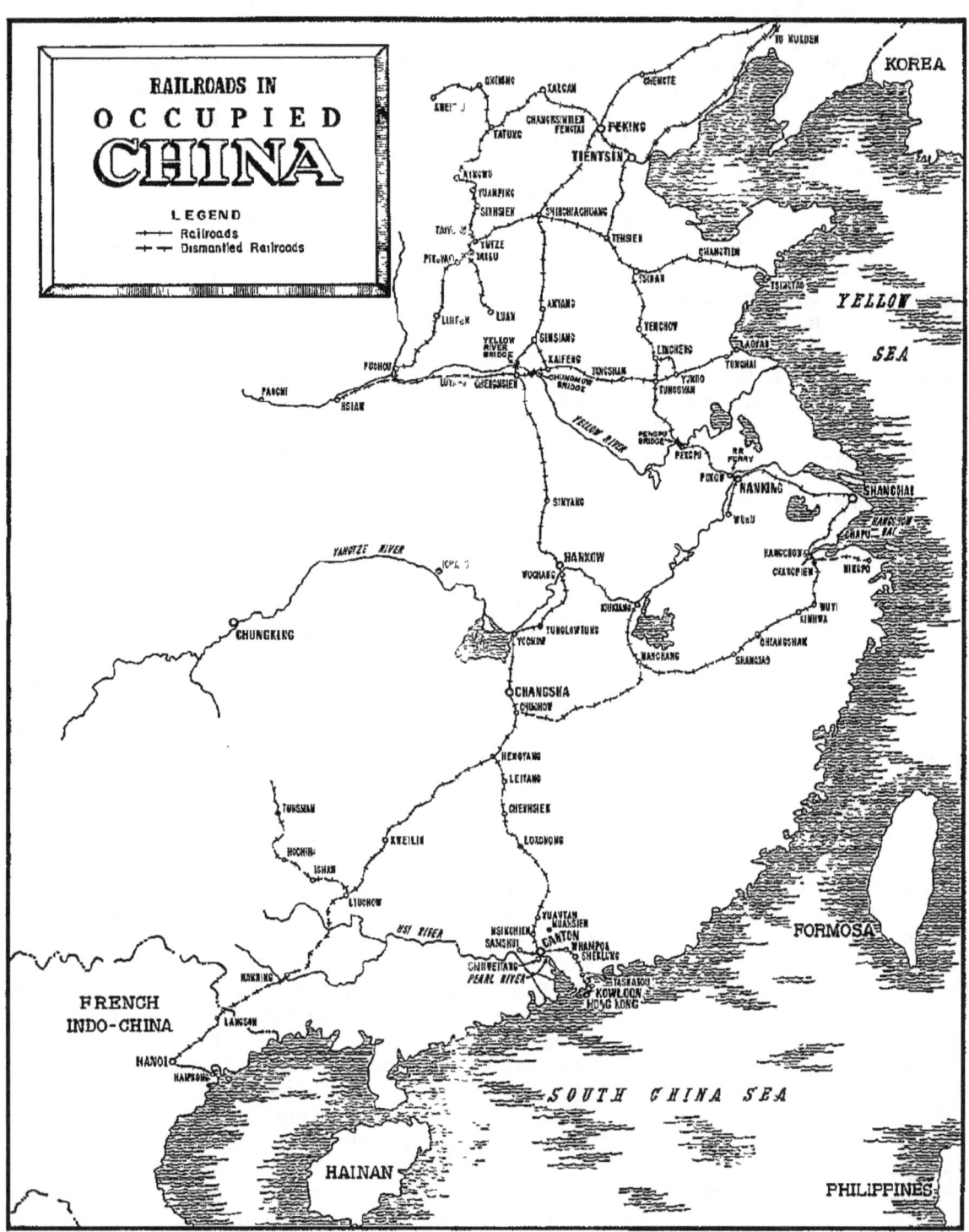

Map No. 5

75 locomotives, 535 freight cars, and 196 passenger cars. During the period of Japanese management, the rolling stock available must have been at least equal to this, and was probably greater. Also, the Japanese used a number of diesel or gasoline-powered cars, imported from Japan, for the movement of troops. Nine marshalling yards of importance were found on the line, with an additional 31 sidings of one or more tracks. Major repair shops were located at Shanghai and Nanking.

The Hainan had connections with three main lines. At Shanghai there was a junction with the Shanghai-Hangchow-Ningpo, at Nanking with the short Nanking-Wuhu. Finally, by railroad ferry at Nanking, there was a connection with the Tientsin-Pukow and thereby with the north China and Manchurian railroads. Several minor branches were found in the neighborhoods of Shanghai and Nanking.

The Nanking-Pukow Ferry was not only a vital part of the Chinese railroad system; it was also an ingenious example of engineering. This was the only ferry in China whereby whole trains could cross the Yangtze River. A serious problem of engineering was involved because the water level of the Yangtze varied some 24 feet during the year, with daily variations of as much as 3 feet during the low-water season.

Variations in water level were compensated for by slips on each side of the river, each composed of four spans mounted in tandem on long screws, operated electrically, and automatically adjusted to provide an even gradient to any expected water level. All spans were 152 feet long; the six interior spans were all 20 feet wide, and the two which came in contact with the boats flared out from 20 feet to 44 feet.

Two boats more than 300 feet long carried trains across the river between the two slips. Each had three 300-foot lengths of track for loading cars on the upper deck and could carry a load of 1,000 tons. A locomotive was carried on a platform at the after end of the upper deck, the platform being mounted on traveling gear so it would move across the deck horizontally and permit the locomotive to shunt cars from each track in turn. These boats were steam-propelled and made 12 knots in still water. Fully loaded, either of them could carry 21 freight cars of 18-ton tare and three locomotives.

Under Chinese management, the Hainan Railroad carried an average of almost 1,000,000 passengers and 154,000 tons of freight a month during the fiscal year 1935-36. The Japanese moved 881,119 passengers and 203,365 tons of freight over the line in the single month of April 1942, and they increased the freight carried to 229,374 tons in May of 1943. As late as November 1944 it was estimated that 200,000 tons of freight a month were moving over this railroad, but this amount was greatly reduced during 1945 as the importance of Shanghai diminished.[11]

Nanking-Wuhu (Kiangnan) This railroad, originally intended to run from Nanking south to Wuhu then southeast to Chapu on the coast south of Shanghai, was completed 22 miles beyond Wuhu, but the last 22 mile segment was later dismantled and never restored. The line covered 55 miles from Nanking to Wuhu and provided a needed rail connection between these two Yangtze River ports.

In 1935-36 the Kiangnan Railroad had 11 locomotives and 194 freight cars. This stock was greatly reduced by 1944, but since little traffic originated on the line, scarcity of assigned rolling stock had little effect under centralized Japanese management. There were no important stations between the two cities, and major repairs had to be made at Nanking. The Kiangnan connected with the Hainan at Nanking, and had one short branch (15 miles) which sent spurs out to various iron mines.[12]

Tientsin-Pukow (Tsinpu). The Tsinpu, which ran north-south from Tientsin in northeastern Hopei Province to Pukow, across the Yangtze from Nanking, was an important part of the all-rail communications between Korea and the lower Yangtze Valley. The distance between terminals was 626 miles. In addition to being a commodity carrier of considerable importance, the Tsinpu carried the major part of the troops and military supplies sent from north China to the depots and garrisons in the Yangtze Valley.

At Tientsin, the Tsinpu connected with the Peking-Mukden Railroad, the major link between China and Manchuria. At Tehsien, the Japanese-built Tehsien-Shihchiachuang ran west to join the Tsinpu with the Pinghan and Chengtai lines. The Shantung Railroad joined the Tsinpu at Tsinan, giving access to the port of Tsingtao and the Yellow Sea. A direct connection with the Lunghai was effected at Tungshan, and a secondary connection was accomplished by a branch which ran from Lincheng, north of Tungshan on the Tsinpu, to Yunho, east of Tungshan on the Lunghai. At Pukow the railroad ferry gave access to the Hainan and Kiangnan Railroads. Ten or more branches, some of them probably dismantled by the Japanese, connected the main line with the Grand Canal and several mining areas.

Ample marshalling yards were available on the Tsinpu, with large yards at the main junction points. Facilities for major repairs were located at Tsinan and Pukow, and locomotives needing major repairs could, if necessary, be sent to Tsingtao or Shihchiachuang. Minor repair shops were available at Tientsin, Tehsien, Yenchow, Lincheng, Tungshan, and Pengpu.

Photographic reconnaissance of the Tsinpu in early 1945 led to an estimate of 200 locomotives and 3,100 cars in service on the railroad. This line carried more than 4,000,000 tons of freight in 1935-36 under Chinese management, and under Japanese control this total was surpassed annually by a wide margin.[13]

Tsingtao-Tsinan (Shantung). The Shantung Railroad originated at Tsingtao, the leading Japanese-controlled port of north China, and ran westward 245 miles to Tsinan. It carried a large volume of strategic mineral ores east to Tsingtao for shipment to Japan and Korea and provided a route inland for the shipment of military and industrial supplies. Changtien, 176 miles west of Tsingtao, was an important source of coal, iron ore, and aluminous shale for Japanese war industries.

At Tsinan the Shantung made connection with the Tsinpu, thus gaining access to Shanghai, the Yangtze River, and the rail networks of north China and Manchuria. A number of branches connected the main line with mines along the way.

The Shantung was part of the north China rail system under centralized Japanese management and thus had an abundance or shortage of cars and locomotives according to the overall status of rolling stock in north China. Photographic reconnaissance in early 1945 led to an estimate of 102 locomotives, 95 passenger cars, and 1,620 freight cars (two-thirds ore carriers) in service at that time. One of the largest railroad shops in China was located at Tsingtao, and another large shop was found at Tsinan. Traffic to Tsingtao for export was known to be about 112,000 tons per month during 1944, and inbound traffic was believed to be considerably less.[14]

Other Chinese railroads. The railroad lines described above were the most important lines in China from the Fourteenth Air Force operational point of view. Among minor lines in north China, the Chengtai from Shihchiachuang to Taiyuan was sometimes a target, and the railroad from Shihchiachuang to Tehsien received some attention. The Peking-Suiyuan (Pingsui) ran west from Peking to Tatung and Kweisiu. A number of minor railroads ran from mines to shipping points on the Yangtze, and some of these were attacked occassionally.

The two railroads connecting China and Manchuria were extremely important to the Japanese, but because of the distance from Fourteenth Air Force bases, they did not enter into air operations in China. The most important of these by far was the Peking-Mukden line, which ran southeast from Peking to Tientsin and then northeast along the coast to Mukden. This railroad carried almost all the rail traffic between China and Manchuria. A second line ran from Peking into Manchuria through Jehol, but because of poor construction and steep grades, its capacity was very low when compared to the Peking-Mukden.

The Manchurian railway net was far more extensive than that in China proper. A complex of north-south and east-west lines, almost comparable in density to the railway systems of the United States or western Europe, linked principal cities with one another, with important industrial areas, and with areas which produced raw materials. Construction was of good quality, and there was considerable length of double-tracked line with double-track bridges. Besides connections with China proper, as already noted, the Manchurian system had connections with the Korean railway network and with the Trans-Siberian Railroad of the U.S.S.R. The Manchurian railway network was fully adequate to meet all military and economic requirements, and it was out of range of Fourteenth Air Force bases in China.[15]

RAILROAD ADMINISTRATION IN OCCUPIED CHINA

The railroads in Occupied China were under three different administrative sections during most of World War II. Those roads in newly-occupied territory, or in areas where fighting was going on, were administered directly by the appropriate Japanese army. Chinese civilian employees might or might not be used as members of the operating crews, depending upon advisability and availability, but even under the military, Chinese coolies were used extensively for upkeep and repair work. During 1944-45, the Pinghan south of the Yellow River, the Canton-Hankow, the Hunan-Kwangsi, and the Nanchang-Kiukiang were directly under Japanese armies.

In 1937, at the time of the invasion of China, all railroads in occupied territory had been placed under military control. In 1938, two corporations, partly owned by the Japanese government, were formed to exploit Chinese resources—the Central China Development Company and the North China Development Company. These were technically holding companies, having as their object the creation and control of affiliates for the exploitation of different sectors of the Chinese economy. Among the 35-odd affiliates, the Central China and North China Transportation Companies were created to administer the railroads. Some attempt was made in late 1944 to give the puppet Chinese government at Nanking a voice in railroad management, but this voice, if it spoke at all, had no effect on operations. The presidents of both companies were Japanese, former officials of the Manchurian railway system. More Chinese were employed than Japanese, but the Japanese held the key positions, and the Chinese officers had little opportunity to affect policy. Both Chinese coolies and Japanese soldiers of railway regiments were used for maintenance and repair.

The Central China Transportation Company had monopoly control of all railways south of the Yangtze River and those up to but not including the Lunghai. This included complete control of the Shanghai-Nanking, Shanghai-Hangchow-Ningpo, Nanking-Wuhu, and Chekiang-Kiangsi. The Central China Company also controlled the Tsinpu Railroad from Tungshan south. The Lunghai and all railroads to the north were controlled by the North China Transportation Company.

Ultimate control of the railways, despite the essentially civilian organization of the companies, lay with the Japanese military. The North China Development Company and the Central China Development Company were matched by officers on the general staff of the China Expeditionary Army (the highest Japanese military headquarters in China) whose duties were to supervise the railroads in order to coordinate railroad operations with military plans. A meeting of these officers, officials of the two holding companies, and representatives of the Japanese government were held every three months.

On a lower level in north China, an army railroad corps, essentially a corps of railway engineers, under a lieutenant general, matched the North China Transportation Company. Orders from Expeditionary Army Headquarters were frequently submitted to the company through the railroad corps. The North China Transportation Company had eight branch offices (central bureaus) in major cities, and the railroad corps had a corresponding subordinate headquarters in each of the eight cities. Also, the railroad corps had a military representative at each station. A similar system prevailed on the central China railroad lines.

As their military situation in China worsened, the Japanese Army again took over full control of the railroads as of 1 April 1945. In central China, the military actually operated the lines while the Central China Transportation Company functioned merely as an advisory organization. In north China, where the rail network was much more extensive and where nominal civilian control had been in effect a longer time, the transition back to military control was slow. This was due not only to the factors listed above, but also to the fact that the army lacked personnel well-enough trained in railroad operation to replace Japanese civilian personnel on higher levels or Chinese civilian employees on lower levels. The conversion from civilian to military control in north China had not been completed by the end of the war.

The central bureaus mentioned above were responsible for railroad operation within their various areas, subject to policy decisions, priorities, and control of through trains from company headquarters. Each of the bureaus had locomotives and repair and maintenance facilities assigned to its area and was responsible for upkeep of the lines under its jurisdiction. Defense of the lines against air and guerrilla attacks was a responsibility of the railroad corps.[16]

INTERDICTION OPERATIONS

Introduction. From early in 1943, aircraft of the Fourteenth Air Force delivered occasional blows at the railroads in Occupied China. Some of the strikes were sweeps which found good targets of opportunity on the railroads; others were intended to support Chinese ground forces. After the beginning of the Japanese offensive of 1944, attacks on the rail lines became more frequent as the Fourteenth Air Force desperately struck at any and all available targets in a vain attempt to check the enemy advance.

By the end of 1944, the loss of eastern bases to the advancing Japanese had, for all practical purposes, made continuation of the Fourteenth Air Force campaign against ocean shipping impossible. At the same time, Allied advances into the Philippines promised new bases for attacks on shipping along the China coast. It was obvious that a new target system must be given priority, but no theater directive assigned a new mission to the Fourteenth Air Force. However, a fourth priority task as assigned by theater directive of 1 December 1944 was air support of ground forces defending the Kunming area by "interfering with and interrupting enemy communications and supply installations. . . ."[17] A tactical directive to wing commanders from air force headquarters on 1 January 1945 gave no priority to interdiction or attacks on enemy communications (except Yangtze shipping), but the covering letter informed wing commanders that "Nothing in the enclosed directive rescinds any special mission or tactical instructions . . . by the CG of this air force. Attacks upon railways . . . rolling stock . . . bridges, etc. are continuing objectives of this air force and will be accomplished."[18]

On this somewhat dubious authority, the Fourteenth Air Force effort against railroads in Occupied China was built up until railway interdiction became the chief air activity in the theater. In April 1945, a detailed program for interdicting the railways was drawn up and distributed to wing commanders as a tactical directive. Insofar as fuel supplies permitted, this was the plan followed in rail interdiction operations for the remainder of the war.[19]

For purposes of discussion, the interdiction operations against the railroads may be divided into operations against marshalling yards, repair shops, open track, rolling stock, and bridges. It must be kept in mind, however, that these various kinds of attack complemented one another Attacks on bridges not only interrupted traffic, but also created concentrations of rolling stock in marshalling yards. Strafing attacks against locomotives filled the repair shops with damaged locomotives and made the shops more lucrative bombing targets Destruction of shop facilities, on the other hand, increased the effectiveness of strafing attacks on locomotives by lengthening the time required for repairs.

Operations against marshalling yards. During 1943 the Fourteenth Air Force made only seven attacks on marshalling yards in Occupied China. Yochow was the target for five of these attacks, one in May, the remainder in November and December. Yochow, 130 miles south of Wuchang, was the railhead for Japanese forces in the Tungting Lake area and therefore the base for the Changteh offensive of 1943. During November and December of that year, 55 P-40 and 36 B-25 sorties were flown to bomb the Yochow yards in an attempt to disrupt communications with and supply to the front.

The short Nanchang-Kiukiang Railroad received attention in February and March of 1944 with a strike at each terminal. The Kiukiang mission of 24 February was reported by Chinese sources to have destroyed five locomotives and seven railroad cars. The credibility of these sources was reduced somewhat, however, by the assertion, wildly improbable, that 1,000 enemy troops had been killed in the bombing. Nevertheless, an American liaison officer reported a few weeks later that only one locomotive was then in operation on the whole Nanchang-Kiukiang line.

As the Japanese began their summer offensive, strikes were delivered against Sinyang and Chenghsien, the delivery points north of Hankow and south of the Yellow River for equipment for the reconstruction of the Pinghan Railroad. A 5 May raid on Sinyang by nine B-25's damaged a locomotive repair shop, probably damaged the turntable, and definitely destroyed 22 storage buildings adjacent to the yards. Threatening Japanese movements to the south led to a 24-plane B-24 strike against the Canton marshalling yards on the night of 14/15 June 1944.

In July, as the Japanese offensive reached Hengyang, 10 strikes were flown against yards on the Pinghan and on the Wuchang-Hengyang section of the Canton-Hankow Railroad. Yochow was bombed four times, Wuchang twice, Yunglowtung and Sinyang once each, and Kaifeng, through which supplies shipped west on the Lunghai reached the Pinghan, once. A total of 51 B-24, 42 B-25, and 105 fighter-bombers attacked these targets. August effort, 47 B-24, 16 B-25, and 101 fighter-bomber sorties, consisted of nine strikes against six yards, including Kiukiang and Kinhwa. Twenty-three B-24's which attacked Yochow on 3 August, burned eight railroad cars, derailed six others, scored a direct hit on the turntable, and temporarily halted movement in and out of the yards. A strike by 24 B-24's on 29 August was not so successful, since 75 percent of the bombs missed the target. Two August strikes against the Kinhwa yards of the Shanghai-Hangchow-Ningpo Railroad were reported to have destroyed nine locomotives, though this was probably an exaggeration.

For the remainder of 1944, operations against yards followed the same pattern, with chief emphasis on the Wuchang-Hengyang and southern Pinghan lines, though yards as far apart as Nanking and Samshui were bombed. Results, insofar as they were revealed by photo-interpretation and intelligence from Chinese sources, were not impressive. For example, the only damage reported from rather accurate bombing of the Yuncheng yards by six B-25's and 10 P-51's was the destruction of two locomotives and damage to two more. Twenty strikes, made up of 9 B-24, 77 B-25, and 145 fighter-bomber sorties, bombed 15 railroad yards between 1 September and 31 December 1944.

The 1945 effort against railroad yards was heavier, in keeping with the program of railroad interdiction. Between 1 January and the end of the war, more than 900 sorties hit such targets in Occupied China. B-24's flew more than 225 sorties, B-25's something under 300, and fighter-bombers more than 400. Most strikes were carried out by small numbers of fighter-bombers and/or B-25's, but the B-24's made seven strikes in group strength against Shihchiachuang, Sinsiang, Tsinan, and Chenghsien, and a two-squadron strike against the Wuchang yards. Eighteen B-25's and 12 P-40's struck the Yochow yards on 29 March, and 20 B-25's, 16 P-51's, and 4 P-47's bombed the important Shihchiachuang yards on 19 July.

It is noteworthy that yards on the Pinghan were bombed more heavily than any others during the course of the war. About 364 sorties struck yards which served the Pinghan alone, and about 270 sorties, including a great part of the total B-24 effort against yards, struck junctions of the Pinghan with other lines. The 90-odd sorties directed at Kaifeng might also be considered as blows against the Pinghan, since the Kaifeng Cutoff provided, with the Lunghai, an alternate route across the Yellow River for Pinghan traffic.

The yards on the Wuchang-Hengyang section of the Canton-Hankow also received a heavy weight of attack, some 580 sorties. Yochow, victim of 368 sorties, and Yunglowtung, which was the target of 90 sorties, were the chief targets on this railroad. Only some 118 sorties were flown against yards on the Tungpu, and well under 100 against Tsinpu yards. Approximately 150 sorties were flown against yards on other rail lines.

Because of the limited effort which could be applied, and because yards could quickly be restored to use after attack, Fourteenth Air Force commanders sent missions against marshalling yards only when large concentrations of rolling stock were believed to be present. Interrogation of Japanese railway officials after the end of the war confirmed the belief that attacks on yards slowed traffic very little. Usually through traffic could proceed as soon as the bombs stopped falling; attacks on Sinsiang on three successive days in June 1945 did not halt traffic. The capacity of yards was greatly reduced by strikes such as those on Kaifeng and Shihchiachuang, but this caused the Japanese little grief because other forms of air attack had reduced traffic to such an extent that the yards were not overburdened.

The amount of damage done to rolling stock by the bombing of a marshalling yard depended upon the number of cars in the yard, the accuracy of the bombardiers, the kind of bombs dropped, and pure chance. Even when cars were damaged, much of the freight they contained might still be salvaged and, of course, many cars in the yards were empty. It is worth noting, however, that damage done to locomotives in yards was, in general, much heavier than damage inflicted by strafing attacks on the roads.

A table prepared by the North China Transportation Company main office in Peking showed the effect of 23 strikes on railroad yards during the period March-July 1945. This table did not include all strikes during these months, and there are a number of errors in dates. Some of the strikes listed, moreover, amounted to no more than one strafing pass by fighters sweeping the rail lines. As can best be determined by comparisons of Fourteenth Air Force and Japanese records, approximately 90 B-24, 70 B-25, and 100 fighter-bomber sorties were involved in the tabulated strikes. In all, 126 locomotives and 1,076 freight and passenger cars were damaged. This amounted to less than one locomotive per two sorties, and only four cars per sortie. For a small air force such as the Fourteenth, especially one plagued by a chronic shortage of aviation fuel, attacks on marshalling yards were an unsatisfactory means of interrupting traffic or reducing rolling stock.[20]

Operations against railroad repair shops. No definite or even approximate number of missions or sorties flown against railroad repair shops in Occupied China can be determined, because some attacks on marshalling yards hit repair shops and many bombs intended for repair shops fell in adjacent marshalling yards. Suffice it to say that occasional missions against shops were flown from November 1944 until the end of the war, and that from March through June 1945 these facilities received considerable attention.

In all, there were 14 shops capable of major repairs available to the Japanese in north China, and 19 others suitable for medium repairs or major repairs in an emergency. Approximately 50 minor facilities were capable of routine maintenance and minor repairs such as patching bullet holes. Fourteenth Air Force estimated the total capacity of the major shops as 136 repair jobs of all kinds per month, and thought that the remaining facilities increased this capacity to 200 per month, or 2,400 repair jobs of all kinds per year Information secured after the close of hostilities indicated that this estimate was exceptionally accurate. Since there were only some 1,200 to 1,300 locomotives in north China, and since in normal operation not more than 400 major or medium repairs were necessary per year, it is evident that some excess capacity existed. This was an argument against undertaking missions against repair shops It was also true, however, that damage to a repair shop in one locality made it necessary to move locomotives damaged in that area over longer distances to another shop, thus increasing the time the locomotive was out of service. Also, reduction of repair capacity at the same time a large number of locomotives were being damaged might well result in rate of damage outstripping rate of repair. If this could be brought about and maintained for a short time, then a moderate rate of damage thereafter might keep the shops behind in their work and keep a large number of locomotives out of service Eventually Fourteenth Air Force planners decided to attack repair shops when aircraft and fuel were available and when reconnaissance showed large numbers of locomotives in the shops or awaiting repairs nearby.

The Japanese reported after the war that air strikes against Taiyuan and Tsinan had reduced monthly locomotive repair capacity from 21 to 12 at the former and from 16 to 7 at the latter. Car repair capacity was reduced as much or more. At Shihchiachuang, which was bombed more heavily, it was the fortune of war that although freight car repair capacity was reduced almost 50 percent, from 90 per month to 46 per month, few bombs hit the locomotive shops, and locomotive repair capacity was little affected Overall, the reduction of capacity in the major shops was about 25 percent insofar as locomotives were concerned. Reduction of capacity in smaller centers must have been at least as great. Since locomotives were being damaged at the rate of 250 or more per month during the last four months of the war, it is evident that this reduction in repair capacity was a serious problem for the Japanese.

In spite of the effective Allied raids Japanese ingenuity managed to keep enough locomotives in operation to move essential military traffic Damage to repair shops was repaired as quickly as possible, and equipment was dispersed so as to reduce the chances of hits. At Shihchiachuang considerable progress had been made in moving the shops underground when the end of the war came. Plans had been made to move equipment from some shops to nearby coal mines, but actual implementation of these plans had not begun by the time of the surrender. More practical was the practice of building revetments for the protection of locomotives awaiting repairs, and the equipping of mobile repair shops on flat cars, which could make light repairs and perform routine maintenance anywhere on the railroads.

It might be noted that in several instances major railroad repair shops used electrical power from municipal power plants Repair operations could have been halted just as effectively and probably with less effort by bombing out these power plants. Such procedure would not have damaged the already-damaged locomotives awaiting repair, however, and was not attempted.[21]

Track breaking. A minor and largely experimental phase of the Fourteenth Air Force's campaign against railroads in Occupied China was the breaking of tracks between stations. The idea behind these missions was that breaks on lonely stretches of track would wreck trains before they were discovered, and that at any rate considerable time would be required for repair since equipment would have to be moved from the nearest station. Also, where a highway did not parallel the railroad, there was some expectation that multiple breaks in the track would keep the road out of use for a considerable time, since the Japanese would find it necessary to repair one break before they could move on to repair others.

Comparatively few sorties, probably less than 50, were devoted primarily to track breaking. Sometimes, however, tracks were broken during bombing attacks on targets near the railroad, and sometimes trackage was bombed as a target of last resort. Finally, unsuccessful attacks on bridges often resulted in breaks near the bridge from near misses.

Practically all of the sorties sent out for the primary purpose of track breaking were by B-25's, though the bombers were sometimes escorted by one or two fighters. Most attention was devoted to the Pinghan and the Hengyang-Wuchang section of the Canton-Hankow, but several very successful missions claimed 37 breaks in the Tungpu during May 1945. Track breaks in Occupied China claimed by Fourteenth Air Force from all types of air action except bridge damage and attacks on marshalling yards numbered 254. All of the 26 breaks claimed before March 1945 were incidental; 204 breaks were accomplished deliberately during March, April, and May 1945, 128 of them in May. Shortage of fuel and doubts as to the effectiveness of these missions led to their abandonment in June, and all track breaks from 1 June to the end of the war were incidental.

B-25's used four methods of breaking track. Ordinary skip-bombing was one of these, but few hits were made because the bombs skipped away from the tracks before exploding. The addition of spikes to the nose of the bombs brought more hits but still not enough to justify the effort expended. Next an attempt was made to break track with the 75-mm cannon carried by the B-25H. It proved easy to secure hits on the roadbed with the cannon, but photography revealed that only those shells which struck within a few inches of a rail did any damage. The next tactic was to use a Norden bombsight and drop 100-lb. bombs singly from 1,000 feet, with the bombardiers using Norden low-altitude procedure. This method was more accurate than skip-bombing, but the bomber was vulnerable to automatic weapons fire at this altitude, and the necessity for constant and fairly slow airspeed on the bomb run increased the danger from ground fire. The last method tried, and the most effective and least dangerous of all according to the units which flew the missions, was to drop parachute-suspended demolition bombs from minimum altitude. Such bombs did not skip, and they effected complete breaks when they exploded on the tracks. Best results were obtained against railroads running into cuts through hills, because the banks of the cuts guided the bombs onto the tracks.

Track breaks brought fairly good results although, paradoxically, the Japanese credited all of them to guerrilla action. The Japanese mistake can perhaps be explained by the fact that cuts were intentionally made as far from stations as possible, and the added fact that such missions were frequently flown late in the afternoon in the hope of wrecking trains at night. The Japanese admitted that several trains had been wrecked by running into track breaks at night, and they stated that despite a severe rail shortage it had been necessary to keep a small supply of rails at stations 5-7 kilometers apart along all the exposed rail lines.[22]

Attacks on rolling stock. One of the most successful phases of the Fourteenth Air Force's program of interdiction of railroads in Occupied China was the campaign against locomotives and, incidentally, railroad cars. In effect, this was a campaign against locomotives, because Fourteenth Air Force commanders realized that since some 19,000 cars were available to the Japanese in Occupied China, the limited Allied air capability could not destroy enough cars to have any serious effect on the overall Japanese transportation capacity. Many cars were attacked, but only as targets of opportunity, targets of last resort, and on occasions when they were concentrated in railroad yards. Locomotives, on the other hand, were known to be relatively scarce in Occupied China, 1,250 being estimated as the number available.

As noted earlier, the Fourteenth Air Force program of railroad interdiction resulted largely from the Japanese conquest of eastern bases which made continuation of China-based air attacks on ocean shipping impractical. Naturally, there had been some attacks on locomotives and freight cars prior to autumn 1944. From 1 January 1943 to 31 October 1944, destruction of or damage to locomotives and railroad cars was reported as 129 and 85 respectively. These claims resulted from fighter sweeps over the Hankow-Yochow region, from bombing of marshalling yards in the same area, and from aerial destruction of rolling stock abandoned by the Chinese in the Hengyang-Liuchow corridor When reconstruction of the Pinghan and the beginning of reconstruction of the Hankow-Canton and Hunan-Kwangsi Railroads made it clear that the Japanese were going to depend upon the railroads for supply, it immediately became apparent that attacks on the railroads would be a useful method of supporting the Chinese armies. Since rolling stock was correctly believed to be a critical item, it was the first to go on the target list. Later, as the capture of the Philippines made sea sweeps from China bases relatively unimportant and a major interdiction effort against the railroads developed, locomotives remained high on the target priority list.[23]

In the beginning, Fourteenth Air Force pilots, commanders, and intelligence officers were overly optimistic concerning the destructive effect of machine-gun fire on locomotives. During the period 1 November 1944 through 28 February 1945, claims were for 607 locomotives destroyed and only 207 damaged. Apparently all units which were strafed very heavily, or from which steam was seen to escape under fire, were considered destroyed during this period. Experience in all theaters during World War II demonstrated that locomotives are practically indestructible except by a direct hit or very near miss with a large demolition bomb. Even when such a hit has been accomplished, many parts of the "destroyed" locomotive can be used in making repairs on other units. Small demolition bombs, fragmentation bombs, rockets, 75-mm. shells, and machine-gun fire were all capable of inflicting light to severe damage, but such damage could always be repaired if time and facilities were available. The time required for repair was determined by the extent of damage, the location of the locomotive when the damage was inflicted, and the quality of the repair facilities used

Thus the number of locomotives actually destroyed was so small that for the purpose of this study it will be realistic to consider them as only damaged by air attack. The same is true of railroad cars, which were more resistant to damage and destruction than locomotives and easier to repair.

During the last two months of 1944, sorties by 49 B-25's, 316 P-40's, 203 P-51's, and 2 P-47's reportedly damaged 200 locomotives and 529 railroad cars. The Japanese were slow in taking measures to limit the effectiveness of these attacks, and in January, as greater weight was put on railroad targets in north China, the score mounted. During the month pilots of 148 P-40's, 287 P-51's, and 20 P-47's, and 5 B-25 crews reported damage to 358 locomotives and 392 cars.

During February, March, and April 1945, the effort exerted against railroads in general and locomotives in particular continued to be heavy. Rolling stock was attacked by approximately 1,300 fighters and 90 B-25's during the 90-day period. More than half the sorties were flown by P-51's which had range enough to cover, from the various Fourteenth Air Force bases, the entire rail system south of Peking After January, however, Japanese defense against locomotive attacks improved and the score of units damaged was reduced. For the three-month period, claims amounted to 782 locomotives and 1,288 cars

The period 1 May through mid-August 1945 saw a reduction in Fourteenth Air Force operations against railroads That recurrent handicap of the Fourteenth Air Force, the shortage of fuel, again forced a reduction in effort. Total sorties reported to have damaged rolling stock during these last months of the war were about 950 by fighters and 100 by B-25's. One B-24 crew reported destroying a locomotive which ran on to a bridge which was being bombed. Claims remained high, amounting to 859 locomotives and 1,341 cars.

In addition to the claims reported in the paragraphs above, it should be noted that Fourteenth Air Force pilots also claimed to have damaged 51 flange-wheeled trucks. These were diesel trucks equipped with flanged wheels for operation on railroads; they were used in both Burma and China. Truck locomotives in China were found mainly on the Hunan-Kwangsi and Canton-Hankow lines, where they were useful in pulling a few freight cars over sections of track not open to through traffic.[24]

Damage to rolling stock was brought about by attacks on marshalling yards and by fighter sweeps of the rail lines in Occupied China. Also, rolling stock was frequently damaged in attacks on repair facilities, and bombers and fighters bombing bridges usually strafed any rolling stock found in the vicinity. Attacks against marshalling yards and repair shops have been described earlier. Normally, fighter sweeps were carried out by two or four aircraft. The latter number was usual in late 1944 and early 1945 when Japanese interception was still possible, but by the summer of 1945 the Japanese Air Force no longer had to be reckoned with.

When a sweep was made by four fighters, two of them usually remained at 4,000-5,000 feet to provide top cover for the strafing aircraft. The two planes in the lower element flew down opposite sides of the track being swept, strafing one at a time. When about three-fourths of their ammunition had been expended, the lower element climbed to 4,000-5,000 feet and provided top cover while the former cover went down to strafe. When the sweep was made by only two fighters, each of them acted as an element, each providing cover for the other in turn.

The great majority of railroad sweeps were daylight missions, but P-61's flew 16 night sorties against rolling stock along the southern Pinghan and the northern section of the Canton-Hankow rail line. B-25 night intruders in the Hsiang Valley attacked trains when the opportunity offered. The 4th Bombardment Squadron of the Chinese-American Composite Wing (CACW) reported blowing up an ammunition train between Hengyang and Changsha on the night of 27/28 June 1945 and made attacks on three other trains between Puchi and Sienning the following night. A B-25 north of Chuchow reported causing violent explosions and very large fires among the 30 cars of a train attacked on the night of 24/25 July 1945.[25]

The Japanese had few active defenses for locomotives in Occupied China. Until late 1944 or early 1945 fighters were stationed at Hankow and Sinsiang, but the Japanese had great difficulty keeping these aircraft in existence and they seldom intercepted railroad sweeps. The air units at Nanking and Peking were able to offer stronger resistance for a longer time, but they too were eliminated well before the end of the war. For reasons too numerous to list here, the Japanese were unable to replace pilots or aircraft lost in China in late 1944 and 1945.

Antiaircraft defenses grew stronger as the war continued, but they were never adequate to check or even hamper attacks on locomotives. Most antiaircraft weapons were sited to defend railroad yards, repair shops, and vital bridges, thus affording no protection to trains in open country. Such protection was sometimes afforded by armed railroad cars, of which there were two types. One was a common box car with a round hole cut in the roof to permit a machine gun mounted inside to fire at aircraft. The other was a flat car with automatic weapons mounted on it. It is interesting to note that when sufficient warning had been received, the guns aboard these cars were dismounted and set up in adjacent fields. Some further defense was provided when troops were aboard the attacked train, since their light weapons could be used against aircraft.

These defenses were not very effective. On all attacks against railroad targets in China, Fourteenth Air Force lost only 95 aircraft from all causes. Only 37 of these planes were lost on missions which did not make passes at bridges or marshalling yards. Since the number of sorties reporting damage to rolling stock was 3,909, the loss rate was probably less than 1 percent from all causes. During 1945, when Japanese ground defenses were strongest, only 71 aircraft out of 5,744 sorties were lost from all causes on all strikes against railroad targets, an over-all loss rate of only 1.2 percent Since a considerable number of aircraft were lost because of weather, navigation error, or pilot error, it is evident that the Japanese defenses were not enough to protect rolling stock to any significant degree It should be added, on the other hand, that some of the major bridges were very dangerous targets, and that some of the major marshalling yards were well enough defended that rolling stock could find fairly safe shelter there.

Of necessity, the Japanese depended mainly upon passive defenses to protect rolling stock. After mid-1944, trains never ran in daylight south of Wuchang except in very bad weather, and eventually trains on the southern Pinghan were restricted to night runs. Strafing attacks on locomotives practically ceased when trains moved only at night, but obviously a heavy penalty was paid in the amount of supplies transported over the railroad concerned.

The Japanese had a fairly effective warning system, based upon radar warning stations and ground observers. The ground observers included all military guards and some 700 civilians Communication was by telephone, and filter rooms were located at Peking and at each of the eight regional headquarters of the North China Transportation Company. Shihchiachuang, for example, received up to 37 minutes warning when planes were sighted over Japanese-held territory. When Allied aircraft took off from Hsian, which was the main base for railroad sweeps in 1945, observers on the north bank of the Yellow River informed Kaifeng or Shihchiachuang almost immediately.

When warning of an impending attack was received, locomotives were rushed into revetments. The Japanese began building revetments in the fall of 1944, preparing three different kinds. The most common type was comprised of brick or mud walls three feet thick at the base and tapering to two feet at the top, as long and as high as a locomotive Sometimes the top of such a revetment was covered or camouflaged, but lack of materials made this uncommon though it was a successful measure when used. Even when a pilot identified a covered revetment, he had no way of knowing whether or not it contained a locomotive. Some of these shelters were spaced along the right of way in open country where a locomotive could seek shelter when hostile aircraft were sighted. Others were placed on sidings in railroad yards to prevent bomb blast and fragmentation damage.

A second type of shelter was an excavation into which tracks were laid, frequently augmented by low walls or sandbagging along the edge. This revetment was most often found on spurs built especially for dispersion of rolling stock. Sometimes the entire spur was camouflaged, and the excavation was often long enough to give protection to several locomotives.

A few revetments were built of brick in the form of a tunnel. This barrel-like structure was high enough and long enough to shelter one locomotive, but it was not so effective as the other types Though it gave fairly good protection against strafing, it was easily demolished by bomb blast which knocked the bricks out of the walls.

At the end of the war, dispersion spurs with revetments for one or more locomotives had been built at 40 to 50 locations and more were planned. The Japanese averred that these shelters cut damage to locomotives by 50 percent when they were first built, but that the damage rate climbed again to 60-70 percent of what it had been originally as Allied pilots gained skill in finding and strafing locomotives in revetments.

None of the other defensive measures tried by the Japanese achieved any great success. All locomotives were painted a light pinkish tan in the hope that they would be harder to see, but this apparently had no effect. Experiments were made in locating locomotives behind and among the cars in trains, but no change in the rate of damage was secured A number of wooden dummies were built, but only one of these was ever attacked. The most successful decoy measure was to leave damaged locomotives in the open while operational units were sheltered, but this, of course, resulted in additional damage to the units awaiting repair. Fourteenth Air Force intelligence officers had long suspected that engineers on locomotives let off clouds of steam when under attack in the hope that attacking pilots would conclude that the target was sufficiently damaged and go on their way. The Japanese denied this, pointing out that when a locomotive was under attack, the engineer was as far away as he could get.[26]

The student of the Fourteenth Air Force campaign against railroads in Occupied China is fortunate in having available an evaluation of this effort from the Japanese point of view. Japanese officers and civilians at various offices of the Japanese-controlled railroads were interviewed at the close of hostilities, and the records of many of the offices concerned were made available to the questioners. The results of this survey could not be absolutely precise, due to missing records, poor bookkeeping on the part of the Japanese, and the relatively limited time available for interrogation. Nevertheless, the survey was sufficiently complete to serve as a firm basis for conclusions regarding the over-all effect of the air campaign. In conjunction with Fourteenth Air Force records, it provides information for valid conclusions on the results of particular phases of the railroad interdiction effort.

In the case of locomotives, this survey affords an opportunity for a really close check of Fourteenth Air Force claims. As noted earlier, claims of locomotives destroyed must be discounted almost completely; the Japanese records in north China showed only 10 locomotives scrapped. The Allied observers reported that some of the locomotives carried on the Japanese books as damaged were, for all practical purposes, destroyed, but even if three times as many were destroyed as the Japanese admitted, the resulting 30 would be a far cry from the 793 reported destroyed in the Fourteenth Air Force Intelligence Summary. It is also noteworthy that practically all of the locomotives destroyed or severely damaged received their hurt in railroad yards under bombing attack. Damage from strafing was nearly always light.

Fourteenth Air Force claims of locomotives destroyed and damaged in Occupied China came to approximately 2,340. The North China Transportation Company reported 1,791 of its locomotives damaged between 1 May 1944 and 31 July 1945. At Hankow, from whence the Japanese Sixth Area Army administered the Pinghan south of Sinyang and the railroads to the south and west, no figures were available on the total damage to locomotives. It was stated, however, that all the locomotives on the rails between Wuchang and Liuchow had been damaged at least once. Since there were 72 locomotives south of the Yangtze, the total damage in Occupied China thus rises to 1,863, even if none of these locomotives had been damaged more than once. Officials of the Central China Transportation Company at Nanking stated that after January 1945 about 20 locomotives a month were damaged on lines under their control, but it was also stated that 300 were damaged in one month. A check of Fourteenth Air Force mission claims indicates that the lower figure, approximately 140, was nearer correct. This brings the total number of damaged locomotives confirmed by the Japanese to 2,003. If this figure is increased by 34 locomotives claimed damaged before 1 May 1944 and 99 claimed during August 1945, the grand total is 2,136. In other words, claims of locomotives destroyed and damaged exceeded the probable number of locomotives damaged by only about 200. In all likelihood, strafing damage to already damaged units would account for a considerable part of this discrepancy.[27]

At the end of the war, the Japanese had 1,688 locomotives in China in all conditions ranging from very heavily damaged to operational. No information is available as to the number operational on the Central China Transportation Company's lines or on the lines under Sixth Area Army control. In north China, 319 locomotives out of a total of 1,321 were inoperational as a direct result of air attack. In all probability, a higher proportion of those in the Sixth Area Army zone and a lower proportion of those in central China were out of order for the same reason. For the purpose of evaluating Fourteenth Air Force attacks on locomotives, however, north China may be considered alone.

Thus 319 locomotives, approximately 24 percent of those assigned to the North China Transportation Company, were out of order as a result of damage inflicted by aircraft as of 14 August 1945. In addition about 36 percent of the total was inoperational because of mechanical breakdowns of one kind or another. Part of these mechanical breakdowns must be credited to the air campaign, because in 1942 only 20 percent and in 1943 only 24 percent of the locomotives in north China were, on the average, out of use on account of maintenance. In other words, damaged locomotives so overloaded repair facilities which had themselves been reduced in capacity by air attack that maintenance problems could not be dealt with as they arose. If the figure above for 1942 be accepted as normal, then 521 locomotives in north China had been rendered useless to the Japanese by air attack. If there had been no air interdiction of the railroads, 1,057 locomotives would have been available for use in north China. As a result of the interdiction campaign, the number available for use in August 1945 had been reduced to 536.

It must also be noted that the efficiency of these surviving locomotives had been adversely affected. In the first place, because of the campaign against bridges, they required more time to transport a given tonnage a given distance. Secondly, any of them had once been damaged, and hasty repairs, such as sealing off damaged boiler tubes, had left them less efficient—unable to pull heavy loads. Lack of maintenance brought about by the repair situation also reduced the efficiency of those locomotives which remained operational. Thirdly, air attacks drove many trained employees away from the rail lines. Despite the fact that the number of locomotives in use was much smaller, the experience level of engineers and other crewmen was lower in 1945 than during previous years. Bombing attacks on marshalling yards and repair shops had much the same results; skilled employees decamped and their replacements, when there were any, were less skilled and could not repair locomotives so well or so rapidly.

Emphasis must be placed on the fact that the effects of the locomotive campaign were cumulative. The usual damage to a strafed locomotive was light and required, at most, only three days for repair once it had arrived at the shop. Out of the 1,063 units damaged in north China from 1 April through 31 July 1945, 1,033 could have been repaired in less than three full days if shop space had been available. They were not repaired in two or three days because the number of locomotives damaged and the number requiring maintenance soon exceeded the capacity of the repair shops. Therefore, as time went by, more and more locomotives accumulated at the shops and the backlog of work to be done grew larger and larger. More locomotives were reported damaged in January 1945 than in any other month, but the high point of sortie effort against rolling stock was reached in April. Thereafter, as a result of the fuel situation, fewer sorties were flown each month than during the month before. Claims of locomotives damaged likewise decreased each month. Had it been possible to continue operations against locomotives at the April level and to continue bombing attacks against repair shops, it is conceivable that a dearth of locomotives might have made the north China lines useless to the Japanese.

Fourteenth Air Force never mounted a major effort against freight cars and claimed only 3,632 as destroyed or damaged in Occupied China during the war. The North China Transportation Company possessed a total of approximately 19,000 cars during the struggle and had about 14,000 at war's end, of which some 12,500 were operational. Thus about 5,000 cars were lost to the north China system during the war, and there can be no doubt that air attack, and especially the bombing of marshalling yards, had accounted for some of these. However, normal wear and tear must have led to the scrapping of quite a few cars during a five-year period, particularly since many of the cars were obsolete when World War II began. Also, the North China Transportation Company probably lost some cars to the central China and Sixth Area Army railroads.

The fate of these 5,000 cars is of some moment because, contrary to Fourteenth Air Force opinion during hostilities, the Japanese in China were critically short of freight cars. In 1944 it had been necessary for the North China Transportation Company to borrow 2,800 cars from Manchuria in order to supply the Honan campaign. By 1945, the condition of the railroads had greatly increased turn-around time, thus making the shortage of cars more stringent. By 1945, replacements from Korea and Manchuria were not available—in fact, it was impossible to move some high-priority materials over the undamaged railroad from Mukden to Peking because cars were so scarce in Manchuria.

Nonetheless, it was wise in view of the limited resources available to the Fourteenth Air Force to concentrate on locomotives rather than to divert more effort to the destruction of cars. This was true simply because the total number of locomotives was far less than the total number of cars. Since a locomotive was at least as vulnerable as a freight car to strafing attack, and since the damaging of a locomotive put a greater part of the total number out of service, locomotives made a better target.[28]

Attacks on railroad bridges. The purpose of railroad interdiction in China was to impede the movement of troops and military supplies, to prevent Japanese exploitation of Chinese resources, and to disrupt Japanese administration of Occupied China. Attacks on railroad bridges were the most important means of accomplishing these aims. It must be remembered, however, that all of the various kinds of attack on the railroads complemented one another, and bridge destruction would have been far less effective if not accompanied by the bombing of marshalling yards and repair shops and by the strafing of locomotives.

Fourteenth Air Force attacks on railroad bridges were few before the Japanese offensive of 1944. From the beginning of the war until the end of March 1944, only 28 bridges were bombed, and only 136 sorties participated in the bombing. If destruction of a bridge be defined as knocking out one or more spans, pilots on these missions claimed no bridges destroyed. The Puchi bridge on the Canton-Hankow Railroad south of Wuchang was damaged twice, however, and two bridges at Sheklung, on the Canton-Kowloon Railroad, were damaged severely in January 1944 and further damaged the next month. Nine strikes were made on bridges on the short Nanchang-Kiukiang Railroad, and six of these strikes resulted in some damage to the targets.

As the Japanese began their 1944 offensive, it was immediately apparent that the Pinghan bridge across the Yellow River north of Chenghsien was a prime target. Later, when the Lunghai had been extended west to Chenghsien, an alternate route across the river was available, but in mid-1944 all supplies for the Honan front had to come across the Yellow River bridge on the Pinghan. The first strike on this structure was made by B-24's, but only one of the wooden spans was destroyed, and repairs were effected in one day. An attack by P-40's on 3 May 1944 accomplished little more, but on 24 June B-25's smashed one pier and collapsed two spans, doing so much damage that the bridge could not be used again until 16 July. Two subsequent missions did no appreciable damage, but on 3 August three B-25's destroyed three spans and one pier, damage sufficient to keep the bridge out of operation for 30 more days. Another span was destroyed on 20 September, and on 26 October a pier was demolished and six spans collapsed under the bombs of 2 B-25's and 12 P-51's. The bridge was out for 19 days after this strike.

Without recounting all missions against what the Fourteenth Air Force considered the most important bridge target in China, the over-all effect of air attack on the serviceability of the Yellow River bridge can be determined. Between 28 April 1944 and 11 May 1945, inclusive, there were 19 attacks on the structure. Ninety-eight sorties were flown by B-24's, 45 by B-25's, and the bombers were accompanied by 135 fighters, most of which also dropped bombs. According to the Japanese records, which may not be complete, the bridge was out of service for at least 115 of the 378 days between the dates mentioned above

During the height of the Japanese offensive, through November 1944, attacks on railroad bridges were part of an over-all effort to slow down the Japanese advance by reducing the flow of supplies to the front. Effort was concentrated, therefore, against the Pinghan, the Wuchang-Hengyang section of the Canton-Hankow, and the Hengyang-Kweilin section of the Hunan-Kwangsi. From 1 May through 31 November 1944 there were 17 attacks on the Pinghan bridges, including the Yellow River bridge. These strikes were made by 39 B-25's and 115 fighters, mostly P-40's. Five attacks destroyed one or more spans of the target, seven inflicted damage to some degree, and five missed completely.

During the same period there were 21 bombing strikes against bridges between Wuchang and Hengyang, executed by 6 B-25 and about 150 fighter-bomber sorties. The Hunan-Kwangsi was the recipient of no less than 72 railroad bridge attacks by 43 B-25's, 78 P-40's, and 227 P-51's. On the Wuchang-Hengyang section, three strikes destroyed one or more spans, 14 damaged the target bridges, and 4 missed. Of the Hunan-Kwangsi strikes, 13 destroyed spans, 23 inflicted damage, and 36 missed completely.[29]

Since the systematic Fourteenth Air Force campaign against the railroads as a target system in themselves had its tentative beginnings in December 1944 and continued until the end of the war, it is proper, beginning with 1 December, to take up each line separately and, insofar as possible, trace bridge attacks and their effects on transportation on the line in question.

Bridges on the Pinghan were attacked 211 times during this period, being bombed by 78 B-24's, 292 B-25's, and more than 600 fighter-bombers. Seventy-four of these attacks destroyed one or more spans of the target, 41 inflicted damage to some degree, and 96 resulted in no damage. At the end of the war the chief of staff of the Japanese Twelfth Area Army and various officers who had been involved in railroad administration testified that an average of 15 bridges south of the Yellow River and north of Sinyang had been out of service from air attack at any given time during the last months of the war. They added, however, that seldom if ever had both a main bridge and its bypass been out at the same time.

Some operational bridges were so weak that only three or four cars could be crossed at a time, and those at very low speed. From Peking to the Yellow River on the northern Pinghan, 2,160 hours were consumed in bridge repairs from April through July 1945. The longest time taken to repair a bridge enough for traffic to resume was 280 hours, but this was true only because the Japanese preferred to erect a bypass when repair time for the main bridge was estimated to be more than 10 days. Since only 2,928 hours passed during the four-month period, it is evident that through traffic must have been halted much of the time. According to the Japanese, there were only 68 days between 1 April and 13 August 1945 when through trains could proceed from Shihchiachuang to the Yellow River.

A glance at a map will reveal that shutting off through traffic from Shihchiachuang to the Yellow River did not cut Hankow off from supplies from the north. Goods could move from Peking or Shihchiachuang to Tungshan, then west on the Lunghai to Chenghsien or Sinsiang, then down the southern Pinghan to Hankow. An Office of Strategic Services mission observed traffic on the southern Pinghan near Siyang for 20 days in June and July of 1945. This was at a time when a dozen or more bridges on this railroad were out of commission. Yet, during those 20 days 31 trains averaging 23 cars moved north and 25 trains averaging 25 cars moved south. By June the Japanese retreat had begun and the northbound trains were loaded while the southbound trains were largely empty, but it was evident that the capacity for moving military supplies from the north into Hankow still existed.

Next to the Pinghan, bridges on the Wuchang-Hengyang section of the Canton-

Hankow Railroad were hit most heavily during the last nine months of the war. The total number of attacks came to 173, delivered by 78 B-25 and almost 900 fighter-bomber sorties. The fact that fighter-bombers, often carrying small bombs, made so many of the attacks probably accounts for over half the strikes missing or failing to damage their targets. Forty-seven missions destroyed one or more spans of the target bridges, and 35 inflicted damage to some extent.

Representatives of the Japanese Sixth Area Army, which controlled the Wuchang-Hengyang line, reported that it was never possible for them to run through trains from Wuchang to Hengyang. To begin with, practically all the bridges had been destroyed by the retreating Chinese, and these had to be rebuilt before the line could be used. The reconstruction was accomplished by temporary timber trestles, easily damaged by bombs. The Japanese stated that bridge repair between Wuchang and Hengyang was a highly frustrating experience because, time and time again, when they had almost finished restoring a bridge to service, a new air attack knocked it out again before a single train could cross. For example, an important bridge just north of Changsha, after being rebuilt the first time, was bombed on 31 March 1945 and put out of operation. Another strike on 10 April cancelled the repair work done up to that time, and service was not restored until 31 May. For the next 20 days this bridge was open, but the next bridge to the south was out during those 20 days. An attack of 20 June rendered the former bridge unserviceable until 4 July, and a new strike on 12 July knocked it out for the remainder of the war.

Some freight moved over the Wuchang-Hengyang section, of course. When bridges were out, supplies had to be unloaded from one train, ferried across the stream, then loaded on another train. Where terrain conditions made it possible, bypasses capable of taking care of two or three cars at a time were erected hastily, but these seldom lasted long. During high water, river boats could relieve the railroad somewhat, and probably 60 percent of the goods delivered to Hengyang went by water. The amount delivered by all means, however, was not enough to support a serious offensive, and lack of supply and reinforcements, largely due to attacks on railroad bridges, was an important factor in the failure of the Japanese offensive against Chihkiang. As a matter of fact, the Japanese in the Hsiang Valley were not receiving adequate logistic support for the defense of the occupied area, and this was an important reason for the decision to retreat in the summer of 1945.

Everything said regarding the effect of air attack on the Wuchang-Hengyang section applies with greater force to the Hunan-Kwangsi Railroad. This line was never of any great use to the Japanese. As related above, considerable damage was done to the bridges south of Hengyang before 1 December 1944. Of 88 attacks during the remainder of the war, all by fighter-bombers, 24 destroyed one or more spans of the target and 23 inflicted damage to a greater or less degree. Since construction materials could be moved from north China to Hankow only with difficulty, and since they could hardly be moved from Hankow to Hengyang at all, little progress could be made in repairing bridges on the Hunan-Kwangsi. The Japanese used flange-wheeled diesel trucks for hauling a few captured freight cars between damaged bridges, but conventional trains were of little use south of Hengyang.

In Occupied China the only other railroad which was the object of sustained bridge bombing was the Tungpu, and particularly the narrow-gauge section south of Taiyuan. The Tungpu was not a militarily important railroad, since the Japanese forces in the bend of the Yellow River attempted no offensive action, but it was a convenient target for aircraft based at Hsian. There were five fighter-bomber attacks on Tungpu bridges in December 1944 and January 1945, but only one of these was effective. No attacks at all were made in

February 1945. From 1 March to the end of the war, 99 strikes by 20 B-25's and about 350 fighter-bombers were sent against bridges on the Tungpu. Thirty-eight of these strikes destroyed spans, 39 missed entirely, and 22 inflicted damage.

The conclusion is inescapable that effort expended against the southern Tungpu was largely wasted. The line was of very limited capacity at best, but even so, the Japanese military did not utilize anything approaching its full capacity Therefore, despite air action, garrisons along the line received adequate supplies throughout 1945. These garrisons were largely self-sufficient, so interdiction of the railroad could have had little effect in any case unless complemented by a ground offensive.

Attacks on bridges of the east-west Lunghai line were few, amounting to only 20 during the course of the war. These attacks were directed against bridges on the western end of the line, with chief emphasis on the Chungmow bridge across the Yellow River between Kaifeng and Chenghsien. Overall, eight attacks knocked out spans, one inflicted damage, and eleven missed altogether. All these missions were flown after 1 January 1945; they consisted of 33 B-25 and 52 fighter-bomber sorties.

The Chungmow Bridge was an important target because, when the Yellow River bridge on the Pinghan was out of service, traffic could be routed to Kaifeng along the Kaifeng Cutoff then across the Chungmow bridge to Chenghsien. The bridge was of flimsy wooden trestle construction, made up of 5-meter spans on cribbed crosstie piers which supported tracks two feet above the normal water level. The Japanese did not expect this bridge to survive the high water season, which usually began sometime in July. After an especially damaging attack by B-25's of the 490th Bombardment Squadron on 29 June 1945, the Japanese dismantled what remained of the Chungmow bridge. Part of the material was sent south for use in rebuilding damaged bridges on the Pinghan, and the remainder was stored for rebuilding the Chungmow bridge when the water had receded.

The six strikes sent against the Chengtai, between Shihchiachuang and Taiyuan, made use of 6 B-25's, and 25 fighter-bombers. Damage was inflicted on four of these strikes. The Tao River bridge, which spanned a deep gorge, caused the Japanese much concern. This bridge was damaged in April 1945 and again in June. Had attacks been pressed, the Japanese would have been greatly inconvenienced, because coal for operating the Chengtai, the Shihchiachuang-Tehsien, and the Pinghan from Shihchiachuang to Peking came from mines west of the bridge. This crossing of the Tao River was originally selected as a target because the Fourteenth Air Force was aware of the importance of these coal supplies Yet, unaccountably, the Japanese were allowed to repair the structure and keep it in use while considerable effort was expended against nearby bridges on the Tungpu for little or no benefit.

Few attacks, seven in all, were made against bridges on the Tsinpu. Damage was claimed as a result of three of these strikes, but it must have been slight, since operation of the railroad continued unabated. Much more damaging were the bombs of a lone B-29 which bombed the great 1,800-foot bridge across the Yellow River at Pengpu as a target of last resort on 11 November 1944. A near miss by a bomb from this aircraft cut the line between Nanking and Tungshan for two days and reduced traffic for a week The Japanese feared greatly that this incident heralded the beginning of a campaign against Tsinpu bridges, but their fears proved groundless.

The Tsinpu was the most important line in China to the Japanese. From November 1944 through June 1945, traffic varied from 110,000 tons to 205,000 tons per month. The Japanese regarded 120,000 tons a month as the minimum necessary for supporting their commitments in Hunan and east China. They also stated that they did not have the facilities for repairing major damage to the Pengpu bridge, and that transshipment could have moved only 1,000 tons a day across the river. Thus, destruction of the Pengpu bridge would have reduced the Japanese in east China to one-fourth of their requirements.

Fourteenth Air Force neglect of the Tsinpu in general and the Pengpu bridge in particular is more explicable than the neglect of the Tao River bridge on the Chengtai. Tsinpu targets lay much farther away from friendly bases, for one thing. Secondly, because of the chronic fuel shortage, operations were restricted insofar as distant targets were concerned. On the other hand, if the importance of the target had been appreciated, there is little doubt that fuel could have been diverted from attacks on other targets. Even under China logistic conditions, several group-size B-24 or B-25 missions against the Pengpu bridge could have been profitable. The only possible conclusion is that China Theater and Fourteenth Air Force intelligence officers did not fully appreciate the importance of the bridge as a target.

In connection with the Tsinpu Railroad, some attention must be given to the Nanking-Pukow ferry connection between the Tsinpu and Shanghai-Nanking Railroads. The ferries and terminals were attacked several times by P-51 fighter-bombers which dropped a total of 30 bombs. A hit on the Pukow terminal with a 500-pounder on 8 December 1944 damaged one of the elevators so severely that hand jacks had to be used for six months, with a 50 percent loss of efficiency. One of the ferry boats was hit three times, the other once; neither was sunk, though Fourteenth Air Force entered such a claim temporarily. A hit on one of the boats on 25 December 1944 put the craft out of action for six days. This was the most damaging attack on the boats, though two hits by duds on 20 May 1945 would have done far more damage had the bombs detonated. In early 1945, one of the boats went to Shanghai for overhaul, but this was a result of normal wear and tear, not air attack. The overhaul required only 40 days, but mines in the Yangtze delayed the boat's return to Nanking for some time. The ferry was operating at full capacity when the war ended.[30]

During the course of the war, the Fourteenth Air Force made 591 attacks on railroad bridges in Occupied China. Sorties flown in making these attacks numbered about 3,620, of which some 632 were by bombers (110 B-24, 522 B-25) and almost 3,000 by fighter-bombers (1,941 P-51, 707 P-40, 266 P-47, 70 P-38, 3 P-61). On the basis of Fourteenth Air Force claims, which are largely confirmed by Japanese records and photographic evidence, 176 of these strikes, 29.6 percent, destroyed one or more spans of the target bridges. Damage of some sort was inflicted by 144 other strikes, 24.3 percent of those flown. No detectable damage was inflicted by 271 strikes, or 46.1 percent of the total flown.

The records definitely prove that B-25's were far superior to other aircraft as bridge destroyers. Bridges were damaged or destroyed by 63 percent of the strikes in which medium bombers took part. P-47's, P-40's, and P-51's, respectively, achieved damage in 60, 57, and 49 percent of their attacks. B-24's brought up the rear, damaging only 45 percent of the bridges they attacked.

Tactics used in bombing China bridges were in no sense revolutionary. In the attacks of 1943 and early 1944, medium bombers operated from medium altitude and fighters dive-bombed. Bridges were destroyed by such attacks, but the over-all results were not good enough to justify the expenditure of fuel and bombs. Though fighters continued to make some dive-bombing attacks on bridges throughout the war, from mid-1944 on they devoted a considerable part of their effort to minimum-altitude bombing. Except against heavily defended targets, the B-25's operated at minimum altitude against bridges throughout the first seven months of 1945. Such attacks had two great advantages; they were far more accurate than medium altitude strikes, and they were more likely to damage piers and abutments, damage which took longer to repair.

When bridges were heavily defended, the B-25's might strike from medium altitude—one such strike by the 490th Bombardment Squadron persuaded the Japanese that the Chungmow bridge was not worth repairing. Another tactic used against defended bridges was strafing of the antiaircraft positions by fighters before the B-25's began their minimum-altitude runs, but automatic weapons were often able to bring fire to bear on the B-25's despite the fighter effort. Better results were achieved by the use of three B-25's per strike, two of which strafed while the third made its bomb run. When the bombing plane had exhausted its bomb load, it substituted for one of the strafers, which dropped bombs in turn.

The Operations Analysis Section of Fourteenth Air Force concluded, on the basis of B-25 strikes (including Indo-China) made between 1 January and 1 April 1945, that minimum-altitude attacks were much preferable to medium altitude. Destruction or serious damage to a bridge by medium-altitude bombing required 34 sorties and the expenditure of almost 35 tons of bombs. Minimum altitude bombing, on the other hand, accomplished destruction or serious damage to a bridge for every 9.5 sorties and every 9.48 tons of bombs. Fuel consumption was in rough proportion to bombs expended. Losses were higher on low-altitude missions, amounting to approximately 3 percent of sorties flown, but were not prohibitive. It must be remembered that many, perhaps a majority, of the bridges attacked were undefended, and the defenses of most of the rest were light.

For defense of the north China railroads, the Japanese had assigned 47 antiaircraft guns of 75-mm. size and 83 machine guns, 20-mm. and 13-mm. Assigned for the defense of the seldom-attacked central China railroads were 8 antiaircraft guns and 26 machine guns. The number of weapons sited to defend the railroads under military control is unknown, but it is unlikely that the concentration was greater than that in north China. Troops were under orders to use their rifles and machine guns against low-flying aircraft, and they made a considerable contribution to defense. It is nonetheless evident that the number of weapons available was too small to adequately defend the thousands of miles of railroads in Occupied China. Many bridges necessarily were without defenses.

The Fourteenth Air Force interdiction program, as formalized in April 1945, envisaged breaking and keeping out of service six bridges north of the Yellow River and five south of the river on the Pinghan. Four bridges were to be kept out on the Lunghai, five on the southern Tungpu, and four between Wuchang and Changsha. It is impossible to determine from the Japanese and Fourteenth Air Force records whether this program was accomplished specifically, but with the possible exception of the northern Pinghan and Lunghai it was more than accomplished in effect.

The Japanese countered this damage to bridges by transshipment, by rapid temporary repairs, and by the building of bypasses. Transshipment was resorted to when goods were to be moved across a gap which could not be repaired in a few days or hours. Hasty repairs were effected by building temporary piers of cribbed crossties or rails—in shallow water with firm bottom a new pier of this type could be built in a very short time. When a bridge was damaged so severely that a long time would be required for repair, the Japanese built a bypass. The bypass might be a flimsy wooden trestle on cribbed piers or it might, over a dry stream bed, be a simple earth fill on which tracks were laid. Repairs and bypasses of this nature were necessarily short-lived and inefficient. Most could bear only small loads at low speed. On the other hand, they sufficed to keep some traffic moving—traffic sufficient to supply the minimum needs of the Japanese military forces.[31]

EVALUATION OF RAILWAY INTERDICTION IN CHINA

The Fourteenth Air Force campaign against the railroads significantly reduced the flow of supplies to the Japanese armies south of Hankow. From the beginning of the Hunan campaign to the opening of the southern Pinghan, those armies operated on supplies brought up the Yangtze and stockpiled at Hankow. The Japanese were well aware of what air action was doing to shipping on the Yangtze, and they planned to move 45,000 tons of supplies per month over the Pinghan from north China. The interdiction campaign prevented the carrying out of these plans. No more than 25,000 tons a month ever reached Hankow, and by March 1945 only 10,000 tons a month were arriving at Sixth Area Army supply dumps.

Planned supply of the Japanese forces south of Hankow was reduced to an even greater degree. Though no firm plans had been made for rebuilding the Hunan-Kwangsi Railroad to the Indo-China border or for maintaining the ground offensive so as to capture Kweiyang and Chungking, the Japanese would have had much to gain and little to lose by carrying out these projects. Chinese resistance was hardly a factor in the situation, because it barely existed. The Sixth Area Army sought approval of plans for an advance on Chungking. The plan was rejected because the condition of the Canton-Hankow and Hunan-Kwangsi Railroads made supply of such an offensive impossible and because there was no way of providing the necessary locomotives and rolling stock even if the roadbeds and bridges could be repaired.

It is evident that the China Expeditionary Army was justified in rejecting the Sixth Area Army proposal. The much more limited offensive against Chihkiang in the spring of 1945 failed. This failure was in part due to the better equipment of the Chinese armies facing the Japanese, in part to extensive air support given the Chinese by Fourteenth Air Force. Just as important as either of these factors, however, was the lack of supply experienced by the Japanese forces, and interdiction of the railroads was one of the most important of the measures creating this dearth of men and material. Similarly, the low capacity of the western Lunghai under air attack made it impossible for the Japanese to take Hsian after their conquest of Laohokow.

While interdiction of the railroads was not the only reason for the Japanese withdrawal from east China in the summer of 1945, it was an extremely influential reason. Air attacks on the railroads, combined with air action against Yangtze shipping, had made it impossible for the Japanese to complete reconstruction of either the Canton-Hankow or Hunan-Kwangsi Railroad. Such air action had also made it impossible for the Japanese to plan on further advances into Free China. Finally, in the event of an Allied landing on the south China coast, broken communications would make a Japanese concentration to meet the threat almost impossible. Under these conditions, the only reason the Japanese could have for holding their conquests in east China was to prevent use of air bases in that area for attacks on shipping. The invasion of Luzon and the establishment of air bases on that and other islands of the Philippines provided better bases for shipping sweeps than were afforded by east China. Faced with this situation, the Japanese very sensibly withdrew; they began their withdrawal before it was forced upon them because they feared that waiting until later would result in inability to move troops and equipment over the railroads at all.

In connection with this retreat, it may be stated that interdiction continued to upset Japanese plans. Normally, movement of men from Hankow to Peking required four or five days. Some units and their equipment which left Hankow in May 1945 were still short of Peking at the end of the war. Initially, retreating troops marched north to Chenghsien while their equipment moved by train up the southern Pinghan to Chenghsien, then at Chenghsien or Kaifeng men and equipment boarded Lunghai trains and traveled east to Tungshan and then north to Peking. This route consumed too much time and was so exposed to air attack along the first stages that some units, in desperation, fought their way through the unoccupied territory between Chuchow and Nanchang, moved by train to Kiukiang, then marched down the Yangtze to Nanking. In such retreats it was inevitable that troops should be exhausted and much equipment lost.

The railroad interdiction campaign also succeeded in reducing to a considerable extent the exploitation of Chinese resources for the benefit of the Japanese war economy. When they assumed control, the Japanese found in Occupied China railroads capable of moving 30,500,000 tons of freight a year. By 1942, after increasing the rolling stock, improving roadbeds and terminal facilities, and increasing the efficiency of administration, the Japanese controlled a railroad system capable of moving 41,000,000 tons annually. In 1944, after the interdiction campaign began, the total amount of freight moved dropped to 36,000,000 tons. During the first seven months of 1945, movement of goods was at the rate of only 31,000,000 tons per year and going down. No one can say how much this reduction in Chinese railroad capacity affected the Japanese war economy, because too many other factors, air strikes on the homeland, the mining campaign, and submarine action, affected the total result. Certainly, however, railroad interdiction in China had an appreciable effect on the supply of raw materials from China.

The accomplishments of the Fourteenth Air Force against railroads in Occupied China were brought about with a severely limited effort as compared to other theaters of World War II. Throughout the war, the Fourteenth Air Force devoted a total of approximately 8,700 sorties to attacks on railroads, rail installations, and rolling stock in China. This total was made up of approximately 422 sorties by B-24's, 1,224 by B-25's, 2,234 by P-40's, 4,197 by P-51's, 79 by P-38's, 511 by P-47's, and 18 by P-61's. The Eighth and Ninth Air Forces sent out more sorties in 24 hours in support of the Normandy invasion than Fourteenth Air Force was able to apply to rail interdiction during the whole war.

Criticism of the execution of the railway interdiction campaign in China must be tempered by appreciation of the fuel situation. Much of the apparent failure to press interdiction home can be explained in terms of gasoline shortage. This shortage, from the Fourteenth Air Force point of view, was just as stringent in mid-1945 as it had been during earlier years. Total tonnage of supplies delivered at Kunming showed a steady increase, rising from 5,149 tons in December 1943 to 12,537 tons in June of 1944 to 16,578 tons in December of 1944 to 34,165 tons in July of 1945, but, of course, not all the tonnage delivered to Kunming was gasoline. Aviation fuel received by Fourteenth Air Force at Kunming reached a high of 10,728 tons in March 1945 and actually declined to 6,858 tons in July of 1945. The reasons for this decline were various: more equipment was being provided for the Chinese armies, Chinese troops were being flown back from Burma, and stockpiling was going on for the expected transfer of Tenth Air Force from India to China. There were many good reasons for allocating tonnage as it was allocated, but the result was to cut down the amount of fuel received by Fourteenth Air Force and therefore the amount which could be expended on railroad interdiction.

Even after gasoline had been delivered to the Fourteenth Air Force at Kunming, it was still not available for use against the enemy, except in the case of missions directed at targets in Burma or Indo-China. Two considerations reduced the amount of fuel available for use against the Japanese. One of these was the necessity for moving fuel to forward bases. Much of this movement was by air transport, and delivery of one gallon of gasoline to a forward base required the expenditure of one to one and one-half gallons. This automatically cut by one-half the amount of fuel available for operations against the enemy. A second consideration, particularly during the spring of 1945, was the mass movement of Chinese troops and supplies for these troops by air transport. This program was dictated by the necessity for defending Chihkiang and by the plan for building up Chinese ground forces to such a point that they could undertake an offensive.

The following figures on fuel expenditures show the mounting weight of transport operations as compared to tactical operations. In December 1944, 4,960 tons of gasoline were expended in tactical operations, 2,105 tons in air transport; in January 1945 the figures were 5,150 and 4,236 tons, respectively. Transport operations were low in March 1945, using only 1,895 tons as compared to 6,511 tons used in tactical operations. In May of 1945, however, transport operations consumed 6,134 tons as compared with 3,625 for tactical operations, and in July the figures were 4,408 tons and 3,575 tons respectively. The inevitable result of this allocation of fuel was a significant reduction in the number of sorties which could be sent against the enemy. Some Fourteenth Air Force units, particularly those in north China, were idle weeks at a time because their fuel tanks were dry.

Nevertheless, the execution of the railway interdiction campaign is still open to criticism within the framework of the number of sorties flown. The neglect of the Tsinpu bridges, and the Pengpu bridge in particular, was most unfortunate. For the purpose of breaking down Japanese railroad administration and reducing the supply of Chinese raw materials to the Japanese war economy, this was the most important target within effective range of Fourteenth Air Force Bases. For the purpose of reducing supplies to the Japanese ground forces, the Pengpu bridge was second in importance only to the Yellow River bridge. Yet no determined effort was made to destroy this vital target. After the end of the war, Fourteenth Air Force representatives blamed theater policy for this neglect of the Pengpu bridge, and there was some justification for this excuse. Theater policy determined the availability of fuel and required that air effort be concentrated against targets which would aid the Chinese ground forces. But if the importance of the Pengpu bridge had been appreciated by Fourteenth Air Force leaders and explained to theater headquarters, it is possible that more fuel might have been made available. Even if getting more fuel had not been practical, the target was important enough in a purely tactical sense to have justified the diversion of effort from other railroads, and especially from the Tungpu. The effectiveness of railroad interdiction in China would have increased greatly if the Pengpu bridge had been destroyed.

Similarly, the importance of the Tao River bridge on the Chengtai Railroad was not fully appreciated. This structure across a deep gorge could not be repaired by the customary Japanese methods, and its destruction would have placed a much heavier burden on the northern Tungpu, the Pingsui, and the already overburdened northern Pinghan. The Tao River bridge, moreover, was within easy range of the aircraft which attacked targets in the Taiyuan and Shihchiachuang areas.

It must also be stated that the Fourteenth Air Force effort against the southern Tungpu was out of proportion to that railroad's importance. The road had little tactical or strategic value—even after its capacity had been greatly reduced by air action, it was still capable of carrying more than enough tonnage to supply the small Japanese garrisons along its right of way. Presumably there were two reasons why this railroad became a target for so many strikes. Since its gauge was different from that of other railroads in north China, it was effectively isolated; replacement locomotives and cars could not be secured from other lines. Secondly, the Tungpu, because of its location, was a most convenient target for aircraft based at Hsian. These were not valid reasons for attacking the Tungpu, however, unless the results of the attacks would further the over-all objectives of the interdiction campaign, and it is difficult to see how the effectiveness of the campaign against the railroads would have been reduced if the southern Tungpu had been allowed to operate without interference.

One initial weakness in Fourteenth Air Force railroad interdiction was corrected during the course of the campaign. In the beginning, bridge targets were selected on the basis of length and location only. This was a faulty system, since long bridges were frequently reparable in less time than shorter ones. Beginning in the spring of 1945, ease of repair was taken into consideration in selecting bridge targets, and bridges of through-truss construction were especially sought after. Postwar Japanese testimony confirmed the belief that attacks on shorter bridges of this and similar types accomplished longer traffic interruptions than the initial attacks on bridges selected for length alone.

Criticism of Fourteenth Air Force's failure to press attacks on major repair facilities is probably unfair. No doubt some of the B-25 effort expended on the Tungpu and railroad yards elsewhere could have been turned against repair shops with profit, but basically the destruction of major repair facilities required group-size formations of heavy bombers. Such a mission involved the expenditure of approximately 450 tons of fuel more or less, depending upon the distance to the target. To justify the continuation of such costly missions in the China Theater would have required arguments more powerful than could be made without Japanese testimony.

When Japanese testimony was taken at the end of the war, the arguments in favor of attacks against railway shops were greatly strengthened. Such damage as was actually done to shops, complemented by strafing attacks on locomotives, had resulted in swamping the remaining repair facilities and piling up a great number of damaged locomotives to await repair. Additional damage to the shops would have increased the backlog of damaged locomotives and locomotives awaiting maintenance. The resulting loss of locomotive utility would have been great and would have mounted with every passing day, because locomotive and repair shop damage had a cumulative effect. One more benefit to the Allied cause derived from attacks on repair facilities was the desertion of skilled Chinese employes. The shops at Tsinan, Kaifeng, Taiyuan, and Shihchiachuang were all shorthanded after being bombed, and this had added to the loss of repair capacity brought about by the air action.

Had the number of repair facility attacks in the spring of 1945 been increased sufficiently to have reduced capacity by another 20 percent, and had the program of strafing attacks on locomotives been carried out in the same manner as was the case in reality, the Japanese would have faced a dilemma. The cumulative effect of locomotive strafing, neglected maintenance, and inadequate repair capacity must soon have so reduced the supply of operational locomotives on the Tungpu, Chengtai, Pinghan, and western Lunghai that shipments to Hankow would have decreased almost to the vanishing point. This could have been avoided only by bringing in locomotives from other rail lines. Had the Japanese chosen the first alternative, the primary purpose of the interdiction campaign, cutting off supplies to the Japanese ground forces in east China, would have been accomplished. Had locomotives been withdrawn from the Tsinpu and from other lines in north China, Manchuria, and Korea in order to keep supplies moving into Hankow, reduction of the flow of raw materials from China to Japan, a secondary object to the interdiction campaign, would have been accomplished. These are might-have-beens, of course. Even had Fourteenth Air Force commanders and intelligence officers been so far-seeing as to appreciate the results which could have been achieved by continuation and intensification of attacks upon repair facilities, such attacks probably could not have been carried out under the logistical conditions which existed.

That Fourteenth Air Force railway interdiction could have been improved does not in any respect imply that it was a failure. On the contrary, in view of the effort expended, it was remarkably successful. Like all interdiction campaigns, it failed to accomplish the ultimate, and military traffic continued to move. As a result of air attacks, however, this military material moved in reduced volume at reduced speed. Troop movements were, for all practical purposes, slowed to the speed of the walking infantryman, and even so, the men sometimes had to wait on their equipment. The flow of raw materials to Japan was reduced by millions of tons a year, and although Japanese railway administration did not break down, its resources were strained to the utmost. Thus the Fourteenth Air Force's interdiction of the railroads in Occupied China accomplished what it was intended to accomplish. That more could have been done with more fuel and better intelligence does not detract from the success which was achieved.[32]

CHAPTER VI.

CONCLUSIONS

1. THE RESULTS of the Fourteenth Air Force campaign against ocean shipping were disappointing. Daylight missions against shipping off the China coast, even though claims exaggerated the results, were recognized as not worth the effort expended. Sea sweeps by SB-24's with special low altitude bombing equipment were thought to be very fruitful during the course of operations, but postwar assessment revealed that these missions were less efficient than daylight sweeps. Fuel devoted to SB-24 operations could have contributed to more damage to Japanese shipping if it had been expended in mining operations.

2. Mines were more effective against Japanese shipping than were bombing or strafing attacks. Experience in Japanese home waters as well as in China bore out this conclusion. Mines not only sank shipping; they disorganized schedules, closed harbors, and prevented delivery of cargo to its intended destination. In the Fourteenth Air Force zone of operations a limited number of mines closed the port of Haiphong before the end of 1943, eventually closed the Yangtze to ocean shipping, and prevented the movement of ships into and out of Shanghai, Hong Kong, and other harbors for weeks at a time.

3. A requirement existed for mines designed for river interdiction. Fourteenth Air Force asked in vain for a light, floating contact mine for use against river shipping. Existing mines were all too large for use against the smaller vessels on Chinese rivers, and, of course, magnetic mines were not effective against wooden boats of any size. A small contact mine of approximately 100 pounds weight, designed to float just under the surface of the water, could have been dropped in the Yangtze, Hsiang, and Hsi Rivers in sufficient numbers to greatly hamper if not cut off the movement of the steamers, barges, junks, and sampans which delivered the greater part of Japanese supplies to the front.

4. There was a requirement in China for an air-dropped land mine for road and railroad interdiction. This would have been a more radical innovation than the river mine described above, but the need was quite as real. The appropriate weapon would have been light, so as to permit the loading of large numbers in an aircraft, but it would have been powerful enough to destroy a truck or a tank. The same mine or a heavier version could have been used on railroads to destroy locomotives. Such mines needed tamper-proof fuzes so as to inhibit sterilization by enemy personnel, and they needed a device to insure detonation at the proper time. Perhaps some could have had time fuzes, some anti-disturbance fuzes, some magnetic fuzes, and others fuzes sensitive to the proximity of an internal combustion engine. Needless to say, no such weapon existed during World War II.

5. Road interdiction failed in part because Fourteenth Air Force aircraft did not have night capability to match their day capability. Daylight fighter sweeps could almost completely interdict the movement of vehicles on the roads in good weather, but so long as trucks could move freely at night, supplies could be delivered to troops at the front. Fourteenth Air Force used B-25's and, to a limited extent, P-61's for attacks on motor vehicles at night, but at best such missions did little more than harass road traffic. Movement of trucks from supply dumps to the front could have been halted only if the night intruders had

had the same ability as day fighters to locate and then destroy motor vehicles.

6. Successful railroad interdiction demanded good intelligence and constant pressure. Railroads were tempting targets for aerial action, but sheer destruction of the most convenient targets was unlikely to halt or seriously reduce vital traffic. Most of the Fourteenth Air Force's effort against the Tungpu Railroad, for example, was wasted. Interdiction of even a primitive railroad system like that of Occupied China required careful target selection. Effort devoted to less important targets went for naught or brought smaller returns when the more important targets were neglected. In China, destruction of the Pengpu bridge on the Tsinpu Railroad would have increased the effect of other missions against the railroads. Good intelligence was also essential to placing correct emphasis on the various components of the railroad target system.

Constant pressure was also a necessity if the railroad interdiction campaign was to achieve its objectives. Fourteenth Air Force had almost beaten the railroad system of Occupied China to its knees when the declining supply of aviation fuel forced a relaxation of pressure. As a result of this easing of pressure, the railroads were able to continue moving a minimum of military supplies to the front and to move a large (though much reduced) tonnage of material in rear areas. Complete interdiction was an unattainable goal, but constant pressure was necessary if the results achieved were to be as nearly complete as possible.

7. Shortage of fuel was the chief factor limiting Fourteenth Air Force operations. Throughout its combat life, this organization had more aircraft and crews than it could use to fullest effect. Fuel conservation was partly responsible for the substitution of night for daylight sea sweeps, and it was almost wholly responsible for the use of fighter-bombers rather than the more accurate B-25's on bridge targets. Fuel shortage made it necessary to ease the pressure on Japanese-operated railroads after March 1945. Probably the Japanese offensive of 1944 could not have been halted by air action alone under any circumstances, but the advance could have been slowed and losses inflicted to such a degree as to make the Japanese victory Pyrrhic if only more fuel had been available.

8. Diversion of effort was a serious handicap to Fourteenth Air Force interdiction operations. Any effort which was devoted to operations other than interdiction, except counter-air action, reduced, sortie for sortie, the effort which could be applied to interdiction. Likewise effort applied to one form of interdiction detracted from what could be devoted to other types. Possibly, and even probably, effort devoted to the direct support of ground troops in east and north China was worth-while. If the same amount of fuel and munitions had been expended on interdiction, little more and perhaps less over-all damage would have been inflicted on the enemy.

Thousands of sorties, however, were devoted to interdiction in Indo-China and air support of the Chinese troops on the Salween front. Once the Indo-Chinese ports had been closed, additional effort directed against that colony was largely wasted. It must be added that Allied commanders could not see into the future, so they could not know that their efforts were useless insofar as bringing the war to a close was concerned. But the fact remains that that part of Indo-China within effective range of Fourteenth Air Force operations had no material to ship to Japanese forces in Burma or Thailand, and closure of the ports had adequately cut off the shipment of raw materials to Japan. Adequate intelligence would have revealed that Japanese forces in northern Indo-China had no offensive capability or intentions. Operations against Indo-China succeeded in destroying the railroads, but they did not hasten the defeat of Japan.

Diversion of effort to the Salween front was decreed by the theater command, not by Fourteenth Air Force. Theater policy was to open a land supply route from India to China, and the Salween campaign was necessary to open the last part of this route. The whole policy was mistaken, because air transport was far more effective than the Burma Road as a means of supplying Free China. The air effort expended against the Salween in the summer of 1944 might have made a significant difference if it could have been used in the Hsiang Valley, and the Salween effort in early 1945 could have been applied with profit to the railway interdiction campaign.

9. Fourteenth Air Force failed to carefully check and constantly evaluate its claims of destruction of interdiction targets. Past history makes it obvious that there has been a strong tendency everywhere for claims of results of air action to be somewhat exaggerated. This exaggeration may arise from desire for propaganda material, from the normal optimism of airmen, from failure to check for duplication in crew claims, from overconfidence in some weapon or tactic, from wishful thinking, or from carelessness. In China this tendency toward exaggeration was checked in the case of targets like railroad yards, bridges, and railroad repair shops by the use of photographs for assessment No such objective criterion was available for assessing destruction of shipping, motor vehicles, or locomotives, and it was in these categories that unfounded claims were highest. Parenthetically, it must be noted that although claims of locomotives destroyed were almost wholly unjustified, the total Fourteenth Air Force claims of locomotives destroyed and damaged closely approximated the actual number damaged. Claims resulting from night actions were, naturally, much more difficult to assess than those resulting from daylight attacks, but claims based on visual observation in daylight were inaccurate enough.

Though Fourteenth Air Force was unduly lax in evaluating the accuracy of claims, no great harm was done, perhaps because commanders discounted the claims when laying their plans. No great amount of imagination is required, however, to visualize a situation in which belief in erroneous claims could lead to disaster. Certainly the use of inaccurate reports or results as criteria for planning future operations could lead to wasted effort and perhaps to military defeat.

10. Air action alone could not halt a ground advance in China. For air action alone to halt an enemy advance, air weapons needed the impossible capability to seek out and destroy individual enemy soldiers in any terrain. Air action could slow up a ground offensive, cut off its supplies to a large extent, and kill some of the personnel taking part. But, in the context of the battlefield and the adjacent supply routes, it could not do mortal damage to the enemy unless some ground obstacle, normally an opposing ground force, brought about concentration sufficient to constitute an appropriate target for air action.

11. Tactical interdiction was most effective when a ground front was active. Tactically, Fourteenth Air Force interdiction efforts were most successful during the siege of Hengyang and the Japanese offensive against Chihkiang. Air interdiction achieved a measure of success in these campaigns because the Chinese ground forces were resisting stoutly. Faced with stubborn Chinese defenders, the Japanese of necessity expended more men and munitions, and replacement of expended men and material put a greater burden on their supply lines. When air action destroyed supplies needed immediately at the front, lack of supply was a factor in the outcome of the battle. When supplies were destroyed which troops in advancing units did not need immediately, there was no immediate effect, and if other supplies reached the troops later, there was no effect whatsoever. Fourteenth Air Force interdiction efforts in Hunan after the fall of Hengyang had little effect on the ground campaign because the Japanese were meeting with little or no resistance.

12. A small air force of limited logistic and tactical means proved able to carry out an effective interdiction campaign in China. Once air superiority had been won, Fourteenth Air Force was able to interdict effectively, if not completely, the rivers and railroads of the theater. There were errors of omission and commission, but by and large a remarkably small number of sorties inflicted a remarkably great amount of in-

terdiction upon the enemy communications This campaign not only reduced supplies to the battlefield to a trickle, but also reduced significantly the flow of strategic raw materials to Japanese factories. Mainly by virtue of its interdiction campaigns, the Fourteenth Air Force had made the most significant contribution to victory in China. With its anti-shipping and railroad interdiction operations, it had made a less significant but nonetheless very real contribution to the final defeat of Japan.

CHAPTER VII

TRANSPORTATION IN COMMUNIST CHINA

INTRODUCTION

An interdiction campaign can be successful only under conditions of air superiority. A discussion of the capabilities of the Chinese Communist Air Force, now one of the larger air forces in existence, is outside the scope of this monograph It must be understood, however, that the discussion of interdiction which follows is based on the premise that the counter-air war will have been won before full-scale interdiction begins.

The reader must also bear in mind the fact that much of this chapter deals more with what may happen than with what has happened in the past. The opinions expressed are based insofar as humanly possible on past experience as modified by present capabilities. Such projection of history is, nevertheless, highly vulnerable to errors of omission and commission, and the reader must not confuse opinion with fact.

In World War II the Japanese held the major transportation routes in China, so lessons learned in the interdiction of these routes may still have value. The application of these lessons, however, must take into consideration changes which have taken place in the Chinese transportation system since World War II, weapons systems now available for use, and the fact that friendly bases in future conflict would be located outside of, rather than within, China.

The most important change in the transportation system, and it must be emphasized, is a matter of orientation. Before World War II, Chinese transportation was oriented toward the sea and commerce with Japan, Europe, and America. During most of World War II, the same orientation persisted, though the object was the exchange of goods with Japan alone. Since Shanghai and ports on the Yellow Sea carried on this commerce with the West and Japan, China's internal movement of goods was largely east-west. This orientation enhanced the importance of the Yangtze River and the east-west railroads.

Toward the end of the war, military necessity forced the Japanese to emphasize north-south communications in China. With the destruction of her merchant marine, Japan had to depend upon the north-south railroads of China for supply of her armies in that country and for the transfer of raw materials to Manchuria, Korea, and the home islands.

Communist victory over the Nationalist Chinese armies made it certain that internal transportation would continue its north-south orientation. Just as prewar China depended upon the West, and just as Occupied China depended upon Japan, for those products which could not be produced at home, so Communist China depends upon Soviet Russia. Thus raw materials move north through China proper and Manchuria toward Siberia, and products of Soviet factories move south into China over the same routes This north-south orientation is intensified by the fact that Manchuria is more highly developed industrially than north China even as north China has experienced greater industrial development than south China, leading to a north-south orientation for strictly intra-China movement of goods.

Obviously, the present orientation of transportation in China lessens the importance of the rivers and increases the importance of the north-south railroads. In other words, in China proper, the Tientsin-

Pukow (Tsinpu), Peking-Hankow (Pinghan), Canton-Hankow Railroads are the most vital transportation arteries. In Manchuria the most vital parts of the transportation system are the Peking-Mukden Railroad between China and Manchuria and the junctions of the Manchurian and Siberian railroads.

CHINESE COMMUNIST WATERWAYS

Overseas shipping. By the end of World War II, Chinese merchant shipping in service had been reduced to only some 80,000 tons, of which 30 ships of 1,000 tons or more made up 62,000 tons. Under the Nationalist government, this merchant fleet grew rapidly, amounting to 267 ships of 1,000 tons or more and a total of 842,119 tons by 1949. It is still impossible to determine how much of this fleet fled from the mainland with the Nationalists, but the greater part apparently did so. The Nationalists at one time announced that no less than 500,000 privately owned craft of all types escaped from China, but this figure was almost certainly an exaggeration.

Whatever the size of the Chinese Communist merchant marine, it is unable to provide bottoms for trade between China and other nations; the largest vessel in service is less than 7,000 tons. The resulting dependence of China upon foreign shipping for large-scale overseas commerce is one of her chief weaknesses. This was demonstrated by the embargo on strategic materials in 1951, which drastically reduced overseas service to China ports. Since 1951 there has been a steady increase in overseas commerce with Japan and western nations. Great Britain has the lion's share of this trade, but practically all the major nations of the West, except the United States, take part. Most of this trade is in so-called non-strategic materials

The U.S.S.R. and Soviet-satellite nations carry on regular shipping service to Chinese ports. Polish ships, which had been prominent in this trade, ceased moving goods to north China ports after the capture of two vessels by the Nationalists in 1954, but still deliver cargo, mainly kerosene, to Whampoa, near Canton. Probably the most extensive trade of all is that between Siberian and Chinese ports. This commerce has grown to such an extent that many Russian vessels have been transferred from European to Siberian waters It is interesting to note that although most of these ships came to the East via the Suez Canal, some came during the summer months by way of the Arctic route.[1]

Coastal Shipping. Nearly all the ocean shipping under Chinese Communist registry is used in the coastal trade. Principal services are between Manchuria and north China, between north China and Shanghai, between Canton and central China, and between Canton and other south China ports, including Hainan Island Foreign vessels still carry most goods transshipped from Hong Kong to nearby Chinese ports. Chinese tonnage in the coastal trade has been increased by the addition of about 20 former British vessels, but conventional ships are still not numerous enough to carry all the goods to be transported. For this reason many junks, motorized to a considerable extent, are used for coastal freight service.[2]

River shipping. The previously noted reorientation of Chinese transportation toward a north-south axis has lessened the importance of river transport. River shipping is not likely to become insignificant, however, in a country with 50,000 miles of navigable rivers, 6,400 miles of which can be traversed by river steamers. The Yangtze is reported to have carried 2,500,000 tons of freight during the first half of 1953, and it remains the only good means of communication between Hankow and the Chungking-Chengtu region. Other rivers are less important, but the Hsiang in Hunan, the Hsi in south China, and the Amur and Sungari in Manchuria carry considerable freight. In regard to the Yangtze, it is significant that since 1952, building materials and industrial supplies have replaced agricultural products as the major items of freight carried.

The Chinese Communists are reported making increased use of barge tows on the Russian model with a resulting increase in efficiency. Improved navigational aids have helped increase efficiency, as have several large new river steamers built in Shanghai. As a result of increased efficiency and the relative decline in the importance of river shipping, capacity is more than adequate, and the Communists reportedly are having difficulty in finding cargo to fill the available bottoms. River transport accounted, approximately, for only 5,400,000 ton-kilometers in 1952 as compared with an estimated 20,300,000,000 ton-kilometers in 1936.

Communist plans, some of which are being implemented, envisage flood control on all rivers, dredging of the Hsi River, and rehabilitation of the Grand Canal. Three years of work on these projects, it should be added, did not prevent disastrous floods in 1954. Before the floods, an especially ambitious program of flood control on the Huai River, involving 16 reservoirs and 8 dams, was scheduled for completion in 1955. Also included in these plans is a 106-mile canal from Hungtze Lake to the Yellow Sea which will, if and when completed, be navigable for smaller ocean-going ships.

Vulnerability of waterways to interdiction. In the event of open warfare between China and the United States, interdiction of China's overseas trade could probably be accomplished. A declaration of war should be enough in itself to stop all goods carried in western bottoms. A naval blockade should be enough to cut off all U.S.S.R. and satellite trade with ports of south and east China. Air and naval patrols of the narrow channel between southern Korea and Japan would interdict shipping from Siberia to Chinese ports. Bombing attacks upon harbor facilities and mining of harbors would probably be unnecessary, but mining could be an effective measure in case of temporary loss of air superiority.

Interdiction of coastal shipping might prove more difficult. Air and naval searches and mining of ports could be expected to halt the movement of larger vessels, but a fairly large amount of cargo could still be carried by junks. Presumably a major air and naval effort could interdict junk traffic, but it is doubtful that this commerce is of enough strategic importance to warrant such an effort. Certainly it should be possible to interdict junk traffic in the area of any military action on or near any particular part of the China coast if the tactical situation demanded such a measure.

Interior waterways present a much more difficult problem. During World War II, Fourteenth Air Force operated against the Hsi, Hsiang, and Yangtze Rivers from air bases on the Chinese mainland. Operations against rivers were easier to carry out than operations against coastal shipping. Almost certainly, in any future conflict, aircraft engaged in the interdiction of Communist Chinese transportation would be based at some distance from China—in South Korea, Japan, Formosa, Okinawa, the Philippines, or Southeast Asia. Even though air superiority had been established before the campaign began, it would still remain true that river interdiction would involve rather long flights over enemy territory, which would give an opportunity for antiaircraft defenses to come into play. Certainly river ports and the larger river vessels would be well defended.

Mines proved the best weapon against larger river shipping in World War II. Probably they would again prove their worth, since they could be dropped at night in areas unprotected by concentrations of antiaircraft guns. Conventional mines could be depended upon only to halt larger vessels, however, they would have little effect on the junks, sampans, and barges plying the rivers. For even partial interdiction of this light craft traffic, small contact mines such as General Chennault suggested during World War II would be needed.

It is doubtful that an attempt to interdict the rivers beyond mining to a great enough extent to halt movement of larger vessels would be worth the expenditure of effort required. As has been noted above, the main direction of freight movement in modern China is north-south, and the rivers bear east-west. Proportionately and absolutely, the rivers carry far less traffic today than before World War II; coastal and river traffic combined amount to only 10 percent of the ton-kilometer performance of the Chinese transportation system.

Replacement of larger shipping sunk in an interdiction campaign would be most difficult for the Chinese Communists Shipyards of limited capacity are located at Canton and Shanghai, and it is known that some 2,700-ton river steamers have been built at Shanghai since the Communists came to power There are shipyards capable of building medium-sized mechant vessels at Dairen, but these yards have confined their efforts since 1949 to repairing Soviet ships and building smaller vessels, tugs particularly. Presumably all these yards could be bombed out of existence if such action was found necessary

Almost innumerable facilities exist in China for building junks and sampans Even as it would be impossible to destroy enough of these small craft to seriously reduce the amount of freight they carry on the rivers, it would be impossible to destroy enough of the building facilities to prevent replacement of the boats destroyed.[4]

ROAD TRAFFIC IN COMMUNIST CHINA

The roads World War II, despite the destruction it brought about, resulted in overall improvement of the Chinese roads. The Japanese improved roads along the lower Yangtze, in Honan, and in the Hsiang Valley. The Chinese, with American aid, built new roads and improved old ones in the west, forming three relatively good road nets, centered about Kweiyang, Chungking, and Chengtu. The roads deteriorated somewhat during the civil war, but further improvements have been made since the Communists came to power.

As of 1953, it was estimated that there were 80,000 miles of motor road in China (contrasted with 3,000,000 miles in the United States). Communist plans called for restoring old roads or constructing new ones at the rate of some 5,000-6,000 miles per year, so it may be assumed that 90,000 miles of motor road were available in 1955. Few of these highways are paved, but most have a crushed rock surface of poor to good quality. Ferries and fords are still the most common means of crossing streams, and most of the bridges which exist are of low capacity. New and better bridges on Soviet models are being built, however, and old bridges are being strengthened.

Only a few of the Chinese roads are laid out as independent transportation routes The roads in Manchuria run roughly parallel to the rail lines and complement the railroads. In central China the roads either parallel the railroads or rivers or serve as feeder lines for these more important means of transportation. Roads are the only means of moving freight in most of the mountainous area of southeast, southwest, and northwest China, but there is little freight to be moved in those areas. One object of the Communist road-building program is to forge stronger bonds between these remote regions and the remainder of China.

Some of the most extensive road building in China is being carried out in Yunnan, where the mileage was reportedly increased by half during 1953 alone, with considerable additional construction planned. When the present program is completed, there will be four through highways of comparatively good quality connecting Yunnan with Burma, Indo-China, and Thailand. Complementing these through highways are lateral roads built and being built which, running parallel to the border, connect the principal towns on the highways These roads will permit more thorough Communist control of the largely non-Chinese population of remote Yunnan, and they will permit some additional exploitation of natural resources. Probably more significant, however, is the fact that these roads will facilitate economic, political, and military penetration of Southeast Asia by the Chinese Communists.

Strategically, the roads of China are less significant than the waterways and far less important than the railroads Probably the roads connecting central China with the west have the greatest over-all strategic and economic importance. The roads of Fukien, Kwangtung, and southern Chekiang Province opposite Formosa, which link the coastal region with the railroads, might have considerable significance in case of troop action on the mainland or Communist invasion of Formosa. Likewise, the roads connecting Yunnan and Kwangtung with Southeast Asia might have great importance in case of military action involving Indo-China, Burma, or Thailand. A road now in operation between Chengtu and Lhasa, Tibet, is vital to continued Communist control of that mountainous area.

Motor vehicle supply. The supply of motor vehicles in Chinese hands was almost exhausted during World War II. During the last months of the war a number of trucks were supplied to the Nationalists over the Ledo-Burma Road, and a number of vehicles in poor condition were taken over from the Japanese after the surrender, though the Russians apparently appropriated most of the Japanese motor transport in Manchuria. American aid and the United Nations Relief and Rehabilitation Administration (UNRRA) added to the truck supply in the years immediately following World War II. The Nationalist government reported 39,870 trucks and busses and 16,160 passenger cars in China in 1947.

No doubt the civil war reduced the supply of motor vehicles to some extent, but the Communists took over nearly all of those which remained. Upon gaining power, they began buying American, British, Czech, German, and Russian vehicles, and had built up an estimated inventory of some 52,000 trucks by 1952. The number lost during the Korean War is unknown, but replacements more than kept pace with losses. The number of trucks in service in 1955 was believed to be not quite 100,000, of which perhaps 60,000 were suitable for military use. Western-manufactured trucks still predominated, but increasing numbers of vehicles built in Soviet-block nations were still in use. There may be some significance in the fact that passenger busses in Hunan Province were still using charcoal for fuel in 1954.

China as yet has no factories which produce complete motor vehicles, but some trucks are assembled in China from foreign parts, and some parts are now being manufactured. Parts manufacture is being promoted by the government, presumably with the intention of increasing the use of China-made parts in the existing fleet as a step toward an integrated automotive industry. Even if all present plans succeed, it is highly unlikely that completely Chinese-manufactured trucks could be produced in more than token quantities before 1960.[5]

Vulnerability of the Chinese road system. China's roads, even though improved, have features which make them vulnerable to interdictory air action. Most traffic is, after all, confined to a relatively small number of highways, and on almost any road there are some large bridges located where no adequate alternate routes are available. Junctions of the main roads could be expected to provide good targets, as could many of the ferry crossings, since vehicles would accumulate at these points. Since vehicles and parts are relatively scarce, repair shops and parts manufacturing centers would be important targets. Indeed, if all such facilities could be destroyed, wear and tear would constantly reduce truck transportation no matter how effective the maintenance and repair of roadbeds and bridges.

Despite these vulnerable aspects, there are a number of factors which cast doubt upon the ability of an air force to effectively interdict Chinese roads. In the first place, except in western China, railroads and waterways offer alternate routes and in most instances better routes. Secondly, the enormous Chinese labor force would be available for rapid repair of damage and for portage of freight around points of interdiction. Thirdly, although the main roads have no surfaced alternates, the network of village and country roads does afford short-haul alternates except in the wettest weather. Finally, it may be expected that major bridges and vehicle repair installations will be provided with strong anti-aircraft defenses.

All told, the arguments against a program of road interdiction, except in the case of ground action on the Chinese mainland, outweigh those in favor of such a campaign. Even when it has accompanied and supported ground action, air interdiction of highways has seldom been successful in the past. Success would be doubly difficult where huge labor resources are available to repair damage. The Chinese

Communists, it may be added, demonstrated in Korea that they were capable of organizing roadside labor so as to effect repair of bomb damage in the shortest possible time. Finally, it must be noted that in past campaigns, although intensive fighter sweeps and bridge bombing have halted daylight movement of vehicles, air action has never yet succeeded in halting truck movements at night. Until technology or radically improved techniques promise success in night attacks on vehicles, roadway interdiction can be only half successful at best.[6]

RAILROADS OF CHINA*

Background The destruction inflicted on Chinese railroads during World War II has been discussed in an earlier chapter.† Guerrilla action after the close of hostilities added to the destruction inflicted during the fighting by air action and the retreating Chinese armies. A survey made in 1946 indicated that only 80 miles of track out of the 222 miles between Hengyang and Kweilin on the Hunan-Kwangsi line were operable. On the important Tsinpu, little affected by air action, 310 miles of track were inoperable, and 111 spans of bridges on the line were damaged, some beyond repair. The Pinghan was operable in a limited way in 1946, but all installations, and especially bridges, were severely damaged. On the Canton-Hankow line, all bridges of two or more spans were out, and it was estimated that 50 percent of the total steel on the line required replacement. Damage north of Peking was not so severe, but in Manchuria the Russians had removed some of the rolling stock.

The rolling stock situation was almost as bad as that of installations, though perhaps not so bad as was thought at the time. Almost all, if not all, of the locomotives in Chinese hands at the end of the war were beyond repair, and at least 25 percent of those taken over from the Japanese had to have major repairs before they could be used. In China proper, about 15,000 usable freight cars survived the war, but because of lack of maintenance, most of them were in poor condition. Manchuria added to the available supply of both locomotives and cars, but it is impossible to determine how many were taken over by the Russians and how many fell into Chinese hands.

An almost astronomical amount of material was required for restoration of railroads to their prewar condition. Two thousand miles of rails and ties were needed simply to restore the destroyed sections, and much more to put the whole system in good shape. The magnitude of this requirement is indicated by the fact that 160 tons of rails and 2,200 ties were needed for each mile of track. In addition to the need for ties and rails, many thousands of tons of structural steel were required for bridge repair. Finally, the system needed 200 locomotives immediately, 500 locomotives within a few years, and 10,000 freight cars within a few years. Total cost of restoring the roads, in American currency, was estimated at $400,000,000.[7]

Under the Nationalist government, good progress was made in railroad restoration. By 1947, more than 13,000 miles of track were in use, and ton-kilometers of freight had increased from 3,756,000,000 in 1946 to 5,270,000,000 in 1947. The number of locomotives in service increased from approximately 1,500 at the end of the war to 2,477 in 1948, and the number of freight cars increased to more than 31,000 during the same period. Plans were adopted for building 8,650 miles of new track.

Naturally, the crisis of the civil war interrupted this progress. Track mileage actually decreased some 300 miles between 1947 and 1948, and ton-kilometers of freight decreased almost 500,000,000. However, as soon as the Communist victory was assured, railroad construction and reconstruction began once more and was carried forward energetically despite serious shortages of skilled personnel, steel, and tools. Eighty-eight percent of China's railroad mileage was reported in operation in mid-1950. At the end of that year, for the first time since 1937, traffic ran over the entire length of track between Peking and Hankow and between Wuchang and Canton. Russia aided

*See Map No 6, p 89
†Chapter V.

in this reconstruction with advice, steel, and supervisory personnel. Naturally, much of the work done before 1950 was hurried, and much of the effort thereafter was devoted to bringing all the lines up to standard. This was reported as done by the end of 1952, and Communist statements, observers' reports, and intelligence reports agreed that the rail lines of China were for all practical purposes restored to their 1937 condition.[8]

New construction. The Chinese Communists not only have restored practically all the previously existing railroads in China, but have also embarked on an ambitious program of new railroad construction. Information as to how much of various projects is complete, how much under construction, and how much merely planned is conflicting, since conclusions are based largely on very unreliable Communist announcements rather than on observation In the main, the building program is based upon the plans promulgated by the Nationalists in 1947, with amendments dictated by the fact that Communist China desires better connections with Soviet Russia and by Communist long-range military plans. Strategic and political needs take precedence over economic utility, as is demonstrated by the fact that "there are long-term plans for new railways, particularly in south China, which would give quicker and more substantial economic returns than the projects at present receiving the highest priority."[9]

According to official reports of the Chinese Communist government, about 310 miles of new main track were laid down in 1952 and 350 miles in 1953. During the same two years, 273 miles of branches for factories and mines were laid, and 87 miles of railroad were double-tracked. Plans for 1954 envisaged 354 miles of new mainline trackage. Allied intelligence estimates tend to confirm these figures. At the present rate of construction, using the great Chinese labor pool and increasing supplies of steel from the small but expanding Chinese steel industry, the Communists may succeed in adding 2,000 miles of new track by the end of 1957. The new mileage would be greater were it not for the fact that the remaining terrain to be covered on construction in progress is much more difficult than that already traversed.[10]

Some of the more significant new lines are worthy of special note. A line from Chungking to Chengtu, begun by the Nationalists, has been completed and has been extended north from Chengtu almost half the distance to Paochi and a junction with the east-west Laoyao-Paochi (Lunghai) Railroad. Work is progressing rapidly on the incomplete section, which was originally scheduled to go into service in 1955. Whether service can be established so soon is doubtful, but it will almost certainly be established before the end of 1956. If all planned construction is carried out, this line will eventually connect at or near Chungking with other lines leading to Kunming, Kweiyang, Changsha, and Liuchow. In other words, it will be a western north-south trunk line to compare with the Peking-Hankow (Pinghan) and Tientsin-Pukow (Tsinpu).

The most ambitious project now in hand is the westward extension of the Lunghai. This line was extended from Paochi to Lanchow before the end of 1952, and it has since been pushed about 200 miles to the northwest toward Suchow. As projected, this line will eventually extend some 1,300 airline miles northwest of Lanchow to a junction with the Turkestan-Siberian Railroad of the U.S.S.R. north of Alma Ata. Some reports indicate that the Russians may be building southeast to meet the Chinese line. This grandiose project is not scheduled for completion until 1962, and western experts think that the line will not go into service that soon.

The strategic importance of the new line is obvious, since it will provide a new tie with the Soviet Union remote from hostile air bases. The railroad will also have political importance, since it will facilitate Communist control of remote Sinkiang and Kansu Provinces. Economically, the line will have some value, since it will tap the Yumen oil fields, from which at present crude oil is moved by truck to the railhead northwest of Lanchow. Available reports indicate that the quality of construction up to the present is low, but there is little doubt that the roadbed will be improved with the passage of time. Since this project is an extension of the Lunghai, it will have connections with the contemplated Paochi-Chengtu-Chungking-Kunming line at Paochi, with the Pinghan at Chenghsien, and with the Tsinpu at Tungshan. A passenger ferry across the Yellow River also gives access to the narrow-gauge southern section of the Tungpu.

A third major project is a railroad across the Gobi Desert of Mongolia from Chining (north of Tatung) through Ulan Bator (Urga) to Ulan Ude on the Trans-Siberian Railroad of the U.S.S.R. Details of the construction of this route are somewhat vague, but apparently the Russians are building the longer section across Mongolia while the Chinese build the section to Erhlien on the China-Mongolia border. Reports indicate that the Russian-built section is broad-gauge and that the Chinese-built section is standard gauge. A British intelligence report of May 1955 cites a Communist announcement of the opening of the standard-gauge section in December 1954, but indicates that this section was then in process of conversion to broad-gauge to match the Russian section. Because of the scarcity of water in the Gobi Desert, Russian diesels are to provide most of the traction on this line, but the Chinese are reported to be converting a few steam locomotives to broad gauge for use on the southern section. If the information available is correct, this line is either complete at present or will be so within a few months.

Strategically, this line not only will furnish another connection with the Soviet Union, but will also shorten the distance between Peking and Moscow by some 600 miles. This saving in distance and time will be important economically as well as militarily, since it will facilitate and lower the cost of trade in raw materials and finished products between Russia and China. The railroad will connect with Peking via the Peking-Suiyuan (Pingsui) line, and with Tatung and Taiyuan on the Tungpu, and by way of the Tungpu and Taiyuan-Shihchiachuang (Chengtai), with the important junction at Shihchiachuang. Eventually, if all presently-projected railroads are built, there will be a connection with the westward extension of the Lunghai at Lanchow via a line from Paotou along the course of the Yellow River.

Mention must also be made of a bridge now being built across the Yangtze between Wuchang and Hankow. Completion of this project, scheduled for 1957, will add greatly to the efficiency of the Chinese railway network. Over this bridge, trains will be able to move directly from Peking to Canton via Hankow. At present through trains to Canton must go down the Tsinpu to Nanking, cross the Yangtze on the train ferry located there, go on to Shanghai, then move back east on the Shanghai-Hangchow and Chekiang-Kiangsi Railroads to join the Canton-Hankow at Chuchow. Freight cars can be ferried across the Yangtze at Hankow now, however, and passengers can cross the river by ferry and take a new train on the other side.[11]

The status of other railroad projects is even more indefinite than the status of those already discussed. There is no evidence that construction has begun on the proposed line from Paotou along the banks of the Yellow River. Likewise it is unknown whether construction has begun on the planned line from Kunming north to a junction with the completed Chungking-Chengtu Railroad or on the line from Kweiyang north to a similar junction. It may be that some priority is being given to these projects, since they will provide another badly-needed north-south trunk line.

In the south, from west to east, plans call for a number of new lines. A meter-gauge rail connection between Kunming and Kweiyang already extends approximately 100 miles east of Kunming. Also planned is a railroad, begun before World War II but then dismantled as far as it had been built, from Kweiyang to the Hsiang River, across which a junction would presumably be made with the Canton-Hankow Railroad. Standard-gauge lines from Nanning and Litang on the Hunan-Kwangsi to Chenhsien and Fort Bayard on the coast were reported under construction in 1952, and reports indicate that the line from Litang to Fort Bayard has been completed. A new line from Liuchow, the former Fourteenth Air Force base on the Hunan-Kwangsi Railroad, to Canton is planned. There is another plan for a new line which will depart from the Canton-Hankow somewhere between Canton and Hengyang and join the Chekiang-Kiangsi between Chuchow and Nanchang. Plans also envisage an extension of the Wuhu-Nanking line southward from Wuhu to a junction with the Chekiang-Kiangsi east of Nanchang and then south to Foochow, on the coast opposite Formosa. One other line is planned to parallel the coastline from Canton to the proposed Wuhu-Foochow route, with branches leading to the ports of Swatow and Amoy. References may also be found to a proposed railroad around Hainan Island.[12]

Although it lies outside of China proper, the Hanoi-Langson meter-gauge line in Indo-China has been restored to operation with Chinese help, as has the Hanoi-Haiphong line. At Pinghsiang, on the border, the first-named connects with the standard-gauge Hunan-Kwangsi. Through traffic from Hanoi to Saigon is still not possible, though part of the line south from Hanoi probably has been rebuilt. The railroad from Hanoi to Laokay is still in disrepair; across the border in China, the former Kunming-Laokay meter-gauge line is open only from Kunming south to Pisechai.[13]

These notes on new construction would not give a reasonably complete picture of the present and projected Chinese Communist railroad system if mention were not made of those dismantled sections of the prewar rail system which have not been restored. Reference was made in the preceding paragraph to the still unrepaired Pisechai-Laokay section. The railroad on Hainan Island has not been restored, nor has the prewar track which ran from Chinchengchiang north to a point due east of Kweiyang. The condition of the Canton-Samshui Railroad is unknown. Apparently no attempt has been made to repair the Hangchow-Ningpo section of the Shanghai-Hangchow-Ningpo line.

In north China, the Luan branch of the Tungpu remains in disrepair, as do several branches of the Pinghan and the cutoff from the Tsinpu to the Lunghai east of Tungshan. Whether or not the Kaifeng Cutoff from the Pinghan is still in existence is unknown. A 90-mile section, approximately, of the railroad from Peking through Jehol into Manchuria had not been restored at the time of the last reports.

In Manchuria several lines have been abandoned, perhaps because the rails were needed elsewhere. One of these is the former road from Tumen, on the border between Manchuria and Korea, to Suifenho, on the Manchuria-U.S.S.R. border. Likewise out of use are sections of both lines leading from the Amur River across from the Siberian border town of Blagoveschensk to Peian and Nunkiang respectively.[14]

Capacity of the Chinese Communist rail system. Improvements made in the Chinese rail system since World War II have increased the capacity and the efficiency of the lines, though not a little of the increase in efficiency has been brought about by centralized Communist management rather than by physical improvement. Some ideas as to the changes in the usefulness of the system may be gained by noting the estimated present capacities of some of the lines. The Canton-Kowloon, for example, can now move 11,200 tons per day, as compared with 4,800 tons under Japanese control. The capacity of the Hunan-Kwangsi was reported as 5,900 tons per day when it was opened from Hengyang to Pinghsiang in 1951, and it has no doubt increased since. Some 16,000 tons a day can now move over the Chekiang-Kiangsi from Nanchang to Shanghai, and 12,000 tons a day from Chuchow to Nanchang. In 1952, another 12,000 tons a day could move over the much-abused Canton-Hankow Railroad, and this capacity has no doubt increased during the ensuing years.

In north China it is estimated that more than 37,000 tons a day can move over the double-tracked Peking-Mukden railway. Capacity of the present-day Pinghan is some 9,600 tons per day, while the Tsinpu can move at least 9,800 tons per day. If reported double-tracking of the Tsinpu is carried out, the capacity will be increased considerably. The Pingsui can carry 3,000 tons per day, and the combined routes from Tsingtao via Tsinan, Tehsien, and Shihchiachuang to Taiyuan can carry 4,000 tons a day over-all, while the old Shantung Railroad section from Tsingtao to Tsinan can carry 11,000 tons per day. The Lunghai, finally, can move some 6,400 tons per day on the section between Laoyao and Paochi, considerably less on to the western railhead.

Rough calculations from the estimates given for the various main lines in China proper indicate that in 1952 the system had a capacity of approximately 55,000,000 tons of through freight annually. No figures are available as to the ton miles actually transported in any year since the Communists seized control of China, so no comparison with Japanese or Nationalist Chinese performance is possible.[15]

Probably rolling stock is the most significant limiting factor of the Chinese railway system as it now stands. While estimates vary somewhat, the consensus is that in China and Manchuria there are available some 3,000 locomotives, 4,000 passenger cars, and 40,000 freight cars for the standard-gauge lines, plus some 200 locomotives and more than 2,000 cars for the 600 miles of narrow-gauge lines. The rolling stock now in service is in fair condition, damaged equipment having been discarded or cannibalized since 1950, but many of the cars are old, if not obsolete, and frequent breakdowns can be expected until the older equipment is replaced.

Most locomotive replacements must still come from abroad, but more and more parts are being manufactured in China, and assembly of imported parts in Chinese shops is becoming the rule rather than the exception. Freight cars, probably with some imported parts, are being manufactured in China at a rate of probably 1,000 and perhaps 1,500 per year. The Dairen, Tangshan, and Chishuyen (near Shanghai) shops are almost certainly building cars, and shops at Mukden, Chuchow, Changhsientien (near Peking), and elsewhere are probably also in production.

The industrialization program of the Communists, including new railroad construction, has resulted in the use of rolling stock to the limit of its capacity. No reserve of cars is provided, and loadings are several tons higher than customary for the cars in use. This overloading of necessity increases the wear and tear on both locomotives and cars and adds to maintenance problems. It must be emphasized, however, that repair facilities have not been over-burdened and that ton-miles of freight have increased. Nor is there any indication that the practice will have any deleterious effect on Chinese railroad transportation in general, though it will result in more rapid depreciation of the rolling stock so loaded.

A much more serious problem encountered by the administrators of Chinese railroads since 1950 is congestion on the main north-south lines, particularly at Peking, Tientsin, and Mukden. This congestion is mainly a result of the increase in traffic which overburdens terminals designed for prewar volume and then damaged during the war, but scarcity of skilled track and train crews has played a part. Congestion in the yards has increased the turn-around time for freight cars and thus has lowered the efficiency of the railroad net. For example, although a through train from Anshan to Hankow makes the trip in 8 days, single-car time averages 20 days.

The Communists are taking energetic measures to combat this problem, one of them being the overloading of freight cars described above. Whenever possible, all normal traffic is cleared from the lines before seasonal movement of agricultural products begins, and as much freight as possible is sent by through trains. Work is planned, and may have begun, for double-tracking the Pinghan for some distance south of Peking, and the capacity of the Tsinpu is being increased (also by double-tracking, according to some reports). Strengthening of bridges and the laying of heavier rails on the standard-gauge section of the Tungpu and on the Chengtai will provide alternate routing for some north-south freight. The introduction of automatic signalling on the Peking-Mukden line is expected to increase the capacity of that important link. Marshalling yard facilities are being constantly improved throughout China, but special attention is being devoted to Peking, Tientsin, Shihchiachuang, and Taiyuan. Finally, the experience level of train and track crews rises with every day of operations, and the resulting increase in skill will do much to reduce congestion and increase efficiency.[16]

Repair capacity in Communist China is adequate for present maintenance needs, and some of the shops have added capability for building and assembling parts for freight cars and locomotives. Mukden and Dairen are probably the most important centers, since in addition to extensive maintenance activity locomotives are assembled. Very important shops are, however, located at Harbin, Peking, Tangshan, Shihchiachuang, Tsingtao, Tungshan, Chishuyen, and Chuchow, and the shops at Changchun, Mutanchiang, Linyu, Tientsin, Taiyuan, Tsinan, Chenghsien, Pukow, Hankow, Wuchang, Chungking, Kunming, Liuchow, Canton, and Kowloon are vital facilities

The efficiency of these shops is limited by the age of much of the equipment, by damage inflicted during World War II and the civil war, and in Manchuria by the looting carried out by the Russians in 1945. The machinery is of many varieties; thus the interchange of parts is difficult. The Communists have overcome many of these difficulties, and shortage of repair facilities has not been a limiting factor in rail transportation More efficient shop techniques, more effective distribution of available supplies, cannibalization of machinery when possible, and the routing of cars to the shop best equipped to do the work regardless of geographical location have kept enough rolling stock available for Communist purposes. It was estimated in 1952 that the then available facilities could repair 2,578 locomotives, 19,918 freight cars, and 2,662 passenger cars annually, and there can be little doubt that this capacity has increased during the years since 1952.[17]

Mention should be made of the fact that in rails and bridge members, as well as in freight cars and locomotives, Chinese industry is providing a greater portion of the needed products. Rail production is now sufficient for the normal needs of the existing network, and Chinese mills supply a significant part of the rail tonnage used in the construction of new railroad lines. Bridge parts are fabricated at Peking, Chishuyen, and Linyu, and perhaps in some other shops.[18]

It is evident from the above that the Chinese Communists have succeeded in rehabilitating and improving the railroad system which they took over in 1949, but appreciation of these improvements and the relative efficiency with which the system is operated must not be allowed to obscure the fact that the railroad net of China is still primitive by comparison with that of other major nations. Only in Manchuria is the network reasonably adequate. In China proper, in 1952, there was roughly one mile of railroad for every 394 square miles of territory. Soviet Russia had a mile of railroad for every 148 square miles of territory, and the United States had a mile of railroad for every 13 miles of territory.

Even when the present building program is completed, China will have but three north-south trunk lines and only four east-west trunk lines. Thus the alternate routes for long-distance shipping are few, and for short-haul freight alternate routes are practically non-existent. Furthermore, the rivers and roads offer unsatisfactory alternatives to the major rail movements, because they are generally oriented east-west. At present, even if the line through Ulan Bator is open, there are only two connections with the Soviet railroad system, and a third will not be completed for half a decade. Even where the connections exist, problems arise because the Russian lines are broad-gauge and the Chinese standard-gauge. At present passenger cars move across the border by means of new wheels installed while the train is on a narrowing (or expanding) section of track, but in the case of freight cars this system is applied only to those of highest priority, if to any at all. All other goods must be unloaded from the cars in which they were carried to the border and then loaded on the cars of the country for which they are destined. Even if the transfer system were applied to all traffic, movement across the border would be slow. Connections with Korea are adequate, but there is only one connection with the Indo-Chinese rail system, and that one involves a change from standard to narrow gauge.

There are two serious bottlenecks, or potential bottlenecks, within China. At present only the Peking-Mukden railroad can carry goods between China and Manchuria, and it is unlikely that the opening of the low-capacity line from Peking to Manchuria through Jehol Province will handle the traffic increase to be expected within a few years. To the south, that section of the Canton-Hankow Railroad between Hengyang and Chuchow must handle all traffic moving north from any point of origin between Hengyang and Hanoi or between Hengyang and Canton. Likewise, all freight moving into the area indicated from the north or east must pass over the same section of track.

At present there is serious delay in moving cars, goods, and passengers across the Yangtze between Hankow and Wuchang, but this will end with the completion of the bridge across the Yangtze at this point.

Finally, despite increased home production of railroad materials, China is still heavily dependent upon imports. Almost all locomotives added to the system, a great quantity of rails, and some freight cars must be imported if the expansion of the net is to be continued. Likewise, machine tools and other equipment for railroad repair shops must be brought in from abroad. In view of the fact that the Chinese railroads are the chief means of transportation in the country, essential to the Communist program of industrial growth, the system is extremely thin and highly vulnerable.[19]

Vulnerability of Chinese railroads to interdiction. The Fourteenth Air Force experience in World War II demonstrated that interdiction of even a primitive railroad net like that of China requires careful planning, constant evaluation of results, and constant pressure. Since complete interdiction has never been possible, operations must be planned so as to accomplish carefully evaluated aims. Above all, experience in China as elsewhere teaches that an interdiction campaign should not be undertaken without clear appreciation of what can and what cannot be accomplished. Failure to achieve an impossible but publicized goal may lead to loss of morale and belittlement of real accomplishments.

In the event of hostilities involving the United States with Communist China, much will depend upon the reasons for undertaking an interdiction campaign. Interdiction may be considered desirable as a means of supporting friendly ground forces arrayed against Communist armies. Obviously, attacks against Manchurian railroads might be of great help to friendly ground troops engaged in Korea. In an invasion of the south China coast opposite Formosa, road and river interdiction would be more important than cutting railroads unless the coastal railroad from Canton to Foochow had previously been put into operation. Were an invasion of Hainan Island in progress, interdiction of boat traffic from the mainland would take precedence over railroad strikes, but cutting the Hunan-Kwangsi Railroad and its branches leading to Fort Bayard and Chenhsien would probably be necessary. In case of hostilities in Indo-China or Thailand, interdiction of the Hunan-Kwangsi and Kunming-Pisechai Railroads would be necessary, but more emphasis would probably be given to the roads leading to the area of battle.

Tactical interdiction in China, in other words, would depend upon the area of ground action. It would be, in any case, an effort to stop movement into the battle zone by any means—water, road, or railroad. Possible areas to be interdicted are as many as possible battle zones, and determination of which railroads to attack would obviously depend upon the area to be interdicted. It should be borne in mind that Fourteenth Air Force experience is of limited value in planning such a campaign, because Fourteenth Air Force, though handicapped by shortages of fuel and munitions, had the great advantage of working from bases within China. The fact that aircraft involved in any foreseeable interdiction campaign against Chinese railroads in the future would be operating from bases outside of China creates entirely new problems of planning.

One other statement may be made in regard to possible tactical interdiction of Chinese railroads or other means of transportation. Such an air campaign will accomplish little in a tactical sense unless ground fighting is heavy. Tactical interdiction can be decisive only when the ground side being interdicted has immediate need of the supplies destroyed or delayed by air action. Cutting off 90 percent of the supplies sent to an enemy force will have no tactical effect if the force is able to carry out its plans with the remaining supplies. On the other hand, destruction of only 10 percent of the force's supplies will be decisive if it requires 100 percent to accomplish its aims.

It is conceivable that a war between Communist China and the United States might be an air and naval war without ground force participation Or, again, in the event of Communist aggression against Korea, Formosa, or Southeast Asia, United States policy might be to force China to desist without any intention of bringing about her complete defeat. In such an air war against China, the railroads may prove to be a vital target. They are the chief means of transportation within the country, and in many areas they are the only significant means of transportation. Since it is almost certain that sea routes would be closed in the event of war, substantial quantities of military or civilian materials and substantial numbers of troops could move between Manchuria and north China and between north China and south China only by rail. Also, the railroads provide a target system subject to air action which will not necessarily involve inflicting hundreds of thousands of casualties upon the civilian population. Thirdly, at least two vital components of the railroad system, bridges and repair shops, are susceptible to bombing and destruction by conventional weapons. Finally, present doctrine indicates that comparatively low-yield nuclear weapons will at last make attacks upon marshalling yards worth-while.

The Chinese rail system taken as a whole has many weaknesses which contribute to its vulnerability to air attack. The small number of through and alternate lines reduces the number of targets which must be attacked in order to disrupt traffic throughout the whole system. Interdiction of the Peking-Mukden line would, for all practical purposes, end large-scale movement of material between Manchuria and north China. Interdiction of the Canton-Hankow Railroad between Hengyang and Chuchow would cut all rail communication between north and east China on the one hand and the vast region south and west of Hankow on the other hand. The fact that practically all the railroads are single-tracked will add to the effectiveness of interdiction. Even when the bridge across the Yangtze at Hankow is completed, there will be only two train crossings of the river in all China (there are four crossings of the Mississippi below Cairo), and one of these will still be the train ferry at Nanking. Paradoxically, the great number of major bridges on the rail lines provides an abundance of good interdiction targets. In many areas, particularly near the east coast and south of Hankow, floods frequently disrupt rail transportation during the rainy season (May through September), and air action can certainly take advantage of and increase this disruption Finally, the scarcity of skilled labor will add to the difficulty of overcoming the disruption brought about by air attack.[20]

There are also factors which would tend to reduce the effect of an interdiction campaign against the Chinese rail system. Without doubt, the most important of these is the giant and apparently well-organized labor force available to the masters of China. Masses of coolies can repair much interdiction damage and can be employed for portage of goods around points of interdiction. In central and south China, rivers provide alternate routes in many instances, particularly in an east-west direction, and in Manchuria and near the larger cities throughout the country roads provide alter-

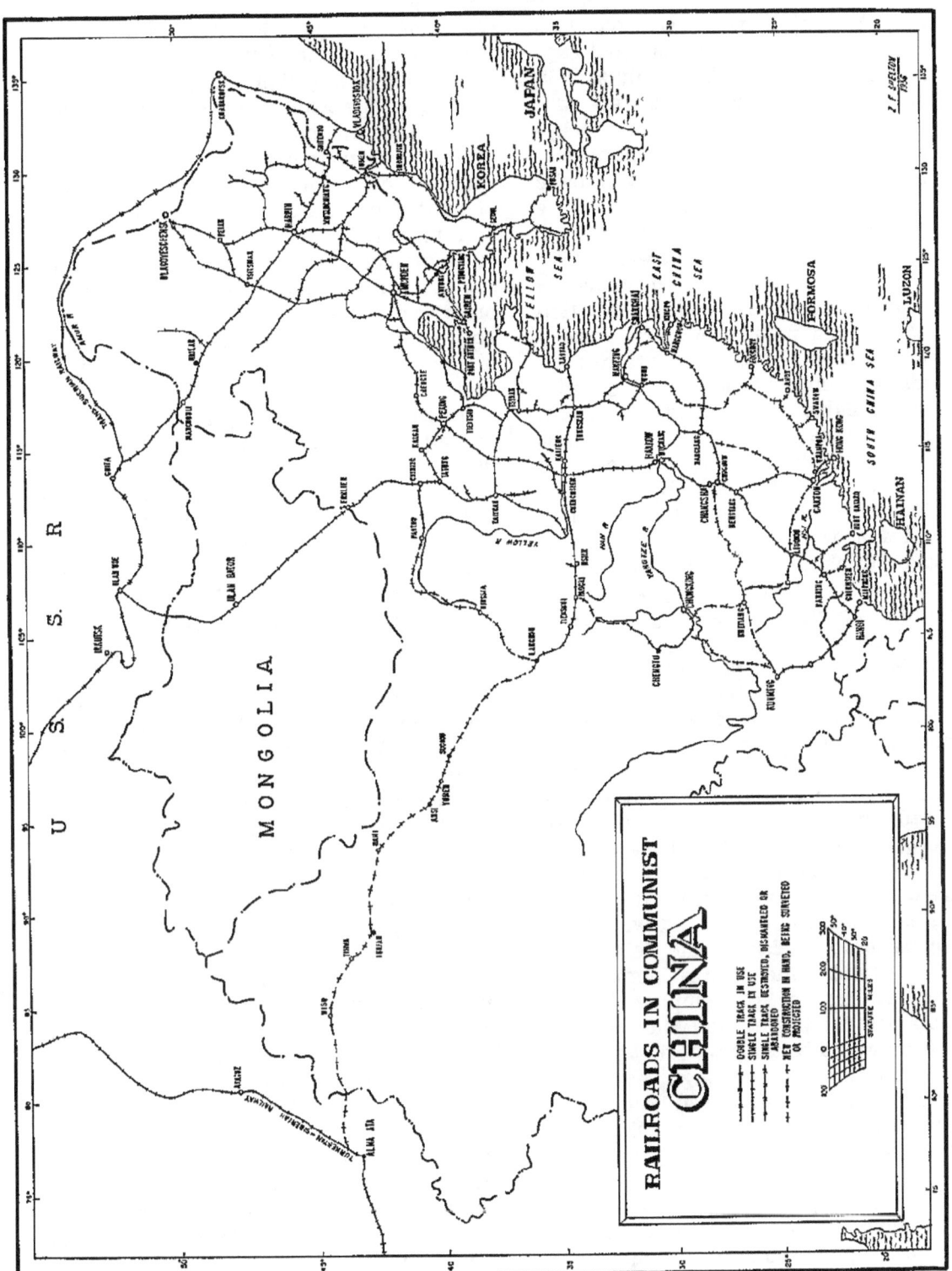

Map No. 6

nate routes of some importance. Coal is so widely distributed in China that fuel supplies are almost invulnerable to air attack. Finally, the major railroad targets are sure to be well-defended by antiaircraft weapons, and the location of most of such targets in the interior of the country will make it necessary for attacking aircraft to fly long distances over enemy territory.[21]

Obviously, the strengths and weaknesses of the Chinese railroad system must be taken into consideration if an interdiction campaign should prove necessary. Experience has demonstrated that attacks on roadbeds are unprofitable when oriental labor is available in quantity. In Korea, track breaks were mended in less than eight hours in almost all instances, and multiple breaks were mended as rapidly as single ones. Unless there is some reason for delaying rail transportation for a few hours only, attacks on trackage would be of little benefit, and even when such a delay was necessary and desirable, a bridge might provide a better target.

Abundant labor can do much to lessen the effects of bridge bombing. During World War II the Japanese demonstrated in Burma and China that superficial repair of damaged bridges and the construction of flimsy bypasses could keep essential military traffic moving. In Korea the Communist forces demonstrated that they were as efficient as the Japanese in this respect. Bridge destruction would lessen the volume of railroad traffic, however, and would impose considerable delay in the delivery of goods. Certainly the bridge across the Yangtze at Hankow (if complete by the time air attacks begin) and the Nanking train ferry would be targets of first priority in any interdiction campaign in China. Many other bridges might well become targets, particularly those between Peking and Mukden and between Hengyang and Chuchow. The Yellow River bridge on the Pinghan is an important structure, but the river's change of course since World War II has presumably reduced the importance of the bridges at Chungmow and Pengpu, though the latter, especially, may still be a good target. The bridge across the new course of the Yellow River north of Tsinan may now be as important as the Pengpu bridge was during World War II.

Most bridge attacks during an interdiction campaign not in direct support of ground action would be concentrated on specific sections of railroad for the purpose of halting or delaying traffic for some specific reason, or they would be carried out so as to bring about concentrations of rolling stock in certain marshalling yards in order to create good bombing targets. Probably a campaign putting chief emphasis on bridge destruction would not bring about decisive results.

Rolling stock, although no particular scarcity exists, probably affords, in conjunction with repair shops, the best target for a full-scale interdiction campaign in China. This would especially be true if nuclear weapons are to be used. Present rolling stock is being used to capacity, and attacks on bridges and other installations, by delaying traffic, would increase the need for rolling stock for movement of the same volume of freight.

A campaign against rolling stock is not likely to include as much locomotive strafing as took place during Fourteenth Air Force operations. Since aircraft engaged in an interdiction campaign against China would be flying from bases outside of China, the range factor would confine locomotive strafing to rail lines fairly near the coast, or to those lines nearest friendly bases in Korea, Japan, Formosa, the Philippines, or Southeast Asia. Since locomotive strafing must be carried out at low altitudes, and since jet aircraft consume more fuel at low altitude, it is probable that range for this type of attack would be less than for most other operations by the same aircraft. Better antiaircraft defenses would also be a factor in reducing the amount of locomotive strafing, but distance would be the main problem. Unless bomber-type aircraft are used, which is unlikely, the interior of China and much of Manchuria will provide a safe haven for locomotives and cars insofar as strafing is concerned.

One possibly effective weapon, reportedly in development, would be a mine so de-

ping, with the probable exception of night junk movements, could be achieved by air and naval action.

3. Complete interdiction of Chinese river shipping is impossible, but mining can destroy, harass, and delay larger vessels. Interdiction of the rivers will not be so vital as it was in World War II, because a smaller proportion of China's freight today is transported by water. Moreover, the rivers generally provide east-west routes, and the main movement of traffic in Communist China is north-south.

4. The Communists have improved the motor roads in China, but the road system remains insignificant except in the mountainous regions of the south and west.

5. Interdiction of motor roads in China would be profitable only as a means of supporting an active ground campaign.

6. Because rivers provide east-west routes and because the roads in most of China are mere supplements to rail and river routes, the railroads are the vital transportation arteries of Communist China. Except in very limited areas, roads and rivers do not provide any alternative means of transportation.

7. The Chinese Communists have made important improvements in the Chinese rail network, and their plans suggest much more extensive improvement in the future, but the railroad system is still primitive by western standards

8. An air campaign against the Chinese railroad system might prove to be a means of bringing the Chinese government to terms without resort to a land campaign or nuclear attacks on population centers.

9. Probably an air campaign directed against rolling stock and repair facilities would bring the best results in interdicting the railway system as a whole.

FOOTNOTES

CHAPTER I

1. Wkly Isum, 14th AF, 17 May 44, 18 Jul 45, 862 607*; Progress Rpts of 14th AF (Correspondence from Maj Gen Claire L Chennault to Gen Henry H Arnold), Aug 44-Jan 45, 862.113; China Area Oprs Rec, 6th Area Army Oprs, Japanese Monograph No 130, Off of the Chief of Mil Hist, Dept of the Army, pp 1-2; Joint Army-Navy Intel Study (JANIS) No. 76, China, East Coast, Nov 44, Chap VII, pp 37-43, 178 1-76; JANIS No. 77, China, South Coast (Kwangtung Province, Including Hainan Island), Mar 45, Chap VII, pp 31-36, 178 1-77; JANIS No 70, Indo-China, Oct 45, Chap VII, pp 46-59, 178 1-70

2. Wesley Frank Craven and James Lea Cate, eds., *The Army Air Forces in World War II*, IV (Chicago, 1950), 422; Charles F Romanus and Riley Sunderland, *Stilwell's Mission to China*, U.S. Army in World War II, The China-Burma-India Theater (Washington, 1953), pp. 187-88; Claire L Chennault, *Way of a Fighter* (New York, 1949), p. 45.

3. Rpt, Chennault to Wendell L Willkie, 8 Oct 42 cited in Chennault, *Way of a Fighter*, pp 212-16

4. Plan of Air Oprs in China, 14th AF, 30 Apr 43, 862.322A; Chennault, *Way of a Fighter*, p 222

5. Chennault, *Way of a Fighter*, p. 225

6. Craven and Cate, *AAF in WW II*, IV, 441, 524; Ltr, Brig Gen Howard Davidson to CG AAF, 27 Jun 43, Plans File, 10th AF, 1942-45, 862 164; Wkly Isum, 14th AF, 23 Feb 44; Tac Directives for Ftr and Comp Wgs, 14th AF, 30 Mar 44: China Oprs, 14th AF, 1942-45, 862 311, Plans of Air Oprs, 14th AF, 1944, 862 317A.

7. An Evaluation of 14th AF Oprs during 1944 with Due Consideration given to the Logistical Problems Involved, Rpt No 9, AAF Eval Bd, CBI, 15 Jun 45, 138 7-9

8. 5th Ind (Rpt, Chennault to Stilwell, Capabilities of VLR, 16 Feb 44) Hq 14th AF to C/S USAF CBI, Fwd Ech, 21 Apr 44, 862 322C

9. Chennault, *Way of a Fighter*, p 223

10. Effectiveness of Air Attack against Japanese Merchant Shipping, Rpt No 4, AAF Eval Bd, CBI, 15 Dec 44, 138.7-4

11. Wkly Isum, 14th AF, 1943-45, Hist, 308th Bomb Gp, 1943-45, Hist, 11th Bomb Sq, 1943-45.

12. Effectiveness of Air Attack against Jap Merchant Shipping, Rpt No 4, AAF Eval Bd, CBI, 15 Dec 44, *passim*, Hist, 308th Bomb Gp, 1943-45, Hist, 11th Bomb Sq, 1943-45; Wkly Isum, 14th AF, 1943-45; Japanese Naval and Merchant Losses during WW II, Joint Army-Navy Assessment Committee, Feb 47 (JANAC), *passim*, 178 2901

13. Wkly Isum, 14th AF, 23 Feb 44, 1943-45; Eval of 14th AF Oprs, Rpt No 9, AAF Eval Bd, CBI, 15 Jan 45, *passim*; Effectiveness of Air Attack against Jap Merchant Shipping, rpt No. 4, AAF Eval Bd, CBI, 15 Dec 44, *passim*, Sea Sweeps (Radio Rpts), 308th Bomb Gp, 14th AF, 13 Jan-19 Mar 44, 862 162A; Strongpoint Oprs, 14th AF, Nov 44-Jan 45, 862 04F

14. Wkly Isum, 14th AF, 1943-45, JANAC, *passim*; Effectiveness of Air Attack against Jap Merchant Shipping, Rpt No 4, AAF Eval Bd, CBI, 15 Dec 44, *passim*

15. Effectiveness of Air Attack against Jap Merchant Shipping, Rpt No. 4, AAF Eval Bd, CBI, 15 Dec 44, *passim*; Hist, 11th Bomb Sq, 1943-44; Craven and Cate, *AAF in WW II*, IV, 531

16. Intops Rpts, 308th Bomb Gp, 17 Aug 43-30 Jan 44, GP-308-SU-OP (BOMB); Gp Mission Rpts, 308th Bomb Gp, 16 Nov 43-30 Aug 44, Gp-308-SU-OP (BOMB), Wkly Isum, 14th AF, 1943-44

17. JANAC, pp 37-60; Wkly Isum, 14th AF, 1943-45, Effectiveness of Air Attack against Jap Merchant Shipping, Rpt No 4, AAF Eval Bd, CBI, 15 Dec 44, *passim*, Gp Mission Rpts, 308th Bomb Gp, Oct '43-Nov 44, Strongpoint Oprs, 14th AF, Nov 44-Jan 45, Hist, 11th Bomb Sq, 1943-45; Hist, 23d Ftr Gp, 1944-45, Hist, 51st Ftr Gp, 1944-45

18. Ltr, Davidson to CG AFF, 27 Jun 43 Plans File, 10th AF

19. Effectiveness of Air Attack against Jap Merchant Shipping, Rpt No 4, AAF Eval Bd, CBI, 15 Dec 44, p 21

20. *Ibid.*, pp 21-24

21. *Ibid*, pp 13-24; Wkly Isum, 14th AF, May 44-Jun 45, Ltr, Chennault to Arnold, 10 Oct 44: Progress Rpts, 14th AF, Aug 44-Jan 45

22. Effectiveness of Air Attack against Jap Merchant Shipping, Rpt No 4, AAF Eval Bd, CBI, 15 Dec 44, p 14A, Ltr, Comdr U S. Naval Unit, 14th AF, to CG 14th AF, 3 Sep 44 Shipping Rpt, 14th AF and USN, 25 Sep 44, 862.490; Msg, Lt Gen Albert C Wedemeyer, CG USF CT to Gen Douglas MacArthur, CG SWPA, 13 Feb 45 China Oprs, 14th AF, 1942-45

23. Gp Mission Rpts, 308th Bomb Gp, Nov 43-Oct 44; Effectiveness of Air Attack against Jap Merchant Shipping, Rpt No 4, AAF Eval Bd, CBI, 15 Dec 44, pp 13-20

---

*Except where otherwise indicated, all file numbers refer to the Archives of the USAF Historical Division, Maxwell Air Force Base, Alabama

24. See note above.

25. Effectiveness of Air Attack against Jap Merchant Shipping, Rpt No. 4, AAF Eval Bd, CBI, 15 Dec 44, pp. 21-24.

26. Wkly Isum, 14th AF, 1944-45; Gp Mission Rpts, 308th Bomb Gp, Nov 43-Oct 44; JANAC, pp. 60-99.

27. Intel Rpt, Gp Mission No. 95, 308th Bomb Gp, 23 Apr 44; Gp Mission Rpts, 308th Bomb Gp, Nov 43-Aug 44; Wkly Isum, 14th AF, 26 Nov 44; Effectiveness of Air Attack against Jap Merchant Shipping, Rpt No 4, AAF Eval Bd, CBI, 15 Dec 44, pp. 16-19; JANAC, pp. 60-99

28. Effectiveness of Air Attack against Jap Merchant Shipping, Rpt No 4, AAF Eval Bd, CBI, 15 Dec 44, pp. 29-40; The Offensive Mine-Laying Campaign against Japan, USSBS, Naval Analysis Div, 1 Nov 46, pp. 77-80, 137.716-78.

29. See note above.

30. Offensive Mine-Laying Campaign against Japan, USSBS, pp. 77, 79-80.

31. *Ibid.*, p. 1.

32. Offensive Mine-Laying Campaign against Japan. USSBS, pp. 1, 48-49, 108-09; Ltr, Chennault to Brig. Gen S. W. Fitzgerald, Pres AAF Eval Bd, CBI, 1 Feb 45; China Oprs, 14th AF, 1942-45, Capt. Rokuemon Minami, IJN, Intg No 256, USSBS, 1 Nov 45, 137 73; Effectiveness of Air Attack against Jap Merchant Shipping, Rpt No 4, AAF Eval Bd, CBI, 15 Dec 44, pp. 29-40.

33. Offensive Mine-Laying Campaign against Japan, USSBS, pp 35-36; JANAC, pp. 60-90

34. JANAC, p ii.

35. The Imperial Japanese Navy in WW II A Graphic Presentation of the Japanese Naval Organization and List of Combatant and Non-Combatant Vessels Lost or Damaged in the War, Japanese Monograph No. 116, Mil Hist Sec, Special Staff, GHQ FEC, Feb 52, *passim*, K171.41-116.

Chapter II

1. Joint Army-Navy Intel Study (JANIS) No 71, South-Central China, Chap VII, Jun 47, *passim*, AUL M-27988-C; JANIS No. 76, China, East Coast, Chap VII, Nov 44, pp 41-43, 178.1-76; JANIS No. 77, China, South Coast (Kwangtung Province, Including Hainan Island), Chap VII, Mar 45, pp. 35-36, 178 1-77; The Effect of Air Action on Jap Ground Army Logistics, USSBS, Mil Analysis Div, Apr 47, pp. 23-24, 168-70, 137.715-64; Ltr, Maj. Gen Claire L Chennault, CG 14th AF, to Lt Gen Ira C. Eaker, Dep Comdr AAF, 29 May 45; Gen Chennault's Personal Correspondence File, 7 May 44-21 Jun 45, 14th AF, 862.161B; The War against Japanese Transportation, 1941-45, USSBS, Trans Div, May 47, *passim*, 137.713-54; Wkly Isum, 14th AF, 2 Aug, 23 Aug, 25 Oct 44.

2. JANIS No 76, Chap VII, *passim*; JANIS No. 77, Chap VII, pp. 35-36; Msg, LZ5 (liaison with Chinese Forces at Hengyang) to Hq 14th AF, 18 Jul 44, K28; Radios-Incoming, 14th AF, May 43-Jul 44, 862 162A; China Area Oprs Rec, 6th Area Army Oprs, Jap Monograph No. 130, Off of the Chief of Mil Hist, Dept of the Army, pp. 3-9; Plans of Air Oprs, 14th AF, 1944, pp. 2-3, 862.317A; Effect of Air Action on Jap Ground Army Logistics, USSBS, p. 24; Effectiveness of Air Attack against Jap Merchant Shipping, Rpt No. 4, AAF Eval Bd, CBI, 15 Dec 44, pp. 10-12, 138.7-4; Wkly Isum, 14th AF, 2, 23 Aug 44.

3. Effectiveness of Air Attack against Jap Merchant Shipping, Rpt No. 4, AAF Eval Bd, CBI, 15 Dec 44, pp. 21-24

4. Hist, 449th Ftr Sq, 1944-45; Hist, 312th Ftr Wg, 1944-45.

5. Hist, 11th Bomb Sq, Sep-Oct 43; Activities of 11th Bomb Sq, 14th AF, CBI, 26 May-12 Aug 44, Rpt No. 8, Naval Combat Air Intel, 15 Sep 44; Hist, 11th Bomb Sq, May-Oct 44, App, pp. 10-11; Hist, 2d Bomb Sq (P), CACW, Feb 44; 14th AF Experience with 75-mm Shells and 500 lb GP Bombs, Prepared by 24th SCU, 15 May 44; China Oprs, 14th AF, 1942-45, 862.311.

6. Activities of the 11th Bomb Sq, 14th AF, CBI, 26 May-12 Aug 44, Rpt No 8, Naval Air Combat Intel, 15 Sep 44; Hist, 11th Bomb Sq, May-Oct 44, App, p. 5, Ltr, Chennault to [Maj Gen Barney B.] Giles, Chief, Air Staff, 26 Sep 43; Oprs Ltrs, I, 168.491; Ltr, Chennault to Arnold, 21 Feb 44; Oprs Ltrs, I; Msg, Hengyang to 14th AF, 16 Nov 43; Hengyang Intops, 24 Aug 43-29 Mar 44, 862.162A, 14th AF Experience with 75-mm. Shells and 500-lb GP Bombs, Prepared by 24th SCU, 15 May 44; China Oprs, 14th AF, 1942-45.

7. Hist, 68th Comp Wg, 1 Apr-8 Nov 44, pp. 46-52; Hist, 11th Bomb Sq, May-Oct 44; Hist, 491st Bomb Sq, Oct 44; Hist, 4th Bomb Sq (P), CACW, Mar, Jul, Aug 45.

8. Hist, 76th Ftr Sq, 27 May-7 Nov 44; Hist, 8th Ftr Sq. (P), CACW, Apr 44.

9. Intv with 1st Lt Robert S Clapp, Air Intel Contact Unit, Hq AAFRS No. 1, Atlantic City, N.J., 27 Dec 44, 142.053-165; Intv with Capt Stanley J Trecartin, Air Intel Contact Unit, Hq AAFRS No. 1, Atlantic City, NJ, 29 May 45; Strong point Oprs. 14th AF, Nov 44-Jan 45, pp. 17-23, 862.04F; Wkly Isum, 14th AF, 9 Jun 43; Hist,

28th Ftr Sq (P), CACW, May 44; Hist, 76th Ftr Sq, May 44.

10. Strongpoint Oprs, 14th AF, Nov 44-Jan 45, pp. 17-20; Intv with 1st Lt Russel D Williams, Air Intel Contact Unit, Hq AAFRS No 1, Atlantic City, N J., 30 May 45; Hist, 118th Tac Rcn Sq, Jan 44-Jan 45, Suichwan Incls; Hist, 76th Ftr Sq, 27 May-7 Nov 44; Hist, 23d Ftr Gp, Mar 44-Aug 45; Hist, 7th Ftr Sq (P), CACW, Feb 45; Wkly Isum, 14th AF, 9 Jun 43; Ltr, Col Clinton D. Vincent, Dep Comdr Fwd Ech, 14th AF, to Lt Col M F. Taber, 6 Nov 43· 14th AF Oprs, Nov 43, 862 327; Mission Rpts, 7th Ftr Sq (P), CACW, Aug 44, SQ-7(XIV)-FTR-SU-OPS, Hist, 17th Ftr Sq (P), CACW, Jun, Jul 45; Hist, 29th Ftr Sq (P), CACW, Jan 44, Feb 45; Hist, 8th Ftr Sq (P), CACW, May 45, Intv with 1st Lt Gordon Cruickshank, Air Intel Contact Unit, Hq AAFRS No. 1, Atlantic City, N J., 2 May 45

11 Mission Rpt No. 302, 5th Ftr Gp, 25 Sep 44. Hist, 5th Ftr Gp (P), CACW, Sep-Nov 44; Hist, 426th Night Ftr Sq, Feb-Aug 45, Hist, 427th Night Ftr Sq, Apr-Jul 45.

12 Activities of the 11th Bomb Sq, 14th AF, CBI, 26 May-12 Aug 44, Rpt No 8, Naval Combat Air Intel, 15 Sep 44; Hist, 11th Bomb Sq, May-Oct 44, pp. 10-11.

13. Hist, 5th Ftr Gp (P), CACW, Jun, Jul 45; Hist, 8th Ftr Sq (P), CACW, Jan 45; Hist, 76th Ftr Sq, 27 May-7 Nov 44; Strongpoint Oprs, 14th AF, Nov 44-Jan 45, pp 20-23; Intv with 1st Lt Gordon Cruickshant, Air Intel Contact Unit, Hq AAFRS No. 1, Atlantic City, N J., 2 May 45; Intv with Capt Daniel Schaible, Air Intel Contact Unit, Hq AAFRS No 1, Atlantic City, N.J, 22 May 45, Hist, 74th Ftr Sq, Jan 45; Analysis of Ftr Oprs, 14th AF, Jul 44-Feb 45, Prepared by 24th SCU, 21 May 45, 862 310A; 14th AF Experience with 75-mm. Shells and 500-lb GP Bombs, Prepared by 24th SCU, 15 May 44 China Oprs, 14th AF, 1942-45.

14 Offensive Mine-Laying Campaign against Japan, USSBS, Naval Analysis Div, 1 Nov 46, pp 4, 29-40, 35-36, 48-49, 79-80, 108-9, 137-716-78; Effectiveness of Air Attack against Jap Merchant Shipping, Rpt No 4, AAF Eval Bd, CBI, 15 Dec 44, pp. 10-20, Capt. Rokuemon Minami, IJN, Intg No 256, USSBS, 1 Nov 45, 137 73, Ltr, Chennault to Brig Gen S W. Fitzgerald, Pres AAF Eval Bd, CBI, 1 Feb 45 China Oprs, 14th AF, 1942-45, Effect of Air Action on Jap Ground Army Logistics, USSBS, pp. 23-24; Msg, Hq AAF to Hq 14th AF, 15 Dec 44, WARX 77634: Radios, China Stations to 14th AF, 14 Dec 44-1 Jan 45, 862.162A; Ltr, Arnold to Chennault, 25 Mar 44· Oprs Ltrs, I, Ltr, Chennault to Eaker, 29 May 45, Gen Chennault's Personal Correspondence, 1944-45

15. China Area Oprs Rec, 6th Area Army Oprs, Jap Monograph No. 130, pp 13, 27; Wkly Isum, 14th AF, 1943-45.

16 Analysis of Ftr Oprs, 14th AF, Jul 44-Feb 45, Prepared by 24th SCU, 21 May 45

17. Hist, 68th Comp Wg, 1 Apr-8 Nov 44, *passim*, 9 Nov-31 Dec 44, App; Hist, 5th Ftr Gp (P), CACW, Dec 44, Jan, Feb 45, Hist, 26th Ftr Sq (P), CACW, Nov 44, Hist, 8th Ftr Sq (P), CACW, Jan 45; Hist, 11th Bomb Sq, May-Oct 44

18 Wkly Isum, 14th AF, 10 May 44; Hist, 7th Ftr Sq (P), CACW, Feb 45; Hist, 28th Ftr Sq (P), CACW, May 44; Hist, 76th Ftr Sq, 27 May-7 Nov 44; Effect of Air Action on Jap Ground Army Logistics, USSBS, pp 168-70.

19. Offensive Mine-Laying Campaign against Japan, USSBS, pp. 48-49.

20. War against Jap Trans, USSBS, pp. 4-6, Wkly Isum, 14th AF, 23 Aug 44.

21 Effect of Air Action on Jap Ground Army Logistics, USSBS, pp 23-24.

22. *Ibid*, Wkly Isum, 14th AF, 1943.

23 China Area Oprs Rec, Comd of the China Area Expeditionary Army, Jap Monograph No 129, Off of the Chief of Mil Hist, Dept of the Army, p 9; Field Marshal Shunroku Hata, Intg No 522, USSBS, 8 Dec 45; China Area Oprs Rec, 6th Area Army Oprs, Jap Monograph No. 130, pp. 3-8; Wkly Isum, 14th AF, Jan-May 44; Directive, 14th AF, 30 Mar 44. China Oprs, 14th AF, 1942-45

24 Wkly Isum, 14th AF, Jun-Nov 44; Effect of Air Action on Jap Ground Army Logistics, USSBS, pp. 23-24; Hata, Intg No 522, USSBS, 8 Dec 45.

25 Strongpoint Oprs, 14th AF, Nov 44-Jan 45, pp. 6-11, 20-23, Effect of Air Action on Jap Ground Army Logistics, USSBS, pp. 168-70; Wkly Isum, 14th AF, Nov 44-Jan 45.

26 Wkly Isum, 14th AF, Dec 44-Apr 45; China Area Oprs Rec, Comd of the China Area Expeditionary Army, Jap Monograph No 129, pp. 68-69.

27. Wkly Isum, 14th AF, Apr-May 45.

28 China Area Oprs Rec, 6th Area Army Oprs, Jap Monograph No. 130, pp. 64-65, 85-86; Wkly Isum, 14th AF, Jun-Aug 45; Offensive Mine-Laying Campaign against Japan, USSBS, pp. 48-49; War against Jap Trans, USSBS, pp 4-6, Hata, Intg No 522, USSBS, 8 Dec 45; Effect of Air Action on Jap Ground Army Logistics, USSBS, pp. 23-24, 168-70; China Area Oprs Rec, Comd of the China Area Expeditionary Army, Jap Monograph No 129, pp. 101-13

29. China Area Oprs Rec, Comd of the China Area Expeditionary Army, Jap Monograph No. 129, pp. 8-11, Ltr, Maj Wilfred J. Smith, Asst A-2, 14th AF, to CG 14th AF, 4 Jan 44 Changteh File, 14th AF, Nov-Dec 43, 862 162A; Wesley Frank Craven and James Lea Cate, eds, *The Army Air Forces in WW II*, IV (Chicago, 1950), 534-35

30. Ltr, Vincent to Taber, 6 Nov 43: Ltr, Brig Gen Edgar E Glenn, C/S 14th AF to CO Fwd Ech, 14th AF, 18 Nov 43· 14th AF Oprs 1942-45

31. Wkly Isum, 14th AF, Nov-Dec 43, 28 Jun 44; Ltr, Smith to CG 14th AF, 4 Jan 44. Changteh File, 14th AF, Nov-Dec 43.

32. Ltr, Smith to CG 14th AF, 4 Jan 44: Changteh File, 14th AF, Nov-Dec 43, Oplans, 14th AF, 1943-45, 862 317B, Plans of Air Oprs, 14th AF, 1944, 862.317A

33. China Area Oprs Rec, Comd of the China Area Expeditionary Army, Jap Monograph No. 129, pp. 14-48; Wkly Isum, 14th AF, 26 Jul 44; Claire L. Chennault, *Way of a Fighter* (New York, 1949), pp 268-70

34. Chennault, *Way of a Fighter*, p. 286.

35. Oprs against Chinese Airfields, U S. and U.S.S.R, 1943-45, Jap Monograph No. 78, Off of the Chief of Mil Hist, Dept of the Army, *passim*, China Area Oprs Rec, Comd of the China Area Expeditionary Army, Jap Monograph No. 129, pp. 11-87.

36. Wkly Isum, 14th AF, 26 Jul 44

37. Effectiveness of Air attack against Jap Merchant Shipping, Rpt No 4, AAF Eval Bd, CBI, 15 Dec 44, p 7A; Wkly Status and Oprs Rpts (Form 34's), 14th AF and CACW Sqs, Jun 44; Chennault, *Way of a Fighter*, pp 290-91.

38. Wkly Isum, 14th AF, May-Jul 44; Hata, Intg No 522, USSBS, 8 Dec 45

39. Wkly Isum, 14th AF, May-Aug 45

40. China Area Oprs Rec, 6th Area Army Oprs, Jap Monograph No 130, p 33.

41. Kwangsi-Kweichow-Kwangtung Campaign, 1 Aug 44-1 Jan 45: Radio Correspondence, Kwangsi, Kwangtung, Kweichow, 1944-45, 862 162A; China Area Oprs Rec, 6th Area Army Oprs, Jap Monograph No. 130, pp 3-8, 22-24, 27, 33-36

42. China Area Oprs Rec, Comd of China Area Expeditionary Army, Jap Monograph No 129, pp. 64-72; China Area Oprs Rec, 6th Area Army Oprs, Jap Monograph No. 130, pp 8-9, 15-19, 26, 33-36; Wkly Isum, 14th AF, Aug-Dec 44

43. Wkly Isum, 14th AF, Aug-Nov 44; China Area Oprs Rec, 6th Area Army Oprs, Jap Monograph No 130, pp 2-36; Kwangsi-Kweichow-Kwangtung Campaign, 1 Aug 44-1 Jan 45: Radio Correspondence, Kwangsi, Kwangtung, Kweichow, 14th AF, 1944-45; Effect of Air Action on Jap Ground Army Logistics, USSBS, pp 168-70, Oprs against Chinese Airfields, U S. and U S S R., 1943-45, Jap Monograph No. 78, *passim*; G-2 Periodic Rpt, USF CT, 2 Nov 44, 852.607, Ltr, Chennault to Arnold, 17 Dec 44: Progress Rpts of 14th AF, 1944-45, 862.113.

44. Wkly Isum, 14th AF, Nov 44-May 45; China Area Oprs Rec, 6th Area Army Oprs, Jap Monograph No. 130, pp 33-36, 64-67

45. Wkly Isum, 14th AF, May-Aug 45; China Area Oprs Rec, 6th Area Army Oprs, Jap Monograph No. 130, pp. 64-70; China Area Oprs Rec, Comd of the China Area Expeditionary Army, Jap Monograph No. 129, pp. 100-19

46. Wkly Isum, 14th AF, 1943-45.

47. Jap Naval and Merchant Losses During WW II, Joint Army-Navy Assessment Committee (JANAC), Feb 47, *passim*, Effect of Air Action on Jap Ground Army Logistics, USSBS, p 24; The Imperial Japanese Navy in WW II: A Graphic Presentation of the Jap Naval Organization and List of Combatant and Non-Combatant Vessels Lost or Damaged in the War, Jap Monograph No. 116, Mil Hist Sec, Special Staff, GHQ FEC, Feb 52, *passim*, K171.41-116.

48 JANAC, *passim*, Effect of Air Action on Jap Ground Army Logistics, USSBS, p 24; Offensive Mine-Laying Campaign against Japan, pp 35-36.

49. IJN in WW II, Jap Monograph No. 116, pp. 171-279.

50 Wkly Isum, 14th AF, Aug 44-Sep 45.

51. China Area Oprs Rec, 6th Area Army Oprs, Jap Monograph No. 130, pp. 3-9, 15-19, 22-24, 26; Oprs Against Chinese Airfields, U S. and U.S.S R, 1943-45, Jap Monograph No. 78, No. pp.; Hata, Intg No 522, USSBS, 8 Dec 45; The Offensive Mine Laying Campaign against Japan, pp 4, 48-49; The Effect of Air Action on Japanese Ground Army Logistics, USSBS, pp 23-24.

Chapter III

1 Joint Army-Navy Intel Study (JANIS) No 76, China, East Coast, Chap VII, Nov 44, pp 24-33, 178 1-76, JANIS No. 77, China, South Coast (Kwangtung Province, Including Hainan Island), Chap VII, Mar 45, pp 18-27, 178.1-77; An Eval of 14th AF Oprs during 1944 with Due Consideration Given to the Logistical Problems Involved, Rpt No 9, AAF Eval Bd, CBI, 15 June

Notes

1. 45, pp 8-9, 138 7-9; Wkly Isum, 14th AF, 14 Jun, 4 Oct, 25 Oct 44, 30 May, 20 Jun 45, 862 607

2. JANIS No 70, Indo-China, Chap VII, Oct 45, pp 34-35, 178 1-70

3. Salween-Burma Road, Ground Force PRO Rpt, *passim*, 855 309A, Salween Campaign, May 44-Mar 45, 14th AF, *passim*, 862 04D, Completion of the Salween Campaign, 10 May 44-20 Jan 45, Chinese Combat Command, *passim*, 855 04A, Wesley Frank Craven and James Lea Cate, eds, *The Army Air Force in WW II*, V (Chicago, 1953), 200-201, Claire L. Chennault, *Way of a Fighter* (New York, 1949), p 273

4. Hist, 11th Bomb Sq, 1944-45; Hist, 491st Bomb Sq, 1944-45, Hist, 118th Tac Rcn Sq, Jun 45, Wkly Isum, 14th AF, 1943-45

5. Wkly Isum, 14th AF, 1944; Hist, 308th Bomb Gp, 1944

6. Wkly Isum, 14th AF, 1944-45, Hist, 11th Bomb Sq, 1944-45, Hist, 4th Bomb Sq (P), CACW, Jun 45

7. Air Oprs in China, Burma, India, WW II, USSBS, Mil Analysis Div, Mar 47, *passim*, 137 715-67; Chihkiang Campaign, 14th AF, Apr-Jun 45, *passim*, 862 451C, Hunan Campaign, 14th AF, 1944, *passim*, 862 309D; Medium Bomber Attack on Bridges, Oprs Analysis Sec, 14th AF, n d, *passim*, 862 454E, Wkly Isum, 14th AF, 1943-45, Oprs of 14th AF in Jul 44, Prepared by 24th SCU, 2 Sep 44· China Oprs, 14th AF, 1942-45, 862 311, Chennault, *Way of a Fighter*, p 298, Hist, 11th Bomb Sq, 1944-45; Hist, 76th Ftr Sq, 27 May-7 Nov 44, Hist, 26th Ftr Sq (P), CACW, Nov 44, Hist, 75th Ftr Sq, Aug 44, Hist, 25th Ftr Sq, 1941-45; Hist, 27th Ftr Sq (P), CACW, Mar 45; Hist, 17th Ftr Sq (P), CACW, Oct 44, Hist, 22d Bomb Sq, May 45, Hist, 4th Bomb Sq (P), CACW, Dec 44, Feb, Jun 45; Mission Rpt No 89, 7 Jun 45, 4th Bomb Sq (P), CACW: Hist, 4th Bomb Sq (P), CACW, Jun 45, Hist, 3d Bomb Sq (P), CACW, Mar 45; Hist, 2d Bomb Sq (P), CACW, May 44; Hist, 118th Tac Rcn Sq, Jun 45, Hist, 491st Bomb Sq, Sep 44, Hist, 5th Ftr Gp (P), CACW, May 45, Hist, 3d Ftr Gp (P), CACW, Mar 45, Hist, 81st Ftr Gp, Mar 45, Hist, 68th Comp Wg, 1 Apr-8 Nov 44, May-Jun 45, Hist, 426th Night Ftr Sq, Mar 45.

8. Wkly Isum, 14th AF, 1943-45; Burma Oprs Rec, 33d Army Oprs, Jap Monograph No 148, Off of the Chief of Mil Hist, Dept of the Army, *passim*, K171 41-148, Salween-Burma Road, Ground Force PRO Rpt, *passim*, Completion of the Salween Campaign, Chinese Combat Command, 1944-45, *passim*, Salween Campaign, 1944-45, 14th AF, *passim*; Hist, 69th Comp Wg, May 44-Jan 45

9. Hist, 491st Bomb Sq, Mar 45, Hist, 68th Comp Wg, May-Jun 45, Wkly Isum, 14th AF, 1943-45

10. Changteh File, 14th AF, Nov-Dec 43, 862 162A, Wkly Isum, 14th AF, 1943-44

11. Wkly Isum, 14th AF, 26 Jul, 1 Nov 44; Hist, 2d Bomb Sq (P), CACW, May 44, Oprs against Chinese Airfields, U S and U S S R, 1943-45, Jap Monograph No 78, Off of the Chief of Mil Hist, Dept of the Army, *passim*, China Area Oprs Rec, Comd of the China Area Expeditionary Army, Jap Monograph No 129, Off of the Chief of Mil Hist, Dept of the Army, p 31

12. Oprs against Chinese Airfields, U S and U S S R, 1943-45, Jap Monograph No 78, *passim*; Chennault, *Way of a Fighter*, p 298.

13. Wkly Isum, 14th AF, May-Aug 44, Oprs of 14th AF in Jul 44, Prepared by 24th SCU, 2 Sep 44· China Oprs, 14th AF, 1942-45, China Area Oprs Rec, 6th Area Army Oprs, Jap Monograph No 130, pp. 3-8; Chennault, *Way of a Fighter*, p 298

14. Wkly Isum, 14th AF, Jun-Dec 44; Hist, 75th Ftr Sq, Aug 44; Activities of the 11th Bomb Sq, 14th AF, 26 May to 12 Aug 44, Rpt No 8, Naval Combat Air Intel, 15 Sep 44 Hist, 11th Bomb Sq, May-Oct 44, App, pp, 12-13, Intv with 1st Lt Gordon R Francis, Air Intel Contact Unit, Hq AAFRS No. 3, Santa Monica, Cal, 23 Dec 44, 142 053-128, China Area Oprs Rec, 6th Area Army Oprs, Jap Monograph No 130, pp 8-9, 15-19, 22-24, 26, 33-40, Kwangsi-Kweichow-Kwangtung Campaign, 1 Aug 44-1 Jan 45 Radio Correspondence, Kwangsi, Kweichow, Kwangtung, 14th AF, 1944-45, 862 162A; China Area Oprs Rec, Comd of the China Area Expeditionary Army, Jap Monograph No 129, pp 42-43, The Effect of Air Action on Japanese Ground Army Logistics, USSBS, Apr 47, pp. 168-70, 137.715-64, Japanese Army Mobilization Plan Order, Translation, CINCPAC-CINCPOA Item No 9175, p 49, uncatalogued Archives item; Order of Battle of the Japanese Armed Forces, 1 Mar 45, *passim*, 170 227A, Tables of Organization, Japanese Army, Mil Intel Div, 31 Aug 43, *passim*, 170 227F

15. Oprs against Chinese Airfields, U.S and U S S R, 1943-45, Jap Monograph No. 78, *passim*; Wkly Isum, 14th AF, Jan-May 45; Hist, 7th Ftr Sq (P), CACW, Apr 45; Hist, 2d Bomb Sq (P), CACW, Mar 45.

16. Wkly Isum, 14th AF, Jan-Mar 45; Chihkiang Campaign, 14th AF, Apr-Jun 45, *passim*; Hist, 11th Bomb Sq, Jan-Mar 45

17. Hist, 26th Ftr Sq, Apr-Jun 45; Chihkiang Campaign, 14th AF, Apr-Jun 45, *passim*; Oprs against Chinese Airfields, US and U.S.S.R., 1943-45, Jap Monograph No. 78, *passim*; China Area Oprs Rec, 6th Area Army Oprs, Jap Monograph No. 130, pp. 76-78.

18. Wkly Isum, 14th AF, Jul-Aug 45; China Area Oprs Rec, 6th Area Army Oprs, Jap Monograph No. 130, pp. 70-73, 78-80.

19. Wkly Isum, 14th AF, 1943-45.

CHAPTER IV

1. Joint Army-Navy Intel Study (JANIS) No. 70, Indo-China, Chap VII, Oct 45, p. 1, 178.1-70; Interdiction, a Monthly, Jul 45, 18th PID, Hq 14th AF, pp. 13-23, 862.454A, Wkly Isum, 14th AF, 6 Jun 45; Air Oprs in China, Burma, India, WW II USSBS, Mil Analysis Div, Mar 47, pp 71-74, 137.715-67.

2. Ellen J. Hammer, *The Struggle for Indo-China* (Stanford, Cal., 1954), pp. 14-53; Charles Robequain, *Economic Development of French Indo-China* (New York, 1944), pp 376-77.

3. Wkly Isum, 14th AF, 1943-45; Interdiction, Jul 45, pp. 13-23; JANIS No. 70, Chap VII, p. 1.

4. Wkly Isum 14th AF, 1943-45; JANIS No 70, Chap VII, p. 1; Interdiction, Jul 45, pp. 13-23; Air Oprs in CBI, USSBS, pp 71-74.

5. Interdiction, Jul 45, pp. 10, 13-23; Air Oprs in CBI, USSBS, pp 71-74; JANIS No. 70, Chap VII, pp 1, 10-12; Wkly Isum, 14th AF, 1943-45.

6. Interdiction, Jul 45, pp. 15-23; Wkly Isum, 14th AF, 1944-45; Interdiction, a Monthly, Aug 45, 18th PID, Hq 14th AF, p 10, 862.454A; Air Oprs in CBI, USSBS, pp. 71-74.

CHAPTER V

1. Joint Army-Navy Intel Study (JANIS) No 77, China, South Coast (Kwangtung Province Including Hainan Island), Chap VII, Mar 45, pp 2-18, 178.1-77.

2. *Ibid.*

3. JANIS No. 76, China, East Coast, Chap VII, Nov 44, p. 24, 178.1-76, JANIS No. 77, Chap VII, pp 2-18; Wkly Isum, 14th AF, 7 Feb, 25 Jul, 2 Sep 45, 862.607, Interdiction, A Monthly 18th PID, Hq 14th AF, Jul 45, p. 4, 862.454A.

4. Wkly Isum, 14th AF, 13 Dec 44, 31 Jan 45; China Area Oprs Rec, Comd of the China Area Expeditionary Army, Jap Monograph No. 129. Off of the Chief of Mil Hist, Dept of the Army, p. 49; China Area Oprs Rec, 6th Area Army Oprs, Jap Monograph No 130, Off of the Chief of Mil Hist, Dept of the Army, *passim*.

5. JANIS No. 76, Chap VII, pp. 21-23

6. *Ibid.*, pp. 14-17.

7. *Ibid.*, p. 23.

8. Wkly Isum, 14th AF, 3 May, 27 Sep, 4 Oct, 8 Nov 44, 2 Sep 45; JANIS No. 76, Chap VII, pp 1-9; Interdiction, Jul 45, pp. 3-4.

9. JANIS No. 76, Chap VII, pp 19-20; Wkly Isum, 14th AF, 3, 10 May 44, 18 Apr 45; Interdiction, Jul 45, pp 3-4.

10. Wkly Isum, 14th AF, 3, 10, 24 May 44, 6 Jun 45; Strategic Air Campaign against Railroads in Occupied China, (n d. but ca Apr 45), R&A, OSS, Hq 14th AF, pp 1-11, App I, 862.454B; The Effect of Air Action on Jap Ground Army Logistics, USSBS, Mil Analysis Div, Apr 47, pp. 28-32, 137.715-64; JANIS No. 76, Chap. VII, pp. 1-9.

11. JANIS No. 76, Chap VII, pp. 9-14; Wkly Isum, 14th AF, 10 Jan 45

12. JANIS No. 76, Chap VII, pp. 1-9, 17-18.

13. Wkly Isum, 14th AF, 21, 28 Mar 45; JANIS 76, Chap VII, pp. 20-21.

14. Wkly Isum, 14th AF, 2 May 45

15. Effect of Air Action on Jap Ground Army Logistics, USSBS, pp. 28-32; Wkly Isum, 14th AF, 16 May 45, JANIS No. 76, Chap VII, pp. 23-24; Interdiction, Jul 45, pp. 4-6; An Air Study of China, Air Intel Rpt No 100-35/1-33, 21 Aug 47, pp. 63-64, 142.048-35A.

16. Interdiction, Nov 45, Intel Sec, Hq 14th AF, pp iii-v, 1-4, 862.454A; JANIS No. 76, Chap VII, pp. 1-9, Effect of Air Action on Jap Ground Army Logistics, USSBS, pp 28-32.

17. Oprl Directive No. 1, Hq USF CT to CG 14th AF, 1 Dec 44: Directives, Hq USF CT, 1944-45, 852.327.

18. Ltr, Hq AF to Comdrs, Subordinate Units, 1 Jan 45: Tac Directives for Wg Comdrs, 14th AF, 1 Jan 45; China Oprs, 14th AF, 1942-45, 862.311.

19. Ltr, Hq 14th AF to CO 312th Ftr Wg, CO CACW, and CO 68th Comp Wg, 14th AF, 16 Apr 45: Program for Air Oprs to Stop Jap Offensive, 16 Apr 45, 862 317B

20. Interdiction, Nov 45, pp 17, 34-50, 58-68, Annex II, Tables 8, 13; Air Oprs in CBI, USSBS, pp. 74-80; Wkly Isum, 14th AF, 1943-45.

21. Wkly Isum, 14th AF, 10 Jan, 25 Apr 45; Interdiction, Nov 45, pp. 7-20, *passim*

22. Interdiction, Nov 45, pp 17, 58-68; Ltr, Chennault to Arnold, 26 Feb 45: Progress Rpts of 14th AF, 1944-45, 862.113; Hist, 4th Bomb Sq (P), CACW, Mar-Jul 45; Hist, 1st Bomb Sq (P),

CACW, Mar-May 45; Hist, 3d Bomb Sq (P), CACW, Mar-May 45, Hist, 2d Bomb Sq (P), CACW, Apr 45.

23. Memo for C/S, 15 May 44: Memo, Kuter to Arnold, 11 Oct 44; Misc 14th AF War Plans, 1942-45, WP-IV-D-1a, 145 95; Msg, Yunnanyi to Hq 14th AF, 3 Nov 44. Radios in China Theater, 1944-45, 862 162A, Ltr, Hq 14th AF to Comdrs Subordinate Units, 1 Jan 45; China Oprs, 14th AF, 1942-45; Hist, 68th Comp Wg, Jan-Apr, May-Jun 45; Ltr, Chennault to Arnold, 26 Feb 45; Progress Rpts, 14th AF, 1944-45; Program for Air Oprs to Stop Jap Offensive, 16 Apr 45; Supplement to Directive for Air Oprs to Stop Jap Offensive, 15 Apr 45, 862 317B; Ltr of Instrs No 1, Hq AAF CT to CG 14th AF, 6 Jul 45; Directives, USF CT, Jul-Aug 45, 852 327

24. Air Oprs in CBI, USSBS, 65-66, 74-80, Wkly Isum, 14th AF, 6 Dec 44, 1944-45, Interdiction, Nov 45, pp 7-17; Hist, 2d Bomb Sq (P), CACW, Oct 44, Hist, 7th Ftr Sq (P), CACW, Apr, Jun 45; Hist, 8th Ftr Sq (P), CACW, Jun 45

25. Interdiction, Aug 45, p 6, 862.454A, Wkly Isum, 14th AF, 6 Dec 44, 11 Jul 45, Air Oprs in CBI, USSBS, pp. 74-80, Hist, 8th Ftr Sq (P), CACW, Jul 45; Hist, 7th Ftr Sq (P), CACW, Feb 45; Hist, 4th Bomb Sq (P), CACW, Jul 45; Col Charles G Chandler, Intv, Air Intel Contact Unit, AAFRS No. 3, Santa Monica, Cal, 6 Apr 45, 142 053-160; Intv with 1st Lt Gordon Cruickshank, Air Intel Contact Unit, Hq AAFRS No. 1, Atlantic City, N J, 2 May 45; Intv with 1st Lt Robert C. Lambert and 1st Lt William W. Slaughter, Air Intel Contact Unit, Hq AAFRC, Santa Ana, Cal, 21 Mar 45.

26. Interdiction, Nov 45, pp 7-17, Annex III, I; Wkly Isum, 14th AF, 28 Mar 45

27. Wkly Isum, 14th AF, 1943-45; Interdiction, Nov 45, pp 7-17, 41-45, 51-68

28. Interdiction, Nov 45, pp. 7-17, 51-68

29. Wkly Isum, 14th AF, 1943-44; Effect of Air Action on Jap Ground Army Logistics, USSBS, pp 28-32; Interdiction, Jul 45, pp 1-2, Interdiction, Nov 45, pp 4-5, Annex II, Table 18; Field Marshal Shunroku Hata, Intg No 522, USSBS, 8 Dec 45, 137 73.

30. Interdiction, Aug 45, pp. 7-9, Interdiction, Nov 45, passim; Hist, 530th Ftr Sq, Jul 45; Hist, 490th Bomb Sq, May-Jun 45.

31. Wkly Isum, 14th AF, 3 May 44; Interdiction, Jul 45, pp. 1-2, 10, 12, Interdiction, Aug 45, pp 11-17; Interdiction, Nov 45, passim, Intv with Capt Daniel Schaible, Air Intel Contact Unit, Hq AAFRS No 1, Atlantic City, N J, 22 May 45; Intv with 1st Lt Robert H. Jones, Air Intel Contact Unit, Hq AAFRS No. 1, Atlantic City, N.J., 6 Jun 45, Hist, 75th Ftr Sq, Mar 45, Hist, 3d Bomb Sq (P), CACW, Mar-Jun 45; Hist, 2d Bomb Sq (P), CACW, Nov 44; Hist, 530th Ftr Sq, Jul 45, Incls 5-7; Hist, 528th Ftr Sq, Nov 44-Aug 45; Hist, 490th Bomb Sq, May-Jun 45; Hist, 3d Ftr Gp (P), CACW, Jun-Jul 45; Hist, 81st Ftr Gp, May-Jul 45; Hist, 341st Bomb Gp, Jul 45; Medium Bomber Attacks on Bridges, Oprs Analysis Sec, 14th AF, passim, 862 454E; Program for Air Oprs to Stop Jap Offensive, 15 Apr 45.

32. Hata, Intg No. 522, USSBS, 8 Dec 45; China Area Oprs Rec, 6th Area Army Oprs, Jap Monograph No. 130, passim; Japanese Preparations for Oprs in Manchuria, Jan 43-Aug 45, Jap Monograph No. 138, p 52, K171 41-138; Effect of Air Action on Jap Ground Army Logistics, USSBS, pp. 28-32, China Area Oprs Rec, Comd of the China Area Expeditionary Army, Jap Monograph No 129, pp. 14-15, 54-55, 79, Distribution of Tonnage Received by 14th AF Excluding the Chengtu Area, Jan-Jun 44, 31 Jul 44, Misc 14th AF War Plans, 1942-45; Oprs in CBI, USSBS, pp 65-66; Wkly Isum, 14th AF, 18 Jul, 2 Sep 45.

CHAPTER VII

1. The Economic Development of China through 1957, CIA/RR-33, pp. 121-23, AUL M-30084-S, National Intel Survey (NIS), China, Vol III, Chap III, Sec 36, 1950-53, AUL M-34677-S; Strategic Vulnerability of Communist China, Intel Div, Hq UN and FEC, 15 May 53, p. 42, AUL M-37466-2-S, Notes on Some Aspects of the War Potential of Communist China, Based on Information Received up to Mid-February 1955, Joint Intel Bureau (Melbourne) [JIB(M)] Rpt No 5/1/55, Dept of Defense, Australia, pp. 18, 30-35, AUL M-36760-4-S.

2. Economic Development of China through 1957, p 121, Notes on the War Potential of Communist China, pp 30-35

3. Notes on War Potential of Communist China, pp 30-35; NIS, China, Vol III, Chap II, Sec 33; Economic Development of China through 1957, pp 121-22, In the Wake of the Armies, UNRRA, Mar 46, p. 2, 248 501-30, Strategic Vulnerability of Communist China, p 16; Col F. N. Graves, "Red China, Vulnerability of LOC's," AWC Thesis, May 53, pp. 28-29, 35, AUL N- 32983-S; *Economic Survey of Asia and the Far East. Prepared by the Secretariat of the Economic Commission for Asia and the Far East, United Nations* (New York, 1951), pp. 265-68, Richard L. Walker, *China under Communism: the First Five Years* (New Haven, 1955), pp 227-31

4. Notes on War Potential of Communist China, pp. 18, 30-35; Strategic Vulnerability of Com-

munist China, p 16; Economic Development of China through 1957, p 122

5. Notes of War Potential of Communist China, pp 19, 30-35; Strategic Vulnerability of Communist China, p. 8, NIS, China, Vol III, Chap II, Secs 30, 32, World Area Survey, China, AWC, AU, 1950, Chap II, AUL M-35452-1-S, Rpt on Communist China, RIKU Rpt No. 404, 27 Sep 54, Hq 500th Mil Intel Gp, AUL M-38124-8-S; *Economic Survey of Asia and the Far East* p. 264; Special Study on South China and Adjacent Southeast Asia Areas, FEAF Dep for Intel, n d., pp 3-6, AUL M-39091-S; Physical and Cultural Geography of West China, Kansu Sinkiang, Tsinghai, and Northwestern Szechwan, CIA/RR-G-11, Oct 53, Central Intel Agency (CIA), Office of Research and Reports, pp 33, 105, AUL M-29611-28-C.

6. Strategic Vulnerability of Communist China, p 8.

7. Current Food, Coal, and Trnas Situation Prevailing in China, R&A No. 3433, Dept of State, 2 Jan 46, AUL M-30065-R, NIS, China, Vol III, Chap III, Sec 31, Joint Army-Navy Intel Study (JANIS) No 71, South Central China, Chap III, Jun 47, pp. 3-4, 39, AUL M-27988-C; World Area Survey, China, Chap II, p. 5; China Railways, JIB, UK, Aug 47, AUL M-31155-14-S

8. NIS, China, Vol III, Chap III, Secs 30-31 *Economic Survey of Asia and the Far East*, pp 256-60

9. Notes on the War Potential of Communist China, p. 31

10. Chinese Communist Prospects, 1954-57, Intel Rpt No. 6501, Off of Intel Research, Dept of State, 24 Dec 53, pp 51-52, 72, AUL M-30591-S, Notes on the War Potential of Communist China, pp 30-35; Project Construction in Communist China under the Five Year Plan. CIA/RR PR-90, 17 Dec 54, p 28, AUL M-29611-S

11. Notes on War Potential of Communist China, pp 30-35; *Economic Survey of Asia and the Far East*, p 261; Project Construction in Communist China, p. 29; Intel Digest No. 185 (4-17 May 55), JIB, Ministry of Defense, UK, p. 8, FEAF Intel Roundup No. 145, Sec 53, pp. 30-32.

K720 607A; NIS, China, Vol III, Chap II, Sec 31.

12. Notes on War Potential of Communist China, pp 30-35, App "C"; NIS, China, Vol III, Chap II, Sec 31

13. Notes on War Potential of Communist China, App "C"; The Kunming to Pisechai Railway, Dec 53, JIB(M) Note 821/600/N1, p 1, AUL M-36760-8-S

14. Notes on the War Potential of Communist China, App "C."

15. Railway Targets, China Proper South of the Yangtze, JIB Rpt No. 5/1/53, Dept of Defense, Australia, pp 6-7, AUL M-3670-4-S; Railway Targets, China Proper North of the Yangtze, Based on Information Received up to Oct 52, JIB(M) Rpt No. 5/8/52, pp 4-6, AUL M-36760-4-S

16. Economic Development of China through 1957, pp. 118-19, Some Notes on Chinese Rolling Stock, Based on Information Received up to November 1953, JIB(M) Rpt No 5/2/54, pp 1-4, 19-20, AUL M-36760-8-S; Strategic Vulnerability of Communist China, p. 18; Rpt on Communist China, RIKU Rpt No. 258, 4 May 54, Hq 500th Mil Intel Gp, p. 1, AUL-M-38124-8-S, Intel Digest No 185, JIB, UK, p. 7; Notes on War Potential of Communist China, p. 18.

17. NIS, China, Vol III, Chap III, Sec 31; Strategic Vulnerability of Communist China, pp. 10, 20

18. NIS, China, Vol III, Chap III, Sec 31; Notes on War Potential of Communist China, p 18.

19. Strategic Vulnerability of Communist China, p 10; Notes on the War Potential of Communist China, pp 18, 30-35, NIS, China, Vol III, Chap III, Sec 30; RR Tgts, N China, p. 4; Chinese Communist Prospects, 1954-57, p. 7; Economic Development of Communist China through 1957, pp. 118-19

20. RR Tgts, China Proper South of the Yangtze, pp 5-7; RR Tgts, N China, *passim*; Strategic Vulnerability of Communist China, pp. 19-20.

21. Strategic Vulnerability of Communist China, p. 10.

GLOSSARY

CACW	Chinese-American Composite Wing
CATF	China Air Task Force
CBI	China-Burma-India Theater
Chengtai	Taiyuan-Shihchiachuang Railroad
FEAF	Far East Air Forces
Hainan	Shanghai-Nanking Railroad
JANAC	Japanese Naval and Merchant Losses during World War II, Joint Army-Navy Assessment Committee Report
Kiangnan	Nanking-Wuhu Railroad
LAB	Low Altitude Bombing
Lunghai	Laoyao-Paochi Railroad
Maru	Japanese merchant ship
Pinghan	Peking-Hankow Railroad
Pingsui	Peking-Suiyuan Railroad
SCR-717	Airborne Radar used primarily for sea search
Shantung	Tsingtao-Tsinan Railroad
Tsinpu	Tientsin-Pukow Railroad
Tungpu	Tatung-Puchou Railroad
UNRRA	United Nations Relief and Rehabilitation Administration
USSBS	United States Strategic Bombing Survey

INDEX

A

Aerial photography, 39, 42, 66, 76, 84
Aircraft losses, 4, 36, 68-69, 77
Air Forces (numbered):
    Eighth AF, 79
    Ninth AF, 79
    Tenth AF, 7, 31, 39, 79
    Fourteenth AF, 2, 4-6, 8-14, 16, 20-34, 36-37, 39-44, 46, 48-56, 61-66, 71, 73, 75-84, 88, 94, 97, 100
Air Regiments (numbered):
    22d Air Regiment (Jap), 21
    29th Air Regiment (Jap), 21
Air superiority, 40, 48, 84, 86, 88
Air support, 31, 35, 62, 78
Air transport, 1, 4-5, 23, 79, 84
Allied bases, 5, 23, 42-43
Ammunition, 1, 20, 25, 30, 37, 68
Amoy, 1, 8, 11, 94
Ankang, 24, 30
Antiaircraft, 6, 9, 11, 19, 21-22, 27, 36-37, 68, 76-77, 88, 90, 100
Anti-Submarine Warfare Assessment Committee, 11
Armies (numbered):
    1st Army (Jap), 26
    6th Area Army (Jap), 43, 70, 72, 74, 78
    6th War Area Army (Chinese), 25
    9th War Area Army (Chinese), 30
    11th Army (Jap), 25-29
    12th Army (Jap.), 26
    12th Area Army (Jap), 73
    13th Army (Jap), 26
    23d Army (Jap.), 27, 29, 41
Army railroad corps, 61
Automatic weapons, 22, 36, 66, 68, 77
Automotive industry, 90

B

B-24, 2, 5-7, 10-11, 17-18, 21, 23, 27-28, 36-37, 49-50, 56, 63-64, 72, 76, 79
B-25, 5-7, 17-18, 20, 22-23, 25, 27-31, 36-37, 39-40, 43-44, 49-50, 56, 63-64, 66-67, 72-77, 79-80, 82-83
B-29, 10-11, 13, 17, 26-27, 75
Barges, 7, 16-18, 20, 23-25, 28-33, 54, 82, 87-88
Bombers, 5-9, 13, 17-19, 23, 26-31, 36-37, 39-40, 42, 46, 56, 66, 68, 72, 76, 101 See also individual entries.
Bombing 2, 19, 33, 36-37, 39, 64-65, 70-72, 82, 88, 91, 98, 100, dive, 19-21, 36-37, 76, low altitude, 66, 82; medium altitude, 5, 36, 76-77, minimum altitude, 5, 19-20, 36-37, 66, 76-77; night, 9; radar, 8-10, skip bombing. See "minimum altitude" above; spike, 66
Bomb run, 6, 8, 36, 39, 66, 77
Bombs, 8-10, 12-13, 17-21, 36-37, 39, 44, 50, 63-67, 73-77, 101
Bombsight, 8, 66
Bridges. 29, 34, 36, 39, 41, 44, 49, 51, 53, 56, 61-62, 66-69, 71, 76, 89-91, 95, 100; bypass, 36, 39, 52, 73, 77, 100, Chiengrai, 50, Chungmow, 56-57, 75-76, 100; Dara, 50; Do Len, 52, Hai Duong, 51; Hankow-Wuchang, 93, 97-98, 100, Hue, 50; Kenghluang, 50; Pengpu, 75-76, 80, 83, 100; Puchi, 72, railroad, 36-37, 40, 44, 50, 72-77, 98, repair, 51, 73, 77, 100, road, 35-36, 40-44, 90, road-railroad, 35, 40, 50-51; Sheklung, 72; Song Chu, 52; Song Rang, 51; Tao River, 75-76, 80; Tsinpu, 80, Yellow River, 56, 72-73, 75, 80, 100
Burma, 2, 11-12, 25-26, 30, 35-36, 39, 44, 46, 48, 52-53, 68, 79, 83, 89-90
Buses, 40, 90

C

Camouflage, 22, 69
Campha Port, 5, 49
Cannon, 6, 18, 20, 66
Canton, 1, 5, 11, 15, 23, 26-27, 29, 31, 41, 43, 53-54, 56, 63, 87, 89, 91, 93-94, 96-97
Cap St. Jacques, 1, 5, 7, 10
Cars motor, 40, 90 See also Railroad and Rolling stock
Carts, 39, 42, 44
Casualties, 20, 37, 98
Cavalry, 27, 37, 41
Central China Development Company, 61
Central China Transportation Company, 61-62, 70
Changhsintien, 56, 95
Changsha, 14, 26-27, 31, 41, 43, 54, 68, 74, 77, 92
Changteh, 25, 27
Changteh Offensive, 25, 40, 63
Chekiang Prov, 55, 89
Chenghsien, 40, 54, 57, 63, 72-73, 75, 78, 93, 96
Chengmai, 49
Chengtu, 26, 87, 89-90, 92
Chenhsien, 54, 93, 97
Chennault, Maj Gen Claire L, ix, 2, 4, 18, 21, 88
Chiang Kai-Shek, Generalissimo, 2
Chihkiang, 19-20, 23-24, 27-28, 30-31, 33, 43-45, 48, 74, 78-79, 84
Chihkiang Campaign, 43-44
China Air Task Force (CATF), 2
China Coast, 1-2, 7, 10-11, 26, 62, 78, 97
China Expeditionary Army, 61, 78
China Theater, 12, 76, 81
Chinese-American Composite Wing (CACW), 18, 22, 26-27, 40, 68
Chinese Armies, 4, 7, 13, 23-27, 29-30, 33-34, 42, 44-45, 52, 56, 62, 67, 78-80, 91. See also Armies (numbered).
Chinese Communists. 87-89, 91-92, 95-96, 102; Air Force, 86; announcements, 92-93; Government, 92, 101-2, merchant marine, 87; road-building program, 89; transportation, 88; waterways, 87-89
Chishuyen, 95-96
Chuanhsien, 29, 41
Chuchow, 54-55, 68, 78, 93-98, 100
Chungking, 2, 14, 54, 78, 87, 89, 92, 96
Close support, 42, 44
Commands (Numbered):

XX Bomber Command, 5, 11
Communications: 29, 39-40, 50, 53, 59, 62-63, 69, 78, 85-86, 98; lines, 23-27, 34
Convoys, 8-9, 37, 43

D

Dairen, 89, 95-96
Davidson, Maj. Gen. Howard C., 7

E

East China Sea, 14, 24, 26, 40
Enshih, 23-24

F

Far East Air Forces (FEAF), 8, 10-11
Ferries, 16, 39, 54, 76, 89, 93. See also Railroads.
Fighters, 5-8, 17-21, 23-25, 27-31, 36-37, 39-40, 42, 44, 46, 49, 56, 64, 66-68, 72-73, 75-76, 83. See also individual entries.
Fighter sweeps, 5, 7-8, 37, 49, 67-63, 82, 91
Floods, 54, 56, 88
Foochow, 1, 11, 94
Formosa, 1, 7-8, 11, 21, 29, 88-89, 94, 97-98, 100
Formosa Strait, 2, 5-8, 30
Fort Bayard, 5, 93-94, 97
Freight, 50, 52, 55, 59, 64, 74, 79, 87, 89-90, 96-97, 100-102
Fuel: 4-5, 7, 14, 23, 35-36, 40, 48, 49, 62, 64-67, 71, 76-77, 79-83, 97, 100, charcoal, 90; coal, 60, 75, 100; gasoline, 4, 7, 10, 13, 19, 22-23, 28, 79; kerosene, 87; motor, 28, 34, 42, 90
Fukien Prov., 89

G

Gia Lam, 46, 49
Grand Canal, 60, 88
Ground fire, 17-19, 21-22, 66
Ground support, 10, 39, 83
Groups (Numbered):
  1st Bombardment (CACW), 27
  23d Fighter, 22, 27
  308th Bombardment, 6-7, 17, 27
  341st Bombardment, 17-18, 50
Gulf of Tonkin, 2, 5-8, 49-50
Gun boats, 22-25, 32

H

Hainan Island, 1-2, 7-8, 11, 87, 94, 97
Haiphong, 1, 5, 10-12, 46, 49-50, 82
Hangchow, 55, 94
Hankow, 14, 16, 18-19, 21-24, 26, 29-32, 34, 40-41, 43, 54-56, 63, 67-68, 70, 73-74, 77-78, 81, 87, 91, 95-98, 100
Hanoi, 35, 46, 50, 94, 97
Harbors, 4-6, 13, 82, 88
Hengyang, 14, 18, 23, 25-33, 41, 43-46, 51, 54-56, 63, 67-68, 73-74, 84, 91, 94, 97-98, 100
Highways See roads.
Hochih, 29, 41, 43, 54
Holding companies, 61
Honan campaign, 72
Honan Front, 72
Honan Offensive, 40
Honan Prov., 34, 40, 42, 87, 89
Hong Kong, 1, 5-6, 8, 11, 53, 82, 87

Hopei Prov., 59
Horses, 36-37, 39-43
Hsian, 42, 56, 69, 74, 80
Hsiang Valley, 18-20, 27-31, 37, 39, 40-42, 68, 74, 84, 89
Hump, 4, 31, 35, 48
Hunan-Kwangsi Campaign, 25-30, 77
Hunan Prov., 14, 23, 25, 27, 29, 31, 34, 75, 84, 90

I

Ichang, 14, 16, 24
India, 2, 4, 25, 35-36, 39, 52, 79, 83
Intelligence: 37, 63, 81, 83, 92; officers, 9, 67, 70 76, 81; reports, 49, 92-93
Interceptors. See fighters

J

Japan, 1-2, 14, 21-22, 24, 26, 29, 32, 40, 48, 56-57, 59-60, 81, 83, 85-88, 100
Japanese: Air Force, 1-2, 21, 68; armies, 22-23, 25, 42, 61-62, 77 See also Armies (numbered); defenses, 21, 36, 67-68, forces, 1, 5, 16, 23, 25-26, 28, 33, 39, 43-44, 48, 63, 74, 77-78, 80-81, 83, losses, 33, offensives, 14, 24, 26-27, 35-37, 40-41, 52-54, 56, 62, 72-74, 83-84
Jehol Prov., 60, 94, 97
Joint Army Navy Assessment Committee Report, Japanese Naval and Merchant Ship Losses During World War II (JANAC), 6-7, 11-12, 32
Junks, 6-7, 9, 12, 16-21, 23-25, 28-33, 82, 87-89, 102

K

Kaifeng, 56-57, 63-64, 69, 75, 78, 81
Kanchow, 5-7, 23, 27, 30-31, 42-43
Kansu Prov., 92
Kiangsi Prov., 5, 55
Kiirun, 1, 11
Kinhwa, 55, 63
Kiukiang, 18-19, 21, 55, 63, 78
Kiungshan, 1
Korea, 2, 26, 46, 54, 56, 59-60, 72, 81, 86, 88, 91, 94, 97, 100
Kowloon, 53, 96
Kunming, 2, 4, 8, 27, 35, 39, 46, 48, 50, 62, 79, 92-94, 96
Kwangsi Prov., 5, 7, 24
Kwangtung Prov., 31, 34, 53, 89
Kweilin, 4, 14, 16, 23, 27-31, 41, 54, 73, 91
Kweiyang, 78, 89, 92-94

L

Lanchow, 92-93
Landslides, 36-37, 39
Laohokow, 24, 30, 42-43
Laoyao, 56-57, 95
Lashio, 35-36, 39
Launches, 6, 14, 16-20, 25, 23-31
Liberator See B-24.
Lighters, 16, 28, 33
Lingling, 23, 25, 27-29, 41
Litang, 93-94
Liuchow, 4, 8, 23, 26-31, 41, 43, 46, 51, 54, 67, 70, 74, 92, 94, 96

Locomotives, 44, 48-66, 72, 81-82, 84, 91, 93, 95-97, 100-101
Loyang, 56-57
Luan, 57, 94
Luzon, 7, 10, 78

M

Machine guns, 6, 18, 20, 22, 37, 67-68, 77
Mako, 1, 11
Malaya, 1, 46
Manchuria, 22, 26, 53, 56-57, 60, 72, 81, 86-87, 89-91, 94-98, 100
Marshalling yards, 49-50, 55, 57, 59-60, 62-64, 66, 68-69, 71-72, 96, 98, 100-101
Medium bomber See B-25.
Merchant marine See shipping and Chinese Communists.
Mines, 10-12, 21-22, 24, 32-33, 48, 56, 76, 82, 88, 100-101
Mining, 5, 6, 10-13, 21-22, 28, 32, 46, 79, 82, 88, 102
Mitchell See B-25.
Motor transport, 19, 28-29, 34, 36-37, 40, 90
Motor vehicle companies, 41-42
Motor vehicles. See Vehicles, Buses, and Cars.
Mukden, 56, 60, 95-96, 100
Munitions, 4-5, 13, 16, 22-23, 26-27, 41, 83-84, 97, 101
Mustangs See P-51
Myitkyina, 35, 39

N

Nanchang, 31, 55, 78, 94
Nanking, 2, 14, 16, 21, 23-24, 33, 53, 57, 59, 61, 63, 68, 70, 75-76, 78, 93, 98, 100
Nanning, 4-6, 14, 16, 26-27, 29, 46, 51, 54-55, 93
Nationalist Armies, 86
Nationalist Government, 87, 90-91
Nationalists, 87, 90, 92
Night attacks, 39, 91 See also Bombing and Night intruder
Night intruder, 20, 22, 31, 39, 43, 68, 82, 101 See also Bombing
Ningpo, 55, 94
North China Development Company, 61
North China Transportation Company, 61, 64, 69-72
Nuclear weapons, 97, 100-101

O

Office of Strategic Services (OSS), 73
Okinawa, 7, 88

P

P-38, 5, 17, 76, 79
P-40, 5-6, 17, 19-20, 25, 40, 50, 63, 67, 72-73, 76, 79
P-47, 6, 17, 64, 67, 76, 79
P-51, 5-6, 17, 19-21, 23-25, 50, 63, 67, 72-73, 76, 79
P-61, 6, 20, 39, 68, 76, 79, 82
Pack trains, 37, 41
Paochi, 56, 92-93, 95
Paoching, 43-44
Peking, 26, 30, 40, 53, 55-57, 64, 67-69, 73, 75, 78, 91, 93-97, 100
Pengpu, 60, 75
Philippine Islands, 1, 4, 8, 30, 62, 67, 78, 88, 100

Phnom Penh, 46, 55
Powered craft, 7, 16, 19, 22, 24, 28-29, 31-33
Pukow, 57, 59-60, 76, 96
Pusan, 46, 56

R

Radar, assessment of damage, 9, 12, low altitude bombing (LAB), 5, 7-9, 17, 30, SCR-717, 7, sea sweeps, 5-8, 10, 17, 83; warning system, 69-
Railhead, 63, 92, 95
Railroads 14, 19, 23-24, 26, 34-35, 37, 42-44, 46, 49, 51, 53-81, 83-84, 86, 90-102, administration, 48, 61-62, 73, 78, 80-81, 101; branch lines, 54-60, 92, 94, 97, beds, 34, 41, 54-55, 57, 66, 78, 100; Canton-Hankow, 5, 16, 23-24, 26-27, 30-31, 43, 53-55, 61, 63-64, 66-68, 72-74, 78, 87, 91, 93-94, 97-98; Canton-Kowloon, 53-54, 72, 94, Canton-Samshui, 54, 94, capacity, 48, 51, 53-55, 57, 59-60, 64, 75, 79, 94-97; cars See Rolling stock; Chekiang-Kiangsi, 54-55, 61, 93-94; Chining-Ulan Ude, 93, Chungking-Chengtu, 92-93; coastal (Canton-Foochow), 97; crews, 70-71, 95-96; defense, 65, 67-70; ferries, 59-60, 76, 93, 98, 100, Hanoi-Haiphong, 46, 51, 94; Hanoi-Lao Kay, 46, 51, 94; Hanoi-Na Cham, 46, 51, 94; Hanoi-Saigon, 46, 48, 51, 94; Hunan-Kwangsi, 26, 41, 54-55, 61, 67-68, 73-74, 78, 91, 93-94, 97, Indo-Chinese, 5, 40, 46-52, 94, 97; Jehol (Peking to Manchuria), 60, 94, 97, junctions, 64, 87, 93, Kaifeng Cutoff, 56-57, 64, 75, 94; Korean, 61, Kunming-Kweiyang, 93, Kunming-Pisechai, 97, Kweiyang-Hsiang River, 93, Laoyao-Paochi (Lunghai), 40, 56-57, 60-61, 63-64, 72-73, 75, 77-78, 81, 92-95, maintenance, 48, 53-54, 61-62, 64-65, 71, 91, 95-96, 101; Manchurian, 56-57, 59-61, 87, 97; Mandalay-Lashio, 53; Nanchang-Kiukiang, 55, 61, 63, 72; Nanking-Wuhu (Kiangnan), 59-61, 94; new construction, 92, 95-96, Paochi-Chengtu-Changking-Kunming, 93, passenger cars, 53-54, 59, 64, 95-96; Peking-Hankow (Pinghan), 22-23, 26, 30, 40, 46, 54-57, 60-61, 63-64, 66-70, 72-73, 75, 77-78, 80-81, 91-95, 100, Peking-Mukden, 60, 72, 87, 94-95, 97-98, Peking-Suiyuan (Pingsui), 57, 60, 80, 93, 95, personnel, 101; Pusan-Singapore, 55, repair, 28, 61-62, repair shops, 10, 49-51, 53-54, 56-57, 59-60, 62-65, 67-68, 71-72, 81, 95-98, 100-102; strikes, 53, 97; Shanghai-Hangchow-Ningpo, 55, 59, 61, 63, 93-94, Shanghai-Nanking (Hainan), 55, 57, 59-61, 76; Shihchiachuang-Tehsien, 56, 60, 75; Siberian, 87; system, 48, 53, 79, 83, 95, 98, 100-102, Taiyuan-Shihchiachuang (Chengtai), 56-57, 60, 75-76, 80-81, 93, 95; targets, 39, 43, 48, 51, 67, 100; Tatung-Puchou (Tungpu), 57, 64, 66, 74-75, 77, 80-81, 83, 93-95, Tientsin-Pukow (Tsinpu), 56-57, 59-61, 64, 75-76, 81, 83, 87, 91-95, Trans-Siberian, 61, 93; Tsingtao-Tsinan (Shantung), 60, 95, Turkestan-Siberian, 92; Wuchang-Hengyang. See Canton-Hankow
Railway regiments, 61
Raw materials, 1, 14, 22, 24, 26, 40, 48, 52, 57, 61, 79-81, 83, 85-86, 93
Reconnaissance, 34-35, 37, 39, 42, 49, 51, 57, 60, 64

River ports, 19, 22, 88
Rivers: 37, 44, 53, 82, 84, 86, 89, 96, 102, Amur, 87, 94; Han, 24; Hsi, 14, 16-17, 19, 23, 27, 29-31, 41, 54, 82, 87-88; Hsiang, 14, 16-19, 21-23, 26-33, 41, 43-44, 82, 87-88, Huai, 88, Kian, 31; Kuei, 16, Pearl, 54; Pei, 14, 31, 54; Salween, 27, 35-37, 44, Sungari, 87; Tao, 75; Yangtze, 9-11, 13-14, 16-28, 30, 32-34, 40, 42-43, 53-57, 59-62, 70, 76-78, 82, 86-89, 93, 97-98, 100; Yellow, 26, 40, 42, 55-56, 61, 63-64, 69, 72-75, 77, 93, 100
River sweeps, 19-20
Roads. 14, 19, 26, 28-30, 34-45, 89-91, 96, 102; Burma, 35-36, 39, 84, Chungyang-Liuyang, 41; Hsinghuang-Changsha, 41; Indo-Chinese, 35; junctions, 90; Ledo-Burma, 35, 90, Route Coloniale No 1, 35; system, 40, 90, 102; targets, 36, 39, 43; traffic, 35, 37, 40, 44, 82, 89; transportation, 34, 36; Yochow-Changsha, 41
Rolling stock, 37, 48-50, 53-57, 59-60, 62-64, 66-72, 74, 79, 91, 93, 95-97, 100-102
Russia, 91, 93
Russians, 90-93, 96

S

Saigon, 5, 13, 35, 46, 48-50, 55, 94
Salween Campaign, 35, 39, 42
Salween front, 39-40, 83-84
Samah Bay, 1, 5, 11
Sampans, 7, 16-20, 23-25, 28-33, 82, 88-89
Samshui, 14, 29, 54, 63
SB-24, 5, 7-10, 82
Sea sweeps: 4-7, 13, 17, 49, 67, 83 *See also* Radar
Shanghai, 1, 7-8, 10-11, 13-14, 24, 55-57, 59-60, 76, 82, 86-89, 93-95
Shensi Prov., 56-57
Shihchiachuang, 55-57, 60, 63-65, 69, 73, 75, 80-81, 93, 95-96
Shipping: 1-9, 11-13, 16-24, 29-33, 37, 40, 42, 44, 46, 48, 56-57, 62, 66, 78, 82, 85, 87, 89, 100-101; capacity, 88; claims, 6-7, 9, 11-12, 24-25, 28, 30-33, 82, 84; coastal, 1, 4, 87-88, 102; river, 10, 13, 16-17, 19, 21, 29, 33, 37, 39, 43, 87-88, 102; routes, 1, 52; Russian, 87, strikes, 1-2, 4, 6, 10, 12, 21
Shipyards, 89
Siangtan, 17, 21
Siberia 86, 88, ports, 87; waters, 87
Singapore, 1, 26, 46, 55
Sinkiang Prov., 92
Sinsiang, 55-56, 63-64, 68, 73
Sinyang, 40, 56, 63, 70, 73-74
South China Sea, 2, 5-8, 30, 50
Southeast Asia, 30, 48, 88-89, 90, 98, 100
Squadrons (Numbered):
  4th Bombardment (CACW) Sq., 68
  11th Bombardment Sq., 6, 18, 27
  22d Bombardment Sq., 50
  449th Fighter Sq., 17
  490th Bombardment Sq, 75-76
  491st Bombardment Sq, 19, 50
Steamers, 6, 14, 16-18, 20, 24-25, 28-31, 82, 87-89
Stilwell, Lt Gen Joseph W., ix, 2, 4

Strafing, 5-7, 12, 16, 19-21, 29, 33, 37, 39-40, 44, 49-50, 62, 64, 68-70, 72, 76, 81-82, 100
Submarines, 1, 8, 11-12, 24, 26, 30, 40, 48, 52, 56, 79
Suichwan, 4-8, 23, 27-28, 30-31, 42-43
Supplies, 2, 27-28, 31, 34-36, 39, 41, 43, 55, 59-60, 69, 73, 75, 77, 79, 82, 84-85, 96, 98, 100
Supply line, 14, 16, 22, 26-30, 36, 41, 44, 46, 81
Swatow, 6, 8, 11, 94

T

Taiyuan, 56-57, 65, 74-75, 80-81, 93, 95-96
Takao, 1, 8, 11
Tangshan, 95-96
Tatung, 57, 60, 93
Tehsien, 60, 95
Thailand, 35, 39, 46, 48-50, 83, 89-90, 97
Theater policy, 80, 83
Tibet, 14, 90
Tientsin, 57, 60, 96
Top cover, 19, 68
Tourane, 1, 8
Trains, 19, 50-52, 62, 66, 68-69, 74, 78, 93, 101
Transshipment, 50, 52, 77
Trucks, 37, 39, 40-43, 50, 52, 82, 90, diesel, 53, 68, 74; flange-wheeled, 53, 55, 68, 74
Tsinan, 60, 63, 65, 81, 95-96, 100
Tsingtao, 5, 53, 57, 60, 95-96
Tugboats, 16-17, 20, 25, 28, 31, 89
Tungshan (Suchow), 56-57, 60-61, 73, 75, 78, 93-94, 96
Tungting Lake, 14, 23, 25, 28, 63

U

Ulan Bator, 93, 96
Union of Soviet Socialist Republics (U S S.R.) 61, 87-88, 92-94. *See also* Russia.
United Nations Relief and Rehabilitation Administration (UNRRA), 90
United States, 53, 61, 87-89, 96-98
United States Strategic Bombing Survey (USSBS), 32

V

Vehicles: 14, 37, 39, 41, 82, 91; claims, 39-44, 84, motor, 39-44, 90
Vinh, 1, 49

W

Wenchow, 1, 11
Whampoa, 54, 87
Wings (Numbered):
  68th Composite Wg, 18, 22
  312th Fighter Wg, 17
Wuchang, 28, 54-55, 63, 69-70, 72-74, 77, 91, 96-97
Wuchow, 14, 16-17
Wuhu, 19, 59, 94

XYZ

Yellow Sea, 56, 60, 86, 88
Yochow, 17-19, 21, 28, 31, 43, 54, 56, 63-64, 67
Yunglowtung, 63-64
Yunho, 57, 60
Yunnan Prov., 14, 25, 35, 39, 46, 52, 89

www.ingramcontent.com/pod-product-compliance
Lightning Source LLC
Chambersburg PA
CBHW082126230426
43671CB00015B/2821